College Identity Sagas

College Identity Sagas

Investigating Organizational Identity Preservation and Diminishment at Lutheran Colleges and Universities

ERIC CHILDERS

PICKWICK *Publications* · Eugene, Oregon

COLLEGE IDENTITY SAGAS
Investigating Organizational Identity Preservation and Diminishment at Lutheran
Colleges and Universities

Pickwick Publications
A Division of Wipf and Stock Publishers
199 W. 8th Ave., Suite 3
Eugene, OR 97401

www.wipfandstock.com

ISBN 13: 978-1-61097-308-3

Cataloging-in-Publication data:

Childers, Eric

    College identity sagas : investigating organizational identity preservation and
diminishment at Lutheran colleges and universities / Eric Childers.

    xii + 256 p. ; 23 cm. Includes bibliographical references.

    ISBN 13: 978-1-61097-308-3

    1. Church colleges—United States—Case studies. 2. Church and college—Unit-
ed States. 3. Secularism—United States—Case studies. 4. Learning and scholarship—
Religious aspects—Christianity. I. Title.

LC574 C43 2012

Manufactured in the U.S.A.

For the family

Contents

Foreword

FROM THE EARLY 90S on, the literature on American Christian higher education has expanded exponentially. This flurry was set off by a bombshell article written by James Burtchaell in *First Things* in 1991: "The Rise and Fall of the Christian College." Other writers also sounded the alarm that the American colleges founded, controlled, and deeply influenced by their sponsoring churches were experiencing a dramatic secularization. Secularization meant first of all that control of the colleges by the churches was diminishing, but more seriously it meant that the influence exerted by a particular religious heritage was also waning. The religious ideas and practices specific to the sponsoring tradition—and the people who bore them—were disappearing from those church-related colleges and universities. The situation seemed dire indeed.

But the bad news was quickly followed by more optimistic reports. Among the first was *Models of Christian Higher Education—Strategies for Success in the Twenty-first Century,* edited by William Adrian and Richard Hughes (1996). I wrote my *Quality with Soul—How Six Premier Colleges and Universities Keep Faith with their Christian Traditions* in 2001. Many more analyses have followed that have shown the strengths and weaknesses of Christian higher education.

More remarkable than the production of books has been the resolve by hundreds of religious schools practically to strengthen their religious identities and missions. Most of these are conservative Protestant schools but also include some Catholic schools that have responded to Pope John Paul II's call for strengthening their Catholic character. Even some liberal Protestant schools—Methodist, Presbyterian, Lutheran—have responded to the need for more intentionality in preserving their religious identity.

Yet, we have hundreds of church-related colleges and universities sliding down the path to the kind of secularization that so alarmed Burtchaell. Many slide heedlessly, but some move away from their religious identity intentionally, striving for elite status of a secular sort. Only a few, such as Baylor University, try both to strengthen their religious identity and rise to the elite level.

The literature on this wide variety of schools is vast, but most of it has been written by administrators, historians, and theologians who have been interested in the challenges facing Christian higher education. These writers have been perceptive and wise in their insights, and we have learned a much about both secularization and maintaining a robust sense of religious identity and mission.

No one, as far as I know, has written an analysis of a set of schools of one tradition from the viewpoint of organizational theory. Now we have a new entry in the field, Eric Childers, who is expert in looking at the dynamics of church-related education from a new perspective, from isomorphic and critical events theory, to be exact.

Childers has selected three Lutheran-related schools—Concordia in Moorhead, Minnestoa; Lenoir-Rhyne in Hickory, North Carolina; and Gettysburg in Pennsylvania—that are at various places on the continuum between robust religious identity (Concordia), on the one hand, and a pervasive secularity (Gettysburg), on the other. A third, Lenoir-Rhyne, occupies a point between the two. He examines how each of them has exhibited isomorphic traits, i.e., how they have emulated other schools and agencies, and interprets their trajectory over forty-five years in the light of critical events theory. They are interesting and illuminating stories. Childers backs up his theoretical interpretations with troves of data collected by vigorous research on each institution, as well as with accounts of interviews with key actors on campus, current and past. He shines light on the factors that enable schools to maintain their religious identities and missions, as well as those that lead to secularization.

This fresh perspective will contribute new insights into the organizational dynamics of Christian higher education. It is welcome indeed.

—Robert Benne
Director of the Roanoke College Center for Religion and Society

Acknowledgments

THIS BOOK BEGAN AS a doctoral dissertation for my work at the University of Virginia. A superstar dissertation committee helped to make this project a reality, guiding me and advising me along the long road from start to finish. What great fortune to have been blessed with such a team! David Breneman, committee chair, with his eye on the pragmatic, empowered me to make this study my own and imparted me with this wisdom: "A good dissertation tells a story and is interesting to read." Brian Pusser, my theory and content expert, taught me in his classes how to strengthen an argument and more importantly, how to *listen* to an argument. Dan Duke, one of the greatest teachers I have encountered in my thirty years of school, showed me how to analyze, disassemble, design, and *appreciate* a study. Bob Benne, one of the boldest, most confident voices in Lutheran higher education, lent his expertise in the field of church-affiliated schools and their struggle to maintain quality with soul. For this committee, I am deeply grateful.

I must also acknowledge the participation of all of the characters I encountered during my visits to the three schools described in this book. Their voices, captured in painstaking interviews, tell the narratives of Concordia, Lenoir-Rhyne, and Gettysburg.

PART 1

Research Design

1

Introduction

BACKGROUND

FROM HIS FIRST PUBLIC act, perhaps the one most remembered by history, Martin Luther demonstrated his deep commitment to education and its power to transform. On October 31, 1517, Luther posted his famous Ninety-five Theses for the interest of the community, the audience that would participate in his attempt to reform the Church and ultimately play a vital force in that reformation. By posting the document on the church door, the public bulletin board, Luther was engaging the instrument of education to mobilize his effort for reform. The grievances outlined in the Ninety-five Theses were now a matter of public conversation. As people began to hear about the treatise, Luther recognized the power of Gutenberg's new printing press and its power to distribute his message so that people could read his case for change. From the beginning, education was the key.

History has conferred numerous titles upon Martin Luther—Reformer, Professor, Theologian, Preacher. However, I argue the title that most fundamentally describes Luther is that of educator, for education is at the heart of his work as a theologian, reformer, professor, and academician. After all, at its foundations, the Reformation was a reformation of teaching. Luther's vocation was pastor and professor, but he performed his service with the fundamental faith in the power of education to transform, enlighten, empower, and ultimately emphasize the freedom for one to serve God and neighbor. Even his most significant literary contribution to the German culture—the translation of the Bible into a "new" German language—was an act fueled by the belief that education holds the potential to empower and galvanize an entire people.

Martin Luther was not simply a church reformer—he was an educational reformer. He championed public, accessible education for all, boys and girls alike. He reformed the classrooms of universities, implementing a curriculum that looks very similar to today's liberal arts. He appealed to government leaders and placed upon them the responsibility of funding such an educational system. He emblazoned in the minds of millions the ever-important question repeated throughout the *Small Catechism*: "What does this mean?"

Leonard Schulze, Former Executive Director of the Division for Higher Education and Schools of the ELCA, writes, "[Luther's] insistence that discernment and equipping were necessary for us to empower ourselves to fulfill our vocations and to serve out neighbors have inspired Lutherans throughout the centuries to place a high value on education." Today, the ELCA enjoys a relationship with its twenty-seven colleges and universities that have been founded over the past nearly 200 years, a clear expression of Lutherans' commitment to and support of education. In sum, Lutherans claim a foundational theological command to integrate faith and learning for service in the world.

Luther, a prolific writer, often engaged the subject of education. He proposed his ideas on educational reform through his work, *To the Christian Nobility of the German Nation Concerning the Reform of the Christian Estate*. Luther's foundational reform changes were curricular, implementing a strong foundation of grammar, languages, rhetoric, and the Bible. His affirmation and strong endorsement of a humanist educational curriculum looks very similar to today's liberal arts curriculum at America's Lutheran colleges and universities. In his treatise, *To the Councilmen of All Cities in Germany That They Establish and Maintain Christian Schools*, Luther persuaded government leaders to redistribute funding from defunct Roman Catholic monasteries and convents to support schools. *A Sermon on Keeping Children in School* is a sharply critical treatise in which Luther argues that failure to properly educate young people is a form of neglect. Luther understands education to be an investment in people, the future, and in the faith community.

Perhaps the most significant expression of his commitment to learning came with the writing of the *Small Catechism* and the *Large Catechism*, both published in 1529, which intended to meet the urgent needs of instructing Christian teachers as well as catechizing Christians. The *Large Catechism*, whose origin was a series of sermons, was intended primarily as an instrument for educating clergy; the *Small Catechism* was intended to answer very specific questions about foundational tenets of the church. While both are considered among Luther's most important and significant work, it is the *Small Catechism* that stands as the most important of Luther's contributions to education, except arguably the translation of the German Bible. For Luther, education was the means for service and fullness of life.

The long-standing tradition of Lutheran higher education takes seriously the marriage of faith and learning, which is the basis for the Lutheran commitment to intellectual inquiry and academic freedom (Bunge, 2006). The Evangelical Lutheran Church in America (ELCA) maintains a steadfast commitment to education, demonstrated by the Division for Vocation and Education, one of its eight primary churchwide organizational offices. Moreover, the ELCA publicly affirmed in August 2007 the importance of education in its latest social statement, joining other churchwide statements ranging from the death penalty to healthcare, from famine to the environment. This most recent social statement, entitled "Our Calling in Education," explains the centrality of learning to the Lutheran faith, the potential of education to transform society, the ELCA's commitment to public schools, equitable access to education for all students, and support of Lutheran schools. The statement is particularly interested in how higher education—religious and secular—serves the public good (ELCA, 2007).

THE PROBLEM

Like most institutions of higher education, secularization has influenced the Lutheran academy. During the latter half of the twentieth century—especially since the mid-1960s—nearly all religious colleges and universities, Lutheran institutions included, have experienced some degree of this

5

change, a distancing from the sponsoring denominational church and loss of religious tradition in multiple facets of institutional life (ELCA, 2007). On the other hand, Lutheran colleges and universities have maintained more significant relationships with their religious tradition than most mainline denominational colleges (ELCA, 2007).

While secularization is but one part of the change equation Lutheran colleges and universities face in the twenty-first century, it is a significant issue as these colleges evaluate the role of their religious identity. Colleges and universities of the ELCA must determine if maintaining their religious identity is an institutional priority, especially amidst secularization, faculty professionalization, and efforts to maintain financial viability. Articulating clearly that the academy can take seriously both faith and learning is important if a college or university seeks to maintain a robust relationship with its religious tradition. Simply put, does organizational Lutheran identity still matter to these colleges and universities?

To the point, colleges and universities look to a wide variety of institutions—beyond colleges and universities that share their own identities—as they plan, evolve, and shape identity (Stensaker & Norgard, 2001). In this process, the likelihood for institutional religious identity diminishment emerges. Do institutions preserve or diminish their traditional religious identities in institutional decision-making processes? Are Lutheran colleges changing, and are they preserving their religious identities? What is more, many ELCA colleges and universities have not clearly, confidently, and consistently articulated a rationale, particularly theologically, for functioning as a Lutheran college (Benne, 2003a).

For some Lutheran colleges, the ties to the faith tradition have loosened over time; for others, that religious tradition was never tightly fastened. And for some of these colleges, the issue of organizational identity is intermixed with issues of institutional survival. In 2009, Waldorf College, an ELCA institution plagued with dwindling enrollment and severe financial challenges, was purchased and will function as a for-profit college apart from the ELCA.

RESEARCH QUESTIONS AND CONCEPTUAL FRAMEWORK

In seeking to discover phenomena related to institutional religious identity at the colleges and universities of the ELCA, this study is guided by three central questions:

1. Are colleges and universities of the Evangelical Lutheran Church in America preserving or diminishing their Lutheran identities?

2. Do the status drivers of secularization, financial viability, and faculty professionalization affect Lutheran institutional identity at these colleges and universities?

3. If the colleges and universities described in the case studies are seeking to preserve their Lutheran identities, why and how are they planning this preservation?

Using these questions as a guide, this study will add to the organizational literature—particularly identity literature—and Lutheran higher education literature, both currently lacking empirical data on whether Lutheran colleges and universities seek to preserve or diminish their Lutheran identities. If these schools are seeking to preserve institutional identity, then how and why are they doing this?

This research study is informed by five sources of information: organizational literature, college and university governance literature, Lutheran higher education literature, and literature related to theories of isomorphism and critical events theory. While institutional theory frames the cross-case analysis, critical events theory shapes the chronologies of the three case studies detailed in the fourth, fifth, and sixth chapters. Because of their centrality to the study, both the institutional isomorphic and critical events theories are addressed in detail in the literature review.

PURPOSE OF THE STUDY

This study is worthwhile for several reasons. First, at the theoretical level, this study will add to the literature on the theory of institutional isomorphic change, especially with regard to the particular organizational field of Lutheran colleges. To date, few studies have been conducted that exclusively address institutional identity preservation and diminishment at Lutheran colleges. This study will add a voice to that conversation, especially in organizational mission and identity. The methodology of this study distinguishes it from other similar work on higher education as it examines Lutheran higher education from an organizational perspective.

Perhaps most significantly, this study examines Lutheran college identity through the lens of organizational theory. Organization theorist Paul DiMaggio, a leading thinker on theories of isomorphism, argues that organization theory is well-suited to the study of religion and related religious topics (Demerath et al., 1998). DiMaggio cites a shift in goals of organization theory from fixed to ambiguous, from formal systems to informal social relations, from organizational structure to organizational culture, and from closed systems to open systems.

While the study is informed by a body of organizational literature, it is conceptually imagined through the lens of two organizational theories, isomorphism and critical events theory. Isomorphism is widely found in institutional theory, often called neo-institutionalism; critical events theory is an important tool for framing organizational histories. Moreover, three schools were selected for examination based upon a spectrum of "Lutheranness,"[1] or the extent to which the institution demonstrates criteria intended to measure expression of Lutheran characteristics. Among colleges and universities within these typologies, three were chosen with a diverse geographic representation: one college from the Midwest, one from the Northeast, and one from the Southeast.

Additionally, at the practical level, this study will determine whether Lutheran colleges and universities look beyond institutions that share their own identities for benchmarking, planning, and emulation. The findings of this study can demonstrate to institutional decision-makers how three particular schools have navigated the uncertain path among clearly professing religious identity, obscuring Lutheran affiliation in ambiguous mission statements, and brushing this tradition completely out of sight. The study can also offer findings useful to other small colleges and universities faced with similar challenges, like similar religiously-affiliated colleges, single-sex colleges, military colleges, historically Black colleges and universities (HBCU), and other mission-specific institutions. The narratives traced in this study can serve as testimonies for both the benefits and related trade-offs of identity preservation.

1. I have taken the liberty of using this pseudo-word at various points in the study. By "Lutheranness" I mean the extent to which Lutheran characteristics are displayed.

Finally, the purpose of this study is to address the clear gap in the research on Lutheran higher education, with special attention to identity. The study addresses this deficiency in the literature by exploring the identity histories[2] of three Lutheran colleges and universities, each located at different places along a spectrum of perceived engagement with their own Lutheran tradition. Following these identity chronologies that are built upon critical events over a 45-year period, the study will present a cross-case analysis that compares and contrasts the three institutions through the lens of isomorphism. What influence does secularization, attention to financial viability, and faculty professionalization exert on a college or university's affiliation with the sponsoring religious tradition? This methodological strategy will add a new perspective to the literature on higher education in general and Lutheran higher education specifically.

DEFINITION OF TERMS

Bureaucratization: The systematic process of a government, corporation, administrative group, or other organization to specialize its functions and adhere to a set of standardized rules.

Ethos: Organizational "way of life" (Benne, 2001). Paul Dovre describes ethos as "the power of one's personality, character, and reputation," transmitted through the people of the organization.

Evangelical: The "evangelical" nomenclature of the ELCA, and any Lutheran-related sense, is from the European derivation that sets Lutherans apart from Roman Catholics and emphasizes the gospel in contrast to the mediation of the church for purposes of salvation. In the sense of "(American) Evangelical," the term is defined this way by Bob Benne, Mark Noll, and David Bebbington (Benne, 2001:74): "Evangelicalism as a tradition derives from the renewal movements led by figures such as George Whitefield, John Wesley, Jonathan Edwards, and Nicholas von Zinzendorf. The common impulses in these movements, as cited by Noll and Bebbington, were conversionism (an emphasis on 'new birth' as a life-changing religious experience), biblicism (a reliance on the Bible as ultimate religious authority), activism (a concern for sharing the faith), and crucicentrism (a focus on Christ's redeeming work on the cross)."

2. Throughout this study, I use several terms interchangeably: case study, identity history, saga, identity chronology, and institutional narrative.

Evangelical Lutheran Church in America: Formed from the 1987 merger of the Lutheran Church in America and the American Lutheran Church, the ELCA is the largest Lutheran body in America, reporting some 4.6 million baptized members in 2008. The ELCA consists of more than 10,000 congregations organized in 65 synods and 18,938 rostered leaders (17,652 ordained clergy, 1,068 associates in ministry, 65 deaconesses, and 153 diaconal ministers); nearly 20 percent of ordained clergy are women. Education, an important part of the ELCA mission, is offered through 8 seminaries, 27 colleges and universities, more than 50 lifelong learning centers, 14 high schools, 296 elementary schools, 1,573 early childhood programs, and 145 camp and retreat centers (ELCA website).

Faculty professionalization: In an article on faculty professionalization, Neil Hamilton, University of St. Thomas law professor, defined professionalization: "In the tradition of peer review, the members of a profession form with society an unwritten contract whereby society grants the profession autonomy to govern itself and, in return, the members of the profession agree to meet correlative personal and collegial group duties to society. The members of the profession agree to restrain self-interest to some degree in order to serve the public purpose of the profession (knowledge creation and dissemination, in the case of the academic profession), to promote the ideals and core values of the profession, and to maintain high standards of minimum performance. In return, society allows the profession substantial autonomy to regulate itself through peer review. For the individual professional, this translates into substantial autonomy and discretion in work" (2006:14).

Isomorphism: A constraining process that forces one unit in a population to resemble other units that face the same set of environmental conditions (Hawley, 1968; Hannan & Freeman, 1977; DiMaggio & Powell, 1983).

Organizational change: Change in formal structure, culture, goals, program, or mission of a defined organization (DiMaggio and Powell, 1983).

Organizational field: (Related to theories of isomorphism) organizations that, in the aggregate, constitute a recognized area of institutional life: key suppliers, resource and product consumers, regulatory agencies, and other organizations that produce service or products. The virtue of this unit of analysis is that it directs attention not simply to competing firms or to interacting networks, but to the totality of relevant actors. In so doing, the field idea comprehends the importance of both connectedness and structural equivalence (DiMaggio and Powell, 1983).

Secularization: The notion that religious authority is in decline in the world (Demerath, 1998), shaped, in part, by the desire to become inclusive and pluralistic (Arthur, 2001).

Status driver: The term used in this study to describe organizational "environmental factors" (DiMaggio & Powell, 1983) that influence institutional isomorphism. This study engages three isomorphic status drivers: secularization, (the struggle for) financial viability, and faculty professionalization.

Synod: Districts by which the ELCA is organized, comparable to a diocese in the Roman Catholic tradition.

Theology of the two kingdoms: While the Lutheran doctrine of the two kingdoms is a complex theological construct, the doctrine essentially explains that separate heavenly and earthly realms exist, and humans interact with one another in society in this earthly realm. Founded on the Apostles' Creed, Luther contends that God as Creator rules two realms—the heavenly kingdom and the earthly kingdom. The spiritual realm, where faith is paramount to reason, is manifested by the people of God who are saved by grace through faith in Christ. The earthly realm, or the created kingdom proclaimed by God as "good" but tarnished by sin, is protected by God through the human structures of family, school, and government. Luther's theology of education grew from his concept of the two kingdoms. Education is placed in the earthly kingdom, and its function is to provide a system by which human beings are educated for service that enriches humanity, bringing it to what God envisions it to become. Moreover, he demonstrates that church schools are environments in which students and teachers alike are free to inquire, investigate, research, challenge, and propose, and this work is performed within the earthly realm of God's two kingdoms.

Vocation: Derived from the Latin term *vocat*, which means "call," vocation is interpreted in two ways: as a strong summons to a particular course of action" or "the work in which a person is regularly employed." The Lutheran interpretation—though certainly not an exclusively Lutheran ideal—relies on a sacred combination of the two definitions. Since God calls us through the Sacrament of Holy Baptism, responsibility is placed upon the Christian to answer his or her call through faithful service in some service to family, neighbor, community, and world—one's vocation. Luther understood vocation to be the calling of God's people for service in God's creation, as well as simply the occupation or work—the station—to which one is called.

ORGANIZATION

This volume is organized in three major sections: the research design, the identity history case studies, and the discussion. Part I details the study's purpose and research questions, as well as the literature review and the methodology. Part II presents narrative case studies of three ELCA colleges and universities. These identity histories tell the stories of Concordia College, Lenoir-Rhyne University, and Gettysburg College based upon significant critical events that shaped each institution over a forty-five-year period. Part III includes a cross-case analysis and features a discussion of the isomorphic influence of secularization, financial viability, and faculty professionalization on the institutional religious identity. A conclusion, which includes the study's implications and suggestions for further research, is contained in the final chapter.

2

Literature Review

ORGANIZATION OF THE LITERATURE REVIEW

THIS STUDY IS INFORMED by literature on organizations, college and university governance, and Lutheran higher education; it is framed by institutional theory and critical events theory. Because the literature review so significantly shapes and directs the study, this review begins with a discussion of institutional theory and critical events theory. While isomorphism and the three related status drivers engaged in the study play critical roles in chapter 7, the cross-case analysis, this organizational change theory also heavily influenced the interview questions. Critical events theory guided the data collection, data analysis, and development of chapters 4, 5, and 6. These chapters contain the case studies of the three schools, the "identity histories," or sagas, which follow a forty-five-year chronological narrative path.

The organizational literature engaged in this review focuses on the topics of mission, identity, and strategy. The college and university governance literature discussed here is intended to demonstrate how decision-making influences identity preservation and diminishment at institutions. Finally, literature on Lutheran higher education is reviewed here for two purposes. First, the literature review is intended to create a composite of ELCA colleges and universities as a distinctive organizational field, an important criterion for studying isomorphism. A clear understanding of how a Lutheran college behaves and envisions its mission is critical to establishing a general composite, or model, of Lutheran higher education. This methodological strategy measures the three schools' expression of their Lutheran identity. Second, the literature review focuses on the few studies that do exist on identity at Lutheran colleges, determining where this dissertation can offer new perspectives to the body of literature. Despite the small number of studies conducted on identity issues related to ELCA colleges and universities, the findings of these studies do provide a valuable description of the ethos, logos, and purpose of these schools.

ISOMORPHISM AND INSTITUTIONAL THEORY LITERATURE

Institutional theory is centrally concerned with the life and behavior of organizations and is the basis of isomorphism. In fact, isomorphism is often referred to as neo-institutionalism. The origins of institutional theory are attributed to American sociologist Philip Selznick, who argued that organizations are shaped by and adapt to both internal and external factors (Hatch, 2006). At its center, institutional theory posits that: "Organizations are driven to incorporate the practices and procedures defined by prevailing rationalized concepts of organizational work and institutionalized society. Organizations that do so increase their legitimacy and their survival prospects, independent of the immediate efficacy of the acquired practices and procedures" (Meyer and Rowan, 1977:340). To the point, organizations are dynamic entities shaped by norms and external environments. Organizational theory should be concerned with the life of organizations (how they are formed, grow, and die), the functioning of organizations, and the impact of organizations on society (Perrow, 2000).

Institutional theory rests upon four basic assumptions. First, it is bidirectional in that both culture and behavior work reciprocally on one another in organizational settings. Second, traditional institutional theory assumes that influence of culture is emphasized over the influence of power. It should be noted, however, that some like Yale Professor of Organization and Management Paul DiMaggio (1988) suggest that the role of power should be restored in this theory in order to strengthen its viability. Third, organizations are more apt to be embedded, or entrenched, rather than move toward change. Finally, institutional theory assumes that human behavior within organizations must be understood in relation to the particular situation being examined. Again, critics challenge this assumption, suggesting that institutional theory would be strengthened if theorists minimize situational specificity when applying the theory in favor of a more generalizable application of institutional concepts related to institutional theory.

The work of organization scholars John Meyer and Brian Rowan (1977) reveals that environmental factors within organizational structures tend to become homogenized, and the organizations subsequently begin to demonstrate similarities with them. Moreover, Meyer and Rowan (1977) contend that organizational survival is based upon an institution's ability to legitimize itself by creating symbols and myths about its culture and functions. As these norms are identified and accepted by external audiences, the organization becomes institutionalized. Thus, an organization's legitimacy is based upon external forces.

Similarly, organizational theorists Jeffrey Pfeffer of UC–Berkeley and Gerald Salancik of UI–Urbana-Champaign (1978) presented a resource dependence model in which organizational legitimacy is derived from external organizations. They argue that no organization is self-contained, and since they depend upon their external environments for resources and legitimacy, the successful organization must first adapt externally and then internally (Pfeffer & Salancik, 1978). Thus, the foundational assumption of the resource dependence theory is that organizations are controlled by their environments. While this research helped to establish the importance of external forces in shaping organizations' success and survival, it also determined that an organization's context reveals significant clues about its activities.

Built upon Meyer and Rowan's work is the theory of institutional isomorphism, also called neo-institutionalism. Yale researchers Paul DiMaggio and Walter Powell considered a specific phenomenon or characteristic in organizations, namely the suspected occurrence of homogeneity in them. Stated another way, they sought to understand what makes organizations similar. In attempting this, DiMaggio and Powell looked to the work of Max Weber, and specifically to rationalization, capitalism, and bureaucratization (the systematic process of a government, corporation, administrative group, or other organization to specialize its functions and adhere to a set of standardized rules).

Weber (1952) explained in *The Protestant Ethic and the Spirit of Capitalism* that rationalization, sparked by capitalism and fueled by the process and momentum of bureaucratization, had created an iron cage that imprisoned humanity. Adopting this metaphor, DiMaggio and Powell (1983) published an influential, oft-cited article, "The Iron Cage Revisited: Institutional Isomorphism and Collective Rationality in Organizational Fields." In the study, they hypothesized that when a group of similar organizations are identified collectively as a specific field, the participants make the organizations increasingly similar in the process of changing them (1983).

While Weber contended that marketplace competition and leaders' desire to control workers caused bureaucratization, DiMaggio and Powell (1983) argued that the causes of bureaucratization had changed, though bureaucracy is still the common form of organization. Bureaucratization arises from organizational structuration, increased interaction among organizations in a single field. As a consequence, the participants within these sharply-defined organizational fields behave with rationality to address change and uncertainty in the organization, which leads, ironically, to homogenization within the field (DiMaggio & Powell, 1983). Theoretically, if Lutheran colleges and universities are defined as an organizational field, then one could examine the phenomenon of homogeneity within the field.

The theory best describing this homogenization process is isomorphism, a constraining process that forces one unit in a population to resemble other units that face the same set of environmental conditions (Hawley, 1968; Hannan & Freeman, 1977; DiMaggio & Powell, 1983). Said another way, institutional isomorphism describes how organizations identified as part of an organizational field change over time to look, function, and behave like the perceived leading organization. Thus, the key ingredient to homogenization is the identification of an established organizational field, comprised of organizations that, in the aggregate, constitute a recognized area of institutional life: key suppliers, resource and product consumers, regulatory agencies, and other organizations that produce service of products. The virtue of this unit of analysis is that it directs attention not simply to competing firms or to interacting networks, but to the totality of relevant actors. In doing this, the field idea comprehends the importance of both connectedness and structural equivalence (DiMaggio & Powell, 1983).

Two types of isomorphism have been identified: competitive and institutional (Hannan & Freeman, 1977; Fennell, 1980; Meyer, 1983; DiMaggio & Powell, 1983). Competitive isomorphism addresses market competition and niche change, which is most appropriate for organizational fields operating in an environment of open competition (DiMaggio & Powell, 1983). Institutional isomorphism, however, also considers the presence of other organizations in the field, in addition to market competition. This is to say that organizations compete for market share and resources, as well as political power and legitimacy. While conformity to institutional norms creates structural similarities in organizations, another normative prescriptive for institutional isomorphism is the broader sociocultural environment (Dacin, 1997). For the study of Lutheran colleges and isomorphic change, sociocultural expectations may very well have a significant influence on organizational change and continuity.

Three assumptions about its process and function guide theories of isomorphism (DiMaggio & Powell, 1983). First, coercive isomorphic change occurs from political influence, formal and informal pressures, and cultural expectations. For instance, certain organizational fields may change (toward conformity) due to a response to mandated industry or government regulations. Second, mimetic isomorphic change occurs from organizational responses to uncertainty (March & Olsen, 1976; DiMaggio & Powell, 1983). For example, uncertainty in the American automobile industry might spark domestic auto makers to emulate successful foreign automobile companies.

Organizations will likely emulate those similar organizations in the field perceived to be successful leaders. Third, normative isomorphic change occurs from professionalization (participants legitimize structures) and socialization (acceptance or recognition through formal education). Examples of normative isomorphic change are hospitals and colleges, institutions that often assess themselves positively if the institution is able to perform as well and offer as much as the competitors. Governance and strategic planning literature, discussed later, will assist in identifying which of these isomorphic functions apply to change among the ELCA colleges and universities.

In their study, DiMaggio and Powell (1983) developed a series of predictors of isomorphic change, constructed in the form of hypotheses.[1]

1. DiMaggio and Powell point out that an empirical test of these predictors is not within the scope of the paper. Instead, the value of the researchers' work is its potential

These predictors are based upon *ceteris paribus* [2] assumptions and are divided into two types of change predictors: organizational-level and field-level (1983). Organizational-level predictors pertain to the speed and degree to which organizations in a field change to emulate other organizations, while field-level predictors describe the isomorphic effects of several identified organizational fields on a specific field. Both predictive types are intended to analyze data on the characteristics of organizations in any field, leading to use of institutional theory in diverse areas. Generally speaking, DiMaggio and Powell's predictors of isomorphic change describe how external and internal forces shape the likelihood that an organization will change to behave like another organization (1983:154–56).

It is worth briefly introducing a notable, contrasting perspective on the field of organizational theory. Population ecology, in comparison to isomorphism, takes a view similar to Pfeffer and Salancik's resource dependence model. Influenced by organizational researchers Michael Hannan and John Freeman's 1977 article, population ecologists assume that organizations rely on external forces to function. This view assumes the environment's point of view over against that of the organization, which potentially affords a useful detachment for more objective evaluation of the organization (Hatch, 2006).

Population ecology takes into consideration a group or field of organizations competing for resources within a single environment (Hannan & Freeman, 1977; Aldrich, 1979). From the perspective of population ecology, organizations do not adapt to the environment, but rather the environment—or the population level—competitively selects the successful organizations. On the other hand, theories of isomorphism suggest that organizations do not change by responding to the environment, but rather emulating institutional norms, protocols, and best practices of the perceived leading organizations. Increasingly, isomorphism is preferred as a viable theory for understanding organizational change; population ecology more resembles a structural theory (Demers, 2007).

A study conducted by Erasmus University researchers Pursey Heugens and Michel Lander (2009) showed the effects of isomorphism on an organization's performance, and alternatively, on identity. The researchers employed a meta-analytical technique to determine, among other things,

---

for predicting organizational change.

2. "Other things being equal."

if conformity to organizational norms enhance or diminish the institution's performance. While Heugens and Lander (2009) concluded that isomorphic template adherence does indeed enhance performance, the most surprising finding was that, specifically, "conformity to institutional ordinances simultaneously improves the *substantive* performance of organizations" (p. 77).[3] This finding contradicts the previously held notion that isomorphism ensures the emulating organization performs more efficiently than non-emulating organizations. As a result, implications for institutional identity could be significant; organizations that avoid emulation may simultaneously maintain identity and function efficiently.

In an exhaustive study of the application of coercive, mimetic, and normative isomorphism, University of Michigan researchers Mark Mizruchi and Lisa Fein examined 160 articles in six American journals that engaged DiMaggio and Powell's oft-cited, influential 1983 work, "The Iron Cage Revisited." Hypothesizing that the majority of researchers focus disproportionately on mimetic isomorphism at the expense of the mimetic and normative techniques, Mizruchi and Fein (1999) argued that the mimetic technique had become the central attraction to DiMaggio and Powell's work because of its applicability to organizational theory. The researchers determined that indeed coercive isomorphism was misused, or at least used when coercive and/or normative isomorphism could have adequately served as an explanation.

The point of Mizruchi and Fein's study and its value to neo-institutionalism is confirmation that isomorphic theory is so widely used by organizational researchers for such diverse hypotheses that imprecise use, or outright misuse, is a potential hazard. The implication for my study is that I did not seek to differentiate between the three forms, since the three primary status drivers that I used—secularization, financial viability, and faculty professionalization—fall into to each of three isomorphic mechanisms.[4] Each of the three isomorphic mechanisms could address the three status drivers my study engages.

Institutional theory is a useful resource for understanding organizational change for three reasons (DiMaggio & Powell, 1983). First, the theory helps to explain organizational homogenization in the presence

---

3. Italics added for emphasis.

4. In their study, Mizruchi and Fein differentiate between "type" and "mechanism." Competitive and institutional are the two isomorphic types, while coercive, mimetic, and normative are isomorphic mechanisms.

of irrational behavior and the absence of innovative ideas. Second, the theory helps to explain the role of political struggle in organizational power, which is not adequately addressed by other theories. Third, the theory could help guide policy in public and private organizations seeking diversity and resisting homogenization. Examining the institutional change of Lutheran colleges and universities through the lens of isomorphism is important and useful for understanding how these institutions understand themselves, how they envision their futures, and how they plan for institutional change.

Organizations like colleges and universities are susceptible to isomorphic change, due to the difficulty in measuring institutional quality (Morphew, 2002). To the point, the procedures and outcomes of colleges and universities, including teaching and learning, are difficult to measure. In the absence of suitable measures, these organizations tend to be judged by prestige and best practices, and subsequently, colleges and universities tend to look and behave like the dominant organization (Meyer and Rowan, 1977; DiMaggio and Powell, 1983; Morphew, 2002a).

Theories of isomorphism allowed me to observe how, if at all, ELCA colleges and universities, through strategic planning and administrative decision-making, seek to preserve or diminish their organizational Lutheran identity. Three components of isomorphism—secularization, financial viability, and faculty professionalization—are utilized in this study and referred to as isomorphic status drivers. Each is discussed in chapter 7, the cross-case analysis, with special attention to how the status drivers affect the preservation or diminishment of Lutheran identity. While I define the 27 Lutheran colleges as a specific organizational field, these organizations also interact with other colleges and universities inside and outside the ELCA college organizational field, especially with regard to the isomorphic status drivers of secularization, financial viability, and faculty professionalization. What role, if any, do these isomorphic status drivers play in the preservation or diminishment of organizational Lutheran identity?

Defining and measuring secularization is not an easy task. After all, what is secularization? Essentially, secularization is the notion that religious authority is in decline in the world (Demerath, 1998). James Arthur (2001), professor at the United Kingdom's Canterbury Church University College, defines secularization simply as the desire to be inclusive and pluralist. Arthur asserts that a college of the church does not become secular through the process of institutional decision-making but rather from a process of erosion. This is to say that secularization is not necessarily intended but occurs eventually as a result of slow, incremental steps. This trend in church-related colleges suggests a shift, or rather a slow drift, toward homogeneity among higher education institutions.

George Marsden defines secularization as "the removal of some activity of life from substantive influences of traditional or organized religion" (1992:16). Marsden further distinguishes between methodological and ideological secularization. The former is the systematic suspension of religious beliefs in order to achieve scientific objectivity, while the latter is reflective of a shift in cultural consensus (Marsden, 1992). Methodological secularization is generally affirmed by religious and non-religious people alike, keeping scientific and technical academic pursuits separate from the religious lens. Roanoke College Professor Robert Benne (2003a) suggests that secularization threatens the religious center of church-related colleges that have never clearly articulated their religious missions and purposes.

Claremont School of Theology Professor Scott Cormode claims that "secularization is in the eye of the scholarly beholder" (Demerath et al., 1998). This is to say that the observer must interpret if isomorphism in the form of borrowing or emulating has occurred, if the original form has been changed. It is not surprising then that identifying, judging, or measuring secularization is a subjective task. With regard to isomorphism, it is important to evaluate secular and religious organizations together in the same organization field in order to understand the secularization process. As has already been established, neo-institutional theory predicts that organizations in the same field will more closely resemble each other over time because of coercive, normative, and mimetic isomorphic influence.

In their book, *Remaking the American University*, Robert Zemsky, Gregory Wegner, and William Massy (2005) draw the metaphor of the lattice and the ratchet, perhaps the clearest explanation of the phenomenon of faculty professionalization. The image of the administrative lattice represents the expansion of the administrative body in colleges and universities, the professionalization of higher education. The other component of the metaphor is the academic ratchet, the force that disengaged and distracted faculty members from attention to the institution in place of focus and energy on professional responsibilities and expectations. These new goals and foci include research, publication, professional service, and personal pursuits (Zemsky, Wegner, & Massy, 2005). Briefly stated, this is the central idea of faculty professionalization and the related pressures of balancing attention to one's discipline and service to one's college or university.

The notion of the lattice and the ratchet does not come without benefits. In fact, faculty members benefitted from the inherent entrepreneurialism afforded by the expansion of the administrative lattice. After all, what is the task of a faculty member? For what work is the faculty member paid? Zemsky, Wegner, and Massey insist that, "As long as a few faculty members were advantaged, there was strong, irresistible pressure to lower the average load for everybody, thus advancing the ratchet by another click" (2005:26). The paradox of this lattice and ratchet, as the authors point out, is that professors who were so well-taught at smallish, teaching-oriented colleges seek in their own academic professions institutions in which teaching and mentoring are deemphasized. One can clearly see how these pressures affect faculty and the small, teaching-oriented emphasis of the Lutheran colleges and universities, at the center of which is the liberal arts foundation.

By the mid-1960s, though certainly sparked by the influx of students created by the G.I. Bill, the notion of mass education for the sake of practicality was prominent in American higher education. However, this trend diminished consensus among American college and university faculties as an array of competing academic agendas emerged. This is to say that academic disciplines began to compete more openly with one another. As colleges and universities emphasized academic specialties and technical skills, the more disciplines and departments within the institution emerged.

To the point, this fragmentation was further emphasized by the growing professionalization of the faculty. Marsden asserts, "For faculty, loyalty to one's profession overwhelms any loyalty to one's current institution" (1992:32). One could see how institutional mission and identity also jeopardized when faculty must choose between one's school and one's discipline. The environmental pressure of faculty professionalization or specialization helped move religious issues to the margins of the university (Marsden, 1992).

Because the faculty environment (especially at research universities) is such that quantity and quality are measurements for professors' performance and value, faculty members are much more likely to fulfill the expectations of their disciplines—their professions—rather than those of their institutions' missions (Albert & Whetten, 1985). Growing membership in faculty unions and professional organizations evidences this movement in faculty commitment and focus. With regard to this study, faculty professionalization raises the question of whether the ideology of the professor will be reflected in the calling *to* the academic discipline or the calling *to* the organization. Organization researchers Blake Ashforth and Fred Mael explain, "Individuals have multiple, loosely coupled identities, and inherent conflicts between their demands are typically not resolved by cognitively integrating the identities, but ordering, separating, and buffering them" (1989:36).

The third status driver, in addition to secularization and faculty professionalization, is the issue of financial viability. It is a basic fact that small colleges, often driven by tuition and fundraising, are particularly sensitive to market effects. The struggle for financial viability is common for most small, private colleges. David Breneman, Economist and University of Virginia Professor of Education, outlined six financial challenges for colleges and universities—particularly small liberal arts colleges—in his 1994 book. Although the book is now fifteen years old, Breneman's arguments and predictions have held true. First, small liberal arts colleges like the ones examined in this study face the pressures of shifting demographics, including high school graduation rates per geographic region. Breneman specifically noted the downward trend of graduating high school students in the northeast, the location and admissions field for Gettysburg College, examined in this study. American demographic changes, especially with regard to an increase in Hispanic and Asian students, loom for colleges and universities in the near future.

Breneman's second economic issue facing liberal arts colleges is the rise in tuition. For many of these colleges, administrators must offer increasing amounts of institutionally funded scholarships, which means tuition discounts. In some cases, institutions are devoting as much as 20 percent of total budgets to student aid (Breneman, 1994). Third, institutions have relied more heavily on discounting as applicant pools become more competitive and as federal financial support has waned. Another economic issue these colleges face is recruiting and retaining quality faculty. Such a demand for esteemed faculty is, of course, essential to the mission of educating students. Today, competition for these faculty members, as well as the increasing salaries they demand, adds pressure the financial viability of private colleges.

Fifth, colleges are growing more and more dependent upon ever-increasing philanthropic dollars and fundraising returns. Institutions are perpetually in campaigns with escalating goals and expectations. Combined with tuition, colleges must depend upon endowment returns and annual giving to balance institutional budgets. A final issue facing small, private colleges is the increasing competition with public universities, and now for-profit higher education centers. Small colleges, often emphasizing small classes, attention to students, and close student-teacher mentoring and teaching, are under greater pressure of offering more while having smaller institutional budgets. Successful competition in the secular marketplace has changed higher education (Albert & Whetten, 1985). Not only is the new paradigm increasingly outcome-orientated, but the same challenges of financial viability still confront small, private colleges.

CRITICAL EVENTS THEORY

The identification of institutional critical events, or turning points, during the thirty-three interviews conducted for the study was vital to the development of a chronological narrative. When asked to name critical events in the college or university's history that shaped the Lutheran identity, the interview participants' responses helped me to analyze, sort, and build an "identity history" of each of the schools, resulting in the framework for the three case studies. These events served as hooks upon which the three historical narratives were unfolded and hung.

University of Virginia Professor of Education Daniel Duke (1995:254) defines critical events as "choice points in an organization's history," representing moments of significant decision-making that shaped the organization, both of which call for detailed investigation and explanation.[5] Arguing against the equal appraisal of past events in an organization's history, Duke employed critical events theory in his study of Thomas Jefferson High School in Richmond, Virginia. For his organizational history of the both successful and beleaguered public school, Duke (1995) chose

---

5. Qualitative researcher Elizabeth Chell describes critical events theory, the term I use in the study, as the critical incident technique (CIT).

representative events that demonstrated the development of the school's specific culture, as well as selected events that illustrated challenges to this organizational culture.

Critical events theory boasts several advantages for the organizational historian (Chell, 1998; Chell & Adam, 1994). First, the technique is a useful strategy because it captures the individual realities of the sites and issues studied and explains what goes on in organizations, which give insights into how behavior and decision-making is shaped. Second, the method allows for the researcher to identify and compare common themes and patterns of critical events in one case or among multiple cases. Third, the researcher's focus on uncovering critical events facilitates revelation of the issues centrally important to the interview participant. Fourth, critical events theory enables participants' responses to be understood in the context of their own specific frame of reference, feelings, and perspectives.

Finally, critical events theory allows a structure for thick description of participants' experiences and detailed explanation of these events, allowing for interview participants to offer their unique recollections on the organization's significant incidences. The researcher's understanding and explanation of these organizational events is critically important to building a credible historical narrative. As Duke (1995:254) explained, "Description without explanation is like food consumption in the absence of taste and smell." Thus, the identification and description of critical events in the histories of the three schools not only gave shape to the narratives but also meaning.

ORGANIZATIONAL LITERATURE: MISSION, IDENTITY, AND STRATEGY

Since this study builds a narrative history of three organizations over a forty-five-year period, it is important to note three elements of historical research. In developing an organizational history, the researcher must describe the life of the organization in its various stages of development, select organizational aspects to be described, and to reflect on the meaning of the organization's history (Duke, 1995). This approach to historical research can effectively trace an organization's history, defined by Duke (1995:240) as "systematic inquiry intended to describe, explain, and find meaning in the creation and evolution of particular organizations." Mission, identity, and strategy all play roles in the development of an organization's historical narrative.

In the past 30 years, evidence has shown that isomorphic change processes have affected and continue to affect the diverse field of higher education institutions (Morphew, 2002b). Institutions with very specific missions and purposes—single-sex colleges, private two-year colleges, and colleges that have changed to university status, for instance—have ignored some of their traditional missions and underserved some of their students (Morphew, 2002b). Such evidence could have implications for Lutheran colleges, institutions that similarly profess a specific mission and reflect distinctive institutional characteristics.

Mission statements of colleges and universities of all institutional types appear to be a requirement for either legitimizing the institution, articulating a shared vision for the institution, or both (Morphew and Hartley, 2006). In their study, Morphew and Hartley (2006) examined the content of more than 300 randomly selected mission statements of colleges and universities to determine whether the statements were expressions of institutional distinctiveness or obligatory rhetorical statements made by institutions. Morphew and Hartley (2006) found that institutional type (public or private) is more important at predicting mission statement content than is Carnegie Classification. The researchers also concluded that a few characteristics (commitment to diversity and liberal arts education) appear across institutional types, and that a commitment to service, though understood differently per school, appears across institutional types. In my own study, the analysis of mission statements promises to provide a deeper understanding of institutional self-identification at Lutheran colleges and universities.

Similarly, a study of Roman Catholic colleges and universities investigated mission statements of representative institutions as part of an analysis of their Roman Catholic identity and a categorization of dominant institutional values (Estanek, James, & Norton, 2006). This study was based upon the assumption that all Roman Catholic colleges and universities demonstrate the values and principles of their faith identity, and that the mission statements are the public forums for articulating these values and principles (Estanek, James, & Norton, 2006). The researchers found that the analyzed mission statements reflect a collective vision of Roman Catholic higher education and demonstrate this identity to be embedded in institutions' foundational heritage and sponsorship, the constituents they serve, and their particular definitions of educational experience (Estanek, James, and Norton, 2006). Serving as a model, this study of Roman Catholic colleges and universities proved helpful in my study of the similar, but smaller population of Lutheran schools.

An assessment of Christian institutions of higher education in England highlighted their identities and missions, arguing that church-related colleges and universities must continually evaluate and determine the most appropriate expression of their mission (Arthur, 2001). This is not to say that these Christian colleges should change their mission but instead take seriously how the mission is publicly stated, applied, and lived out. While church-related colleges are not a homogeneous group and do demonstrate their missions and diverse theological perspectives differently, the bigger question of homogeneity among *all* colleges and universities is significant.

Reflecting the previously mentioned theory of isomorphism, Christian colleges show signs of shifting toward homogeneity while paradoxically addressing complex contemporary challenges like pluralism and fragmentation (Arthur, 2001). Within this tension, mission statements, which can sometimes be ineffective and ignored, have the potential to spark inspiration and purpose among members of the organization. For this potential to be realized, administrators must invite faculty and staff to participate in the development and evolution of the statement.

Similarly, Baylor University Management Professor Duane Ireland and Texas A&M University Business Professor Michael Hitt (1992) also advocated the potential of mission statements to provide direction and inspiration to organizations. Their work focused on a small, private preparatory school and its tumultuous process of developing an institutional mission statement. Ireland and Hitt argued that aiding strategic decision-making is the key reason for developing and implementing a mission statement, describing such statements as "the glue that binds organizations together, proclaims corporate purpose, and provides motivation, general direction, image of character, tone, and inspiration" (1992:34). Ireland and Hitt offered two particularly useful conclusions: mission statements must be supported and endorsed by top level managers, and mission statements must be used to consistently guide strategic decisions and action. Given this scholarship on mission and mission statements, how do the two colleges and one university investigated in this study understand and implement their own institutional mission statements?

Related to mission are identity and strategy. While organizational identity discusses an institution's defining attributes, organizational strategy defines how the institution realizes its identity (Ashforth & Mael, 1996). Social interaction, relationships, and social identity theory are the foundation upon which organizational identity research has been conducted (Albert & Whetten, 1985; Ashforth & Mael, 1989; Dutton & Dukerich, 1991; Hatch & Schultz, 2004). Perhaps the best working definition of organizational identity comes from groundbreaking organization researchers Stuart Albert and David Whetten (1985), who explained identity as an organization's self-description of what is central and distinctive about itself.

Interest in individual identity, if not organizational, is not new. Plato argued that a specific identity manifests differently in each individual, while Aristotle believed multiple identities occurred within each person (Gioia, 1998). Twentieth century social science research (Cooley, 1902; Mead, 1934) prepared the path for the eventual work on organizational identity, ushered by Albert and Whetten's pioneering work in the 1980s (Gioia, 1998). Foundational to organizational identity is social identity theory, which describes individuals as defining and ordering themselves based upon self-perceived distinctiveness that distinguishes them from and characterizes them within sets of groups (Erickson, 1964); Steele, 1988; Gioia, 1998).

Arguing that organizational identity is defined by the way internal participants interpret the organization, Dutton and Dukerich (1991) drew the explicit connection between individual identity and organizational identity. Organizations define themselves by identifying institutional themes and locating themselves within these themes. Organizational identity is created over time through articulation of members' needs and experiences, a process that results in an embedding of members' collective identity in the organization. Said another way, organizational identity is self-identified as central to the organization, distinctive to the organization, and enduring to the organization (Albert & Whetten, 1985). Although a strong identity can significantly influence organizational behavior and attitudes, it can also spark resistance to change (Ashforth & Mael, 1996). At ELCA colleges and universities, the degree of Lutheran engagement varies widely (ELCA, 2007), but those institutions firmly grasping the Lutheran tradition may experience difficulty in either initiating change or in the change process itself.

Albert and Whetten (1985) suggest a dual identity organizational model to understand the multiple dimensions of an organization's identity that develop over time, illustrating this duality using the modern research university as an example. They hypothesize that the university embodies a dual identity of a church and a business. The church represents the normative dimension of the organization, the business the utilitarian dimension. They define the concept of normative identity as directed by ideology and centered on the cultural or educational functions of the organization (Parsons, 1960), and the utilitarian organization as managed by information and oriented toward economic production (Albert & Whetten, 1985). In suggesting this duality, the researchers are essentially arguing that organizations like the religiously-affiliated university evolve toward dual identities, thus impeding the ability to fully live out their religious identity.

Similarly, organization researchers Mary Jo Hatch and Majken Schultz (2004) contend that organizational identity results from a dynamic and relational process of both culture and image. This is to say that organizations create their identities through a mirroring process based upon external perceptions of the organization's image and culture, as well as internal perceptions. Further, when internal members critically reflect on the organization's identity, then this identity is more deeply embedded in the organization's culture, or as Hatch and Schultz explain, "we see reflexivity in organizational identity dynamics as the process by which organizational members understand and explain themselves as an organization" (2004:387). Thus, organizational culture and image significantly influence identity through social process.

A study by Pennsylvania State University researchers Dennis Gioia, Majken Schultz, and Kevin Corley (2000) suggests that organizational identity is actually dynamic. This is to say that organizations are not bound to a stagnant identity. Acknowledging the relationship between organizational identity and image demonstrates how flexibility of identity fosters change (Gioia, Schultz, & Corley, 2000). Critically speaking, this view is a departure from traditional literature on organizational identity, though it is shared by University of Michigan researcher Jane Dutton and University of Texas researcher Janet Dukerich (1991), who claim that identity and image function together to influence an organization's actions. Both studies' findings hold promise for understanding how Lutheran colleges can simultaneously adapt to isomorphic changes, emulate non-Lutheran institutions, and preserve their religious identity.

In a 2001 single-case study, researchers investigated a young Norwegian university,[6] using a qualitative design to understand if an institution of higher education adopts innovations and standards for purposes of legitimacy and survival. Despite the study's limitation of analyzing only one particular school, its findings suggest that higher education institutions address the tension of innovation and homogenization in the isomorphic change process, while continually struggling to shape its identity (Stensaker & Norgard, 2001). For my study, the findings can explain how mimetic, coercive, and normative isomorphic forces affect Lutheran colleges in the process of institutional change and the continuity of institutional identity.

Organizational identity holds potential to be valuable as a source of competitive advantage. A clearly defined and understood organizational identity can inform and direct decision-makers' choices about what is most important and in the best interest of the institution (Stimpert, Gustafson, & Sarason, 1998). James Collins and Jerry Porras (1994) echo this notion in their widely-read book, *Built to Last*, in which they point to identity, or core ideology, as a roadmap for institutional strategy and action. Of the venerable and successful Johnson and Johnson, Hewlett-Packard, and Merck, they write, "They articulated what was inside of them—what was in their gut, what was bone deep . . . The key word is authenticity" (Collins & Porras, 1994:78). The articulation of a clear, confident institutional identity can inspire in organizational members—faculty, staff, students, and administrators alike—a sense of mission. Such an understanding of organizational identity can enhance institutional strategic planning and effectiveness (Stimpert, Gustafson, & Sarason, 1998).

In addition to institutional identity, strategic planning has begun to attract greater attention in college and university decision-making. And the relationship between strategic planning and identity is evident. Identity plays a significant role in organizational strategic-planning, decision-making, and action (Gioia & Thomas, 1996). In fact, since the mid-1990s, more and more colleges and universities have begun to rely on institutional strategic planning (Edge, 2004). Strategic planning involves the

6. Stensaker and Norgard studied the first thirty years (1969–1999) of the University of Tromso, Norway's fourth national university.

process of making, implementing, and evaluating decisions intended to assist an organization in fulfilling its mission, including the strategy of responding to future events that affect the organization (Fidler, 1989; Byars, 1991). Additionally, a strategic plan must be systematic and measurable, and it must answer three basic questions: (1) Where are we? (2) Where do we want to be? And (3) how do we get there? (Edge, 2004).

Strategic planning, or strategy, has been perceived traditionally as a positioning issue. However, Harvard Business Professor Michael Porter re-imagines the notion of strategy, distinguishing it from operational effectiveness. In his article, "What Is Strategy?" Porter argues that strategy is not simply operational effectiveness, which means "performing similar activities better than rivals perform them" (Porter, 1996:62). Rather, operational effectiveness and strategy work together to ensure an organization's ability to identify and establish a difference that it can sustain. The organization must find its niche and perform the function or service in a way its competitors cannot duplicate. Thus, Porter is careful to distinguish that operational effectiveness and strategy are not the same thing.

Porter's (1996) central argument is that successful strategy and strategic positioning involve identifying unique business activities, making necessary competitive trade-offs, and crafting an appropriate fit within the organization's activities. First, Porter contends that the successful organization must identify unique activities it can offer, maintaining attention to the specific needs of many customers, the broad needs of specific customers, or broad needs of a large customer segment in a narrow market. Second, strategic organizations must make trade-offs, or decisions, about their activities in the marketplace. In particular, organizations must choose which activities they will adopt and which activities they will discontinue or choose not to adopt. These important decisions, often difficult, are critical to defining the organization's identity and business activity. Third, the strategic organization must coordinate a proper fit among its activities. This means that the decisions the organization has made regarding trade-offs (what it will and will not do) affects the fit between these defined and chosen activities. In other words, the fit must ensure the activities will be strategically coordinated and mutually supportive.

External planning—focusing on outside opportunities and influences—is another method for determining an organization's strengths, weaknesses, opportunities, threats, and overall strategic position (Bommer &

Janaro, 2005). A successful integrative model for college and university strategic planning determines the organizational mission, objectives, recruiting strategy, and student-winners and qualifiers (Bommer & Janaro, 2005). Such a model must include competitive benchmarks, performance measurements, and targets. However, benchmarking and emulating aspirant institutions threatens to diminish the distinctiveness, the *identity*, of organizations (Gioia & Thomas, 1996).

COLLEGE AND UNIVERSITY GOVERNANCE LITERATURE

The responsibilities and expectations of governing boards directly affect how organizations change, especially with regard to how governance directs strategic planning. Governing board responsibilities are wide and varied, including identification of mission, strategic planning, programmatic review, resource development, sufficient institutional management, board self-assessment, and presidential selection, support and assessment (Fisher, 1991; Ingram, 1993). Trustees must also maintain institutional assets, develop policy, ensure that stewardship of assets supports institutional mission, and advocate institutional interests to the legislature and wider public (Altbach, Berdahl, & Gumport, 2005).

Affirming these basic responsibilities, liberal education advocate and former Dartmouth President James Freedman (2004) adds that college trustees and leaders also hold the duties of nurturing tangible assets (endowment, for instance) and intangible (academic freedom) assets. Former University of California President Clark Kerr and research partner Marian Gade (1989) summarize trustees' responsibilities by naming them "guardians." These functions that are expected to be fulfilled by governing bodies, in turn, affect the direction an institution is ultimately steered, which determines its identity and mission.

Given these expectations of governing boards, trustees and presidents are not necessarily in a position to prioritize preservation of religious identity, if that is even an institutional priority. In fact, in the 2001 Survey of Higher Education Governance, governing boards and administrators at private colleges like the twenty-seven ELCA institutions identified traditional spiritual values as the fourth mission and policy priority, after quality, management, and finance (Kaplan, 2004). While for-profit organizations primarily seek to maximize profits, nonprofit institutions identify objective functions based upon institutional mission, which varies from organization to organization (Pusser & Turner, 2004). Governance at ELCA colleges and universities will determine these institutional functions and priorities based upon their missions.

Generally speaking, the principles of governing boards apply both to corporate models and to college and university boards (Hermalin, 2004). Having said this, two studies on governing boards and institutional performance are worth noting. The researchers in the first study sought to link governing boards and corporate performance in a case-based study of three corporate governance theories. Three central themes emerged: (1) boards must clearly understand the needs and mission of the organization; (2) boards must clearly understand the desires and expectations of the organization's stakeholders; and (3) boards of nonprofit organizations must measure institutional performance against their ability to mobilize resources, and more important to this study, to achieve institutional mission (Nicholson & Kiel, 2007). While the findings speak primarily to corporate governance, the results could have implications that could be extrapolated to higher education governance, as suggested by Hermalin (2004).

A second study examined the relationship between board composition—particularly the effects of insider/outsider status of its members—and organizational performance. Most important for a study of ELCA colleges and universities is the finding that a governing board composed of outsiders is more likely to have positive effects on organizational performance (Wagner, Stimpert, & Fubara, 1998). If this finding holds true for higher education institutions, then it could challenge the widely-held policy at some ELCA colleges and universities that governing boards must be composed of a minimum number of Lutherans, or *insiders*. These ELCA board composition policies, though not universally held at all ELCA colleges, are intended to ensure a minimum number of Lutherans (clergy and laypersons) for the purpose of confidently articulating the Lutheran tradition and core institutional mission. Critically speaking, is a non-Lutheran sufficiently considered an outsider for the purposes of this study? Since no similar studies exist in the body of research on Lutheran colleges, both studies' findings could help to reveal connections between Lutheran college and university boards and institutional performance.

LUTHERAN HIGHER EDUCATION LITERATURE

The purpose of Lutheran higher education literature in this review is primarily to explain its nature and characteristics, in general, and of the ELCA colleges and universities, in particular. Embracing a clear understanding of these schools as a specific kind of organizational field is vital to operationalizing theories of isomorphism. Education, alongside worship, is a central tenet of Lutheran theology (Gritsch, 1994). A distinctive institutional mark on Lutheran college and university identity is their connection, at varying levels according to the institution, to the Lutheran tradition.

Institutional theory requires the presence of a distinguishing organizational field, in this case, Lutheran colleges. For the purposes of this study, I argue that the twenty-seven Lutheran colleges and universities constitute a specific organizational field, though institutions may also affiliate with other organizational groups. Literature on Lutheran higher education helps to develop a characteristic composite of this Lutheran organizational field.

The distinctiveness of Lutheran higher education mission is found in its particular theology, calling for the pursuit of knowledge simply for the sake of knowledge and learning for the sake of ultimately serving one's neighbor through vocation, from the Latin term *vocat*, which means "call." Indeed, the clear articulation of, steadfast attention to, and careful development of vocation is at the core of what it means to be a Lutheran college (Benne & Christenson, 2008; Olson, 2006; Dovre, 2006; Christenson, 2005; Bunge, 2002; Schwehn, 1993).

Steeped in paradox, Lutheran higher education holds in tension the Law and the Gospel, Christ and culture, and the two hands of Luther's two kingdoms doctrine (the Lutheran doctrine explaining that separate heavenly and earthly realms exist, and humans interact with one another in society in this earthly realm) (Schwehn, 1999). Lutheran higher education is marked by freedom of inquiry, exploration of vocation, and a commitment to faculty mentoring of students (Christenson, 2004). The Lutheran doctrines of Christian vocation and the two kingdoms motivate education and allow faith and learning to co-exist, underscoring the importance of faithful inquiry open to all at Lutheran colleges and universities, whether the student or faculty member is Christian or non-Christian (Dovre, 2002).

The five central characteristics of Lutheran higher education are the paradoxical nature of Lutheran theology, the Christian freedom of intellectual inquiry, the priesthood of all believers, the theology of the two kingdoms, and the concept of vocation, in which all are called to express—or live out—one's baptism by serving one's neighbor (Solberg, 1997). In light of this literature, the present study seeks to identify the value and incentive, if any, for these specific colleges to preserve Lutheran identity. Moreover, can institutional isomorphism and strategic planning occur in a way that achieves strategic goals, while preserving institutional identity?

In his book, *Quality with Soul*, Roanoke College[7] Professor of Religion Robert Benne (2001) investigates how six colleges and universities maintain strong ties with their faith traditions.[8] A significant contribution of the book is a four-point typology of church-related colleges. Briefly, the typology classifies church-affiliated colleges and universities as orthodox (marked by a unanimous Christian commitment to the institutional ethos), critical-mass (marked by an insistence that *some* believers in the institutional faith tradition populate all constituencies of the college), intentionally pluralist (marked by a tacit commitment to the faith tradition, intentionally placing members of the tradition in important institutional roles), and accidentally pluralist (very little to no commitment to the institution's faith tradition). Benne's typology is particularly important to this study, as it will play a significant role in the empirical design, explained in the next chapter, the methodology.

Whereas Benne outlines four models of the church-related college in *Quality with Soul*, he also speaks to specific characteristics, if not models, of Lutheran colleges in an essay in religious commentator Richard Cimino's book, *Lutherans Today* (2003).[9] Citing the work of H. Richard Niebuhr and James Burtchaell, Benne questions whether the Lutheran center—its core identity—can sustain. Benne (2001; 2003a) points to Niebuhr's (1956) identification of the Christ and Culture in Paradox tradition (expressed by the Lutheran tradition), the Christ Above Culture

---

7. Roanoke is a college of the ELCA, located in Salem, Virginia.

8. Benne's study investigates schools from the Christian Reformed tradition (Presbyterian), the Evangelical tradition, the Baptist tradition, the Roman Catholic tradition, and two schools from the Lutheran tradition.

9. Benne also comments on the characteristics of these traditions in *Quality with Soul* (202).

tradition (expressed by the Roman Catholic tradition), and the Christ Transforming Culture tradition (expressed by the Reformed tradition).

Benne also notes Burtchaell's typologies, or confluences, of the Lutheran tradition: the more liberal East Coast "Americanist Lutherans" of the Lutheran Church in America and the more centrist Upper Midwest "Confessing Lutherans" of the American Lutheran Church (1998:459–61).[10] Of these two groups, Gettysburg College and Lenoir-Rhyne University come from the Americanist Lutheran tradition, whereas Concordia College would be considered to be Confessional Lutheran. Generally speaking, the Confessional Lutheran colleges and universities are historically more closely connected with the church than their Americanist counterparts.

Other scholars of Lutheran higher education have also suggested models of church-related colleges. First, Concordia College Professor of Religion Ernest Simmons[11] (1998) identifies four models of faith and learning, based upon theologian Ian Barbour's (1997) and philosopher Greg Muilenberg's (1997) work. The first is the conflict model, in which issues of faith must prevail over learning; religion and science, for instance, are in conflict. The second is the independence model in which faith and learning are separated and each is given autonomy; such a complete separation, however, is not possible.

Integration is the third model, which seeks to resolve all truth and understanding within the perspective and context of Christianity and God's sovereignty. The Roman Catholic and Reformed traditions are examples of this model. The last model, which is most congruent with the Lutheran tradition of faith and learning, is the dialogue model. Simmons explains, "While each sphere (faith and learning) has its own integrity, there is an overt attempt to make connections, to approach their interaction in a constructive manner that is mutually beneficial. The dialogue model requires academic freedom if each side is to have the opportunity to pursue its respective endeavors with integrity" (1998:6).

---

10. Burtchaell lists a third cohort, which is represented today by the Lutheran Church-Missouri Synod, not included in this study. It should also be noted that the Lutheran Church in America (LCA) and the American Lutheran Church (ALC) merged in 1988 to form the present-day ELCA.

11. Ernest Simmons is included as an interview participant in chapter 4, the Concordia College chapter.

Second, Capital University[12] Professor of Religion Tom Christenson (2004) also traces four models, which he calls prototypes for expressing faith-relatedness in higher education. Type A is exemplified by church-related colleges that maintain identity by the recognizable religious figures within the campus community. For instance, the religious identity might be personified almost exclusively by the chaplain or religion department. The second type is based upon behavioral expectations of the members of the college community. This behavior might include expectations like chapel attendance or restrictions like prohibition of the use of alcohol, for instance. Type C colleges are ones that express their church-relatedness by expecting theological conformity of its faculty, staff, and students.

The last prototype is one in which the identity is defined by the college's epistemology, anthropology, pedagogy, and ethos. Type D best describes the Lutheran tradition of faith and learning. Christenson describes his vision of Lutheran higher education: "A Lutheran college/university is one that pursues the essential tasks of a university in a way informed by Lutheran theology, particularly as it shapes an understanding of what it means to be human (a Lutheran anthropology), the enterprise of knowing and learning (a Lutheran epistemology), and our understanding of community" (2004:11).

A third concept of church-related colleges and universities is offered by Darrell Jodock (2002), Professor of Religion at Gustavus Adolphus College.[13] First, Jodock suggests a sectarian model characterized by religious uniformity within a religious enclave set apart from secular culture. The second model, non-sectarian, mirrors society, seeking to achieve uniformity by diminishing and avoiding religious differences. Jodock argues that Lutheran higher education is best characterized by a third model, which is neither sectarian nor non-sectarian. In this model, the college builds its institutional identity upon its religious-affiliation, but it does so in a way that engages, participates, and serves society beyond the boundaries of its campus. This model also recognizes the religious diversity among its community participants, acknowledges the inherent struggle, and continues to maintain its Lutheran core.

Jodock (2002) also explains Lutheran college identity in terms of internal and external issues. The internal issue involves the institution's

12. Capital University is one of the ELCA colleges, located in Columbus, Ohio.

13. Gustavus Adolphus College, one of the ELCA colleges, is located in St. Peter, Minnesota. Jodock has written and spoken extensively on Lutheran higher education.

self-assessment of identity and values and the way it expresses, or lives out, its purpose. The second issue is the relationship between the colleges and the church. Jodock poses two related questions: Why should the church have colleges at all, and why should the college be related to the church? Jodock (2002) explains that the Lutheran church founded colleges for the purposes of educating lay and clergy church leaders, as well as educating students for community leadership. Both of these purposes are strongly connected to the ideal of vocation and serving God and neighbor. Lutheran colleges are intended to function in a climate of academic freedom made possible by both the restorative power of the gospel message and the tradition of wisdom and reason. Jodock answers the second question by explaining that the college needs a connection to the church because of the Lutheran tradition's bedrock foundation of the liberal arts, "those studies which aim to set people free" (2002:7).

Not simply understanding, but clearly articulating what it means to be a Lutheran college, should be of paramount concern to Lutheran college leaders. The scholarship reviewed here provides a snapshot of Lutheran higher education's character and ideals, which could serve as a useful tool in communicating these ideals to Lutheran college stakeholders and prospective students. Mark Schwehn, Dean of Christ College at Valparaiso University, writes, "evangelicals like Mark Noll and leading experts in the field of Christian higher education like Richard Hughes have recently observed that Lutherans have implicitly and potentially the best theology of higher education in our time, though neither one of these scholars believes that it has yet been articulated with the force and vigor it needs" (2002:214).[14]

SUMMARY

The work addressed in this literature review shows that: (1) institutional players have a significant effect on shaping organizational identity; (2)

14. Robert Benne cautions against too narrowly defining the distinctive marks of Lutheran higher education. Doing so threatens to undercut, or miss, the tradition's Christian mission. At its foundation, though, Lutheran Christianity is Trinitarian, confessional, and embracing of its tradition—a tradition that emphasizes the ideas of vocation, justification by grace through faith, the dialectic of Law and Gospel, the Two Kingdoms, and the messiness of all of these overlapping concepts. Lutheran colleges and universities can be important vessels for preserving and transferring this tradition and its ideals.

institutional identity is dynamic; (3) college governing boards and presidents significantly shape institutional mission through strategic planning; and (4) colleges and universities of the Evangelical Lutheran Church in America (at variable degrees) are institutions committed to freedom of inquiry, exploration of vocation, and faithful inquiry open to people of diverse faith (and non-theistic) traditions.

Missing in the literature are any empirical studies on isomorphic change in colleges and universities of the ELCA. Perhaps most important, this study, unlike previous scholarship, seeks to analyze Lutheran college identity through the lens of organizational theory. This study fills the literature gap by informing how, if at all, institutional decision-making and strategic planning shape isomorphic change due to secularization, financial viability, and faculty professionalization, and whether organizational Lutheran identity is preserved in this process.

3

Methodology

PHASE I: SAMPLING PLAN

THE EMPIRICAL STRATEGY OF this study follows a two-phase mixed methods design. This approach is appropriate because of the nature of the research questions asked; one is suitably answered by a quantitative design (*which* colleges), while the others are better answered by a qualitative design (*why* these colleges and *what* is happening at these colleges) (Strauss & Corbin, 1998). Phase I is the simple quantitative portion of the empirical strategy, essentially the sample selection phase, in which a specific population of schools was examined and three were selected for case studies in Phase II.

The population of this study is primarily the twenty-seven colleges and universities of the Evangelical Lutheran Church in America (Appendix A). A typology model, proposed by religious higher education scholar and Roanoke College Professor of Religion Robert Benne (2001), classifies religiously-affiliated colleges and universities among four categories. In considering a sample selection strategy, I consulted several similar typologies from other studies (Christenson, 2004; Riley, 2005; Morey & Piderit, 2006). However, Benne's typology is most suited for this specific sample because it allows for several illustrative and objective criteria to be used in situating the twenty-seven institutions within the appropriate typology.

Benne's four categories, or types, of church-related colleges include orthodox, critical-mass, intentionally pluralist, and accidentally pluralist. Benne (2001:48) describes this typology model as a method for locating colleges and universities "somewhere between the poles of 'fully Christian' on one side and complete secularization on the other." It should be clearly noted that Benne's typology does not exclusively classify Lutheran colleges, but rather church-related colleges in general.

For the purpose of sample selection in my study, the twenty-seven Lutheran colleges were placed within Benne's four categories based upon their level of church-relatedness, as opposed to their particular demonstration of Lutheran characteristics. Since Benne (2001) suggests that no ELCA college may fit the criteria for the orthodox typology, one college will be chosen for each of the other three typologies of church-related colleges—critical mass, intentionally pluralistic, and accidentally pluralistic—for detailed case studies in Phase II of the research design. These typologies will be explained in greater detail.

Specifically, I employed the classic Benne typology in the following manner. Benne suggests a list of issues, or "major divides," to be used as determinative criteria (2001:49). From this list, I selected six objective criteria for locating the twenty-seven ELCA colleges and universities within the four categories. To help ensure trustworthiness, I vetted the selection of the six objective criteria with administrators at these schools and at the ELCA to determine the appropriateness of these criteria (Creswell, 1994; Krathwohl, 1998). These six objective criteria are chapel attendance policy, presidential denominational (Lutheran) requirement policy, board (Lutheran) membership policy, percentage of Lutheran faculty, percentage of Lutheran students, and financial dependence upon the church. These six objective criteria capture characteristics reflective of institutional priority and are influenced by institutional planning, administrative decision-making, and school policy.

I collected data for the six objective criteria in three ways. First, I collected data regarding presidential selection requirements and Lutheran student percentages from the Vocation and Education Office of the ELCA.[1] Second, I telephoned each of the twenty-seven college and university presidents' offices to determine chapel attendance policies, percentages of Lutheran faculty, board membership policies, and financial dependence

1. I offer special thanks to the ELCA staff in the Division for Vocation and Education, especially Marilyn Olson, Kathy Baker, and Arne Quanbeck, for providing me these data.

upon the church.[2] Third, the Lutheran Educational Consortium of North America (LECNA), an independent group representing the interests of all Lutheran schools from different Lutheran bodies in the United States and Canada, including the ELCA, made available its longitudinal data, though I did not rely upon it heavily.

Upon collection of data from the schools, I completed the sorting and analysis worksheet (Appendix B). Data were analyzed by using simple descriptive statistics, sorting the survey responses into the four typologies of church-related colleges and universities (Miles & Huberman, 1994). The matrix details all twenty-seven ELCA colleges and universities in the vertical column with the objective criteria arranged in the subsequent six columns. Each institution was scored on a scale of whole numbers, one through four, reflecting Benne's four characterizations of church-related colleges (Appendix C). A mark of numeral one indicates *accidentally pluralist*; a numeral two indicates *intentionally pluralist*; a numeral three indicates *critical mass*; and a numeral four indicates *orthodox*. After the colleges and universities were matched against Benne's criteria and thus characterized by typology, I sorted them into the following table for sample selection:

Table 1: Summary Sorting Grid of Schools by Benne's Four Typologies

Orthodox	Critical-Mass	Intentionally Pluralistic	Accidentally Pluralistic
None	Augsburg College Augustana College (SD) Concordia College Finlandia University Gustavus Adolphus College Luther College Pacific Lutheran University St. Olaf College Texas Lutheran College Wartburg College	Augustana College (IL) Bethany College California Lutheran University Capital University Carthage College Dana College Grandview University Lenoir-Rhyne University Midland Lutheran College Newberry College Roanoke College Susquehanna University Thiel College Wittenberg University	Gettysburg College Muhlenberg College Wagner College

2. In some cases, the presidents' staffs directed me to other campus offices for data collection, including the Offices of the Provost or Academic Dean, the Chaplain, and Institutional Research.

Benne (2001) describes orthodox schools as publically and comprehensively affirming Christian life, requiring all members of the community to subscribe to the common statement of belief. To reiterate, Benne (2001) suggests that none of the ELCA schools likely demonstrate characteristics of orthodoxy. Accordingly, this study focuses on the next three typologies. Critical mass colleges, according to Benne (2001), do not maintain that all community members affirm the Christian tradition but rather insist that a critical mass of Christians, defined differently per school, be present throughout all areas of the campus community.

While the orthodox and critical mass schools understand the Christian faith to be a central paradigm for imagining their mission, colleges categorized as intentionally pluralistic and accidentally pluralistic do not envision the Christian faith as normative to their campus communities. Benne (2001:52) explains that the intentionally pluralistic college "respects (the) sponsoring (religious) heritage enough that it intentionally places members of that heritage in important positions, starting with the president," and demonstrates "straightforward or tacit commitment" to the ethos of the sponsoring heritage. Finally, accidentally pluralistic colleges and universities do not function out of specific strategic commitment to their faith tradition, instead leaving any church-relatedness to chance (Benne, 2001). Choosing one school from each of these typologies will facilitate useful comparisons between the institutions (Maxwell, 2005).

Once the institutions were sorted by typology, purposeful selection directed which particular schools within each typology were chosen for Phase II (Maxwell, 2005; Creswell, 2007). Purposeful selection is an appropriate strategy because it can help achieve representativeness, heterogeneity, specific selection critical for engaging the theories of the study, and specific selection for the purpose of comparison (Maxwell, 2005). Whether this strategy is called purposeful sampling (Patton, 1990) or criterion-based selection (LeCompte & Preissle, 1993), purposeful selection is appropriate in this study because the strategy engages panels of people (or institutions, in this case) that are uniquely able to represent a specific perspective or event (Maxwell, 2005). Additionally, I selected alternate colleges and universities for each of the typologies in the event that one declined participation.

After the twenty-seven colleges and universities were sorted into Benne's three categories, I used purposive selection to choose one from each for detailed examination in the case study chapters. From the critical-mass colleges, I chose Concordia, arguably the ELCA college most closely connected to the Lutheran tradition. What is indisputable, though, is that Concordia College boasts the highest percentage of Lutherans among its student body. Additionally, Concordia is home of two of the most significant figures in Lutheran higher education scholarship, Paul Dovre and Ernest Simmons. Their participation would prove to be a windfall to the study. Finally, choosing a Midwestern Lutheran college among the sixteen situated in that Lutheran-rich region would be an attempt to broadly represent the ethos of that region's schools.

The decision to choose Lenoir-Rhyne from the intentionally pluralistic category was based primarily on two reasons. First, the Lenoir-Rhyne Board of Trustees voted in August 2008 to change the institution from college to university status. Strategic planning and decision-making related to this shift would be an interesting and textured backdrop behind the already complex Lenoir-Rhyne saga. Second, Lenoir-Rhyne's geographical distinction as a Lutheran school in the South, a rarity, played an important role in shaping the Lenoir-Rhyne story.

Finally, I chose Gettysburg College from Benne's accidentally pluralistic category based upon several reasons. First, like the Midwestern Concordia and the Southern Lenoir-Rhyne, Gettysburg's inclusion was based upon its geographical location in the Northeast. Incidentally, the other two accidentally pluralistic colleges were also located in the Northeast: Muhlenberg College in Allentown, Pennsylvania, and Wagner College on Staten Island, New York. Second, Gettysburg was the first Lutheran college founded in America in 1832, which provided a rich longevity from which to draw. A third reason, related to its founding, was the college's significant history shaped by early Lutheran leader, Samuel Simon Schmucker, its founder. Last, Gettysburg has built arguably the finest national reputation among all of the twenty-seven ELCA colleges and universities, a distinction that provides yet another interesting facet to its long-storied history.

Upon initial conversation with each of these colleges' presidents—Concordia's Pamela Jolicoeur, Lenoir-Rhyne's Wayne Powell, and Gettysburg's Janet Morgan Riggs[3]—each executive expressed enthusiasm about

3. When I asked President Riggs to participate in the study, she was serving as Gettysburg's interim president, a post she had held since the previous summer. The following day at the college's Board of Trustees meeting, Riggs was officially elected the fourteenth

participating in my study. Generally speaking, this study covered most of the geographical regions in which Lutheran colleges are located, with the exception of two on the West Coast: California Lutheran University in Thousand Oaks, California, and Pacific Lutheran University in Tacoma, Washington.[4] Although this study's design called for only three case studies, I wanted to capture, in part, the perspective of a West Coast Lutheran school. Loren Anderson, president of Pacific Lutheran University, has been a longtime advocate of Lutheran higher education. An abbreviated transcript of selected interview guide questions answered by Anderson is included in Appendix D.

The literature review and research questions provided focus for selection of site and sample (Marshall and Rossman, 2006). Examining the three colleges within these typologies, I addressed whether, during a specific time horizon, these colleges and universities sought to preserve or diminish their Lutheran institutional identity. Specifically, I conducted face-to-face interviews with *current* administrators and faculty and compared them with data from interviews with *former* administrators and faculty who have institutional memories of the 1965–1975 era at their colleges and universities.[5]

Document analysis of the two points in time—today and then (generally the 1965–1975 era)—was also used as an empirical strategy. Observations during my campus visits supplemented the interviews and document analysis. Furthermore, I investigated whether secularization, the struggle to maintain financial viability, and faculty professionalization affect Lutheran institutional identity. Last, I determined why and how, if at all, the colleges and universities described in my case studies are planning the preservation of their Lutheran institutional identities.

---

president of Gettysburg College.

4. One could argue that Texas Lutheran University in Seguin, Texas, a geographical outlier of sorts, could best be represented geographically by the southern schools.

5. In some instances at the three schools, particular interview participants, who are current faculty or staff members or recently retired, were also employed at the school as early as the 1960s. These perspectives, in a few cases, offered a 45-year historical outlook on the institutional timeline.

PHASE II:
DESCRIPTIVE, INTERPRETIVE MULTI-CASE STUDIES

Frederick Erickson (1986), Joseph Maxwell (2005), and Catherine Marshall and Gretchen Rossman (2006) contend that qualitative research designs are most fitting for researchers interested in exploring the complexity of social interaction, processes, action, and meaning-making. Marshall and Rossman argue that qualitative researchers "are intrigued by the complexity of social interactions expressed in daily life and by the meanings that the participants themselves attribute to these interactions" (2006:2). Erikson contends that qualitative analysis is most appropriate when the researcher needs to know more about the specific structure of phenomena, the ways in which participants make meaning in social settings, and causal linkages not uncovered by methodological approaches (Erickson, 1986).

In this project, I am interested in studying the complexities of action and meaning-making in specific institutions of higher education. The most important component of this study is the thick, detailed description of the people's stories and their decision-making. How do people's experiences, perspectives, and stories affect the structures observed in this project and the processes of meaning-making? Only a qualitative design could ask and answer such specific questions about social reality.

Therefore, the second phase follows a qualitative design because I am seeking to understand specific phenomena occurring in a setting, the meaning-perspectives of the particular actors in the particular events, and the identification of specific causal linkages not identified by experimental methods in Phase I (Erickson, 1986). After the three institutions were selected for detailed examination, Phase II adopted case study methods, utilizing a multiple-case descriptive design and containing detailed narratives of institutional change and continuity at each of the three colleges and universities (Yin, 1984).[6]

The structure of the case study reporting followed a time-series analytical approach in which thematic accounts of the schools' critical events were chronicled (Yin, 1984; Duke, 1995). I used the interview data, document analysis, and observations to craft the narratives of the three selected schools with regard to preserving or diminishing identity,

6. Multiple-case descriptive qualitative designs are sometimes called collective studies (Creswell, 2007).

followed by a chapter addressing institutional identity in the face of the three isomorphic status drivers of secularization, financial viability, and faculty professionalization. A case study reporting plan was appropriate in this study for three reasons. First, case studies are particularly helpful in understanding organizations, offering in-depth descriptive and analytical examinations of phenomena and actors in a particular setting (Yin, 1984). Second, case studies can help explain causal links in real-life scenarios that are too complex to study with surveys and experimental strategies (Yin, 1984). Third, the case study allowed for generalization to the theory of institutional isomorphism rather than generalization from case to case within the study (Yin, 1984).

During data collection and later during data analysis, it became clear that each school's narrative exhibited striking characteristics of the organizational saga: heroic leaders,[7] villains, institutional struggle, victories and failures, distinctive campus ethos, clear mission, and stories of creation, decline, and recovery. The three case studies, shaped by themes and critical events of each institution over a 45-year time horizon, detail a saga, or mythic identity history, for each school. Bolman and Deal write, "All organizations rely on myths or sagas of varying strength and intensity. Myths support claims of distinctiveness, transforming a place of work into a revered institution and all-encompassing way of life" (2003:251). Mitroff and Kilmann (1980) describe sagas as epic myths that engage rich narratives of an organization's history and portray its leaders in heroic terms, often creating a corporate myth that establishes organizational tradition and identity.

Yale sociologist Burton Clark studied three elite liberal arts colleges—Antioch, Reed, and Swarthmore—and noted the saga as a central ingredient in each of their stories. Of the organizational saga, Clark wrote:

> (The saga) is explained by relating it to the ideas of organizational role and mission. All organizations have a social role, ways of behaving linked with defined positions in the larger society, but only some have seized their role in this purposive way that we can call a mission. Then, among those that have been strongly purposive, only some are able to sustain and develop the mission over time to

---

7. By heroic, I mean to emphasize the classic archetypal notion, embodying and representing what a culture and/or organization collectively understand about organizational players. They are *examples* of the ideal, including both extraordinary and ordinary people.

the point of success and acclaim. The mission is then transformed into an embracing saga. (1975:8)

Organizational researcher Andrew Pettigrew suggests that social dramas of organizations can serve as a solid foundation for analyzing and studying the longitudinal process of an organization's development. Pettigrew (1979) bases this analytical approach on Clark's definition of saga, "a system of collective understanding of unique accomplishment in a formally established group" (Clark, 1972:179). The three schools examined in this study are served well by tracing their stories in the framework of the organizational saga: the story behind the story that explains and legitimizes.

SELECTION OF THE TIME HORIZON

The researcher-historian is not required to trace an organization's entire life but rather chooses a specific time period for study (Duke, 1995). The development of the chronological, descriptive case studies of the three schools was based upon a time horizon of more than forty years. While all of the interview participants were asked a list of common questions, half of the group was asked questions that focused, in part, on contemporary identity issues at Concordia, Lenoir-Rhyne, and Gettysburg. The other half was asked questions that relied upon their institutional memories to recall events and ethos of the 1965–1975 era. The chronologies were constructed using a framework of participant-identified critical events that shaped the institution's identity over time from 1965 to 2009, a total of forty-four years. Perhaps the most illustrative comments and recollections came in response to the set of common questions. Had institutional identity at the three schools changed or remained constant over this time horizon?

The selection of the time horizon was based upon seismic shifts in religiously-affiliated higher education in the 1960s. George Marsden (1992) outlined three ideological categories that have ordered American higher education since the mid-nineteenth century. Traditionalist Protestantism, the dominant paradigm from the start, was displaced by liberal Protestantism, which lasted until the 1960s. Over the last forty-five years, this liberal Protestantism has given way to a broad pluralistic secularism, fueled by a growing trend toward university departmental division and specialization. In the mid-1960s, developments changed the relationship between higher education and religion in America (Benne, 2003b; Benne, 2001; Burtchaell, 1998; Marsden & Longfield, 1992; Schwehn, 1993).

First, the rise of practicality emerged concurrently with the increased educational opportunity for a larger segment of the American population. This rise of education to meet students' practical objectives sparked competition among university departments for institutional dollars, which ultimately created further fracturing of faculty departments into sub-disciplines. Related to this phenomenon was the rise of faculty professionalization, which often pitted faculty loyalty to discipline over against loyalty to institution (Marsden & Longfield, 1992). The issue of faculty professionalization is addressed in detail in chapter 7.

Second, the decline of this liberal Protestantism was supplanted with a pluralistic secularism that "questions all beliefs as mere social constructions, challenges what is left of the old consensus ideology, attacks the Western-oriented canon, and repudiates many conventional ethical assumptions (Marsden & Longfield, 1992:33). To be sure, this further secularization of the academy was a gradual process, accelerated during the 1960s. My decision to establish an historical era rather than a particular year is based on two points. First, there is no specific year to pinpoint definitively. A second reason is to establish a larger timeframe in which the study's interview participants could more reasonably recall a fuller record of institutional events, ethos, phenomena, and turning points.

A third development that changed the relationship between the church and the academy in the 1960s is the eventual diminishment of *in loco parentis*. Through the end of the 1950s and into the 1960s, the role of *in loco parentis* was understood to be integral at both public universities and church-related colleges (Benne, 2001). To be sure, many religiously-affiliated colleges and universities interpreted their *in loco parentis* responsibility to also include the development of faith and morality. During the cultural shifts of the 1960s, however, the ideal of *in loco parentis* waned, replaced by, as Benne described, a "public health ethic," facilitated by the emerging student affairs profession (2001:14).

DATA COLLECTION

"Primary sources are the historian's grail" (Duke, 1995:249). Data collection consisted of interviews, observations, and analysis of documents.

I interviewed the current presidents, academic deans, faculty assembly chairpersons and campus chaplains from each of the three purposefully selected institutions. To contrast these current perspectives, I also interviewed members of the three campus communities who were either retired or long-serving, who could recall institutional memory invaluable to this study's data collection. I did not limit selection of participants in roles exactly congruent to the current interview participant panel (president, academic dean, faculty assembly chair, and chaplain). Rather, I attempted to select participants who currently serve or previously served in key institutional roles and who were willing and able to recall institutional memory dating back to the first years of the study's established time horizon. In a few cases, I was able to interview participants who held a full, forty-five-year perspective on the institution. This is to say that they were employed at the institutions in 1965 and are employed or actively engaged today in 2009.

These eight people from each of the three selected institutions—totaling twenty-four *initial* interviews—were appropriate for interviewing in this study because they provided a wide range of perspectives from the setting, making it possible to investigate in detail the relationship between individuals and situations (Kvale, 1996). During data collection, I became convinced that additional interviews and follow-up interviews would be necessary. Although the core eight people were interviewed first at Concordia, Lenoir-Rhyne, and Gettysburg, other campus figures were engaged later. These additional conversations occurred as face-to-face interviews, as well as telephone and email communication.

The interview questions were informed by DiMaggio and Powell's isomorphic status drivers, by critical events theory, and by other literature included in this study's review, particularly literature describing the ethos, vision, and purpose of Lutheran higher education. While the research questions influence what the researcher seeks to understand in the study, the interview questions are intended to serve as a way to gain that understanding (Maxwell, 2005). Lists of interview questions, which were pilot-tested with selected people in similar positions as those on my interview list (Maxwell, 2005), are included in Appendices E–I. The in-depth interviews were recorded, transcribed, and the transcripts sent via email to the interviewees for clarification, revision, and verification.

After the questions and protocols were pilot-tested, the interviews were conducted face-to-face as part of site visits to each of the college or university campuses. Face-to-face interviews as part of site visits to each campus allowed me to observe the participants in their settings and facilitated data collection and theoretical saturation (Strauss & Corbin, 1998). All three site visits occurred in March and April 2009 after meticulous, painstaking planning to arrange each campus visit and corresponding interview itinerary.[8] The planning for each of the visits began six weeks before the first visit was made. The Gettysburg College visit was first of the three site visits, occurring on March 19 and 20, during a chilly couple of days at winter's end. The visit to Concordia, which occurred four weeks later on April 15–17, coincided with unusually mild temperatures in Fargo. The Red River Valley, home of Concordia College, was in the midst of historic flooding that threatened Fargo, Moorhead, and the surrounding region. Finally, the Lenoir-Rhyne visit happened during the final days of April, a most beautiful, azalea-adorned time in Hickory.

The interview guides, sent to each participant ahead of the interview, served three primary purposes. First, the questions assisted analysis by creating a common, standardized core question list. Second, the questions were comprehensive of the entire study, and the potential diverse answers from a common set of questions were desired to portray a more accurate depiction of the sites. Third and perhaps most important, the questions were intended to build trust between the interviewer and the interviewee. Given my decision not to ensure confidentiality for participants, the transparent interview guide was more apt to generate honest responses from participants because they had prior knowledge of the set of common questions. Emailed with the interview guide protocols were consent forms and a personal data questionnaire. The central purpose of the data questionnaire was to help in my preparation for each interview and to gather general contact and identity information about the participants.

My access or entry plan to each of the sites relied upon advice from the national church office, existing relationships and networks within the Lutheran college community, and cold calls to presidents' offices. To gain access to the sites, I first contacted the Office of the Executive Director of the ELCA Division for Vocation and Education for guidance on how

8. My gratitude is offered to the three presidents, as well as their staffs for helping coordinate the interviews around the busy schedules of twenty-four college administrators and faculty. Special thanks go to Dee Ann Krugler and Tracey Moorhead of Concordia, Sherry Erikson of Lenoir-Rhyne, and Pam Eisenhardt of Gettysburg.

to best approach each of the presidents. In my preliminary discussions with leaders of the Lutheran higher education community, I had learned that, generally speaking, ELCA colleges and universities would be open to and interested in participating in a proposed study of identity at Lutheran colleges. At each of the colleges and universities, my initial entry was the presidents' offices, unless otherwise advised by the Vocation and Education Office. Likewise, I requested institutional documents for analysis from the presidents' offices, though some these data ultimately came from other campus sources, including the Office of Institutional Research, the Office of Admissions, and the Office of the Provost.

Because this study addresses a relatively small population of schools and universities that are linked together by a common relationship (some more closely than others) to the ELCA, I did not attempt to maintain confidentiality for participants. In fact, I did not cloak the names of the three schools featured in the case studies, for the detailed descriptions of the schools that I will provide in the case study will prohibit anonymity. What is more, intentionally naming the schools and participants will provide more compelling stories in the case studies.

In addition to interviews, the data collection strategy consisted of observations and analysis of institutional documents. Observations, which occurred as self-guided campus tours, were made during each site visit. This intentional and focused wandering about campus served as a surprisingly useful part of my data collection strategy, as the observations reinforced data from the interviews and documents. Prior to the visits, I had reserved a minimum of one hour per school visit to take a self-guided tour of the campus, noting the general climate of each college community. Guiding my observation were several questions:

- Does the college or university have a chapel?
- If so, where is the chapel located?
- Are Christian symbols displayed prominently on campus?
- If so, what are they?
- Are Lutheran symbols displayed prominently on campus?
- If so, what are they?

Prior to the three campus visits, I had prepared forms for recording observations, which I used during each tour for noting data. After the visits,

I filed the notes in folders containing data from each school and later referred to each during data analysis.

Finally, the study relied on a central and supplemental document analysis strategy (Appendix J). Central documents examined were mission statements, current strategic plans, and strategic plans from the late 1960s and early 1970s. Additionally, I reviewed a variety of supplemental documents for context and background, including admission materials, visitor and fact book publications, campus histories, and websites. I retrieved the mission statements from each of the college websites, and I requested the current and historical strategic plans from the presidents' offices. The presidents' staffs at Concordia and Gettysburg mailed and emailed, respectively, these documents, while the Director of Institutional Research mailed me a hard copy of the historical strategic plan and emailed an electronic copy of the current plan. I gathered the supplemental documents during my campus visits, including the college histories: Concordia's *On Firm Foundation Grounded*, Lenoir-Rhyne's *Fair Star*, and Gettysburg's *A Salutary Influence*.[9] These books were both data-rich and engaging.

DATA ANALYSIS AND MANAGEMENT

Qualitative researchers Coffey and Atkinson (1996) contend that data analysis is performed throughout the process of data collection and is essentially part of the study's design. Indeed, during my initial quick scans of the institutional documents, during the self-guided tours of campus, and during the interviews themselves, I began to recognize themes and critical events that would shape the data analysis and case study narratives. Data were coded in light of my theoretical framework, literature, and questions; subsequently, I conducted analysis via sorting, categorizing, and connecting strategies (Maxwell, 2005).

Specifically, in the narrative case studies (chapters 4–6), the cross-case analysis (chapter 7), and interpretations (chapter 8), I relied upon axial coding for data analysis. I based the case study axial coding technique upon thematic critical events and the cross-case analysis upon

---

9. I also used another recently published history of Gettysburg College, a handsome pictorial book called *Gettysburg College* by Professor of History Michael Birkner, who was interviewed as part of this study.

the three isomorphic status drivers. Simply stated, axial coding is a form of data analysis in which categories are identified and developed from the data and then linked to their data subcategories that provide further specification and clarification about phenomena (Strauss & Corbin, 1998). Around each major thematic category, or axis, the subcategories are linked from coded data. The process of axial coding is the reassembly of data that was disassembled and sorted during open coding (Strauss & Corbin, 1998).

While observation and document analysis were both important parts of my study design, the interview transcripts and field notes were the major data source for my analysis. Interviews in qualitative research allow for description and interpretation of themes in the subjects' lived experiences (Kvale, 1996). These first-hand accounts from members of the three campus communities represented their lived experiences over the time horizon and were subsequently rich, illustrative, and invaluable to this study.

All of the face-to-face interviews were digitally sound-recorded; I also scribbled notes during the visits, careful to note the details of setting, mood, and subject reaction. Following each site visit, I quickly transformed my notes into more detailed thematic memos. Furthermore, I quickly prepared transcripts, based upon the interview questions, within days after I returned from each site visit. I found this quick turn-around process of converting notes into transcripts a vital, though arduous task. Following the preparation of transcripts, I sent each record to the participants via email, asking them for verification of data. In some cases, I included clarification questions for respondents; in other cases, I conducted follow-up telephone conversations for clarification and follow-up. The paper generated from field notes, memos, transcripts, and thematic bundles was immense, consisting of hundreds and hundreds of pages. Electronic records of these documents were also created, preserving the data.

As I began the process of coding and sorting data, I soon realized that a few of the interview questions were particularly useful in uncovering data about what was happening at each school. One question, asking interviewees to identify critical events that influenced institutional Lutheran identity over the time horizon, was particularly significant in the initial coding. I addressed each college separately, in turn. For each school, I sorted the critical events that each participant named, which in most cases were three or four items. Clear patterns of critical events emerged quickly at each school. Pondering these patterns over a period of days and weeks, I noted the most common critical events. What were these events, these turning points, saying about Lutheran identity preservation and diminishment at the school?

Answering this question resulted in the development and identification of major themes for each school, based upon the critical events named by participants and corroborated by documents and observations. For the three colleges, I developed four major themes that helped to trace the identity history, the saga, of each.[10] Using these major themes which had been developed from critical events, I painstakingly coded each participant response, where appropriate, to the corresponding theme. This process included a series of thematic marking, sorting, and shifting of data, yielding twelve coded thematic files, complete with interviewees' responses. The themes, based upon the emergent critical events, served as the foundation for crafting the case study narratives.

Observational data were used to reinforce the themes identified from axial coding of interview data. Taking time during each college visit to stroll about the campus and take note of the placement of buildings, the architecture, the art, the classroom structures, and common student spaces was a valuable data collection technique. I was careful to record field notes and responses to my previously prepared observation questions during the tour. Another advantage of the observations is that they provided an opportunity for me to think intentionally about the themes and ideas that were percolating while I was still on the campuses and before I sat down to sort and code data.

Analysis of documents was a useful strategy for verifying themes uncovered in the interviews and observations. As described in the data collection section, two types of documents were identified for analysis: central and supplemental. The central documents analyzed were mission statements (Appendix K), current strategic plans, and strategic plans from the late 1960s and early 1970s. Supplemental documents were reviewed for context and background, including admissions materials, college histories, visitor publications, and websites. A quick initial reading of all the documents provided a general understanding of the three colleges' institutional values and campus climates. To guide the content analysis of

10. I developed a fifth theme for Concordia College, but chose to include it as a discursive footnote rather than a fully-developed theme.

document data content, I developed a list of questions to focus the reading and review of the mission statements and strategic plans. A full list of the thirteen questions is included in Appendix L. Finally, Appendix M details institutional profiles of Concordia, Lenoir-Rhyne, and Gettysburg.

Content analysis helped to identify, sort, and understand "communication messages" within the central documents of this study (Guba & Lincoln, 1988:240). The use of document content analysis is useful in case studies because it aids in corroboration of data from interviews and observations, and its use is unobtrusive (Yin, 1984; Marshall & Rossman, 2006). Four characteristics mark content analysis (Holsti, 1969; Guba & Lincoln, 1988). First, content analysis is guided by rules; my strategy includes a protocol of questions for focusing document analysis. Second and third, content analysis is systematic and seeks to generalize information for comparison. Fourth, content analysis is concerned with capturing the manifest content of the documents rather than interpretive evidence. This is to say that documents are intended to provide content about the setting, and interpretive work follows in the subsequent coding processes.

After a cursory reading of each of the central documents, I turned to a more careful reading of the mission statements and strategic plans, allowing for further adaptation and shaping of my interview questions. During the interviews and site visits, I put the documents aside and returned to them after the major portion of the interviews had been completed. After I had conducted the interviews and prepared the transcripts, I then conducted a third reading of the documents, this one focused on helping to reinforce themes and critical events emerging in the interview and observation data. The closer and more meticulous analytical reading involved identifying themes in the documents and coding these themes, primarily using DiMaggio and Powell's isomorphic status drivers, Lutheran higher education literature, organizational literature, and critical events theory.

Since the data analysis for chapter 7 followed my axial coding for chapters 4, 5, and 6, the cross-case analysis was a bit easier than it might otherwise have been. In this last stage, I bundled the data according to the three isomorphic status drivers: secularization, financial viability, and faculty professionalization. Although I aligned data from each school with the each of the three status drivers, I made the point of emphasizing the college that most clearly demonstrated engagement of the status drivers.

This is to say that I closely tied Concordia to secularization, Lenoir-Rhyne to financial viability, and Gettysburg to faculty professionalization.

Data management was meticulously administered throughout planning, collection, analysis, and writing of the study. All data were saved in either hard copy or an electronic format. While transcripts, thematic field notes, and coded data were manipulated, sorted, and stored in electronic files, other data like observation reflections, emerging thematic ideas, and interviewees' personal data cards were preserved in the form of hasty scribbles and informal notes stored in old-fashioned file folders. To preserve a chain of evidence, these documents—formal and informal, automated or conventional—are stored on the electronic files of my laptop and in the paper folders of my office desk.

TRUSTWORTHINESS OF THE STUDY

Instead of using the conventional validation paradigm—internal validity, external validity, reliability, and objectivity—researchers Lincoln and Guba (1985) employ the analogous term trustworthiness for qualitative case studies. Building readers' trust with regard to a study's ultimate findings can be bolstered by the researcher's careful attention to the study's truth value (credibility), its applicability to other contexts (transferability), its consistency in other similar contexts (dependability), and its neutrality with regard to researcher bias (confirmability) (Lincoln & Guba, 1985). My study follows these four principles, which helped validate my research and findings.

First, to increase the credibility of my analytical decisions and findings, I relied upon several research strategies, which included triangulation, peer debriefing, and member checks. My triangulation strategy relied on data collected from interviews, documents, and observations. Additionally, I relied upon debriefing of peers to review collected data and analytical choices; these independent perspectives offered fresh, useful insights. Member checking was also employed to ensure the accuracy of interview response records. After each interview, I emailed participants the transcripts and asked for their close review of the content. Throughout the process of data collection and analysis, I conferred periodically with participants, primarily by email and telephone, to question and verify data.

Second, to achieve transferability in the study, I used thick description to tell the stories of the three schools detailed in my case studies, as well as in the cross-case analyses. The use of thick description is critical to transferability insofar as the task of the qualitative researcher is to provide adequate description so that the reader can make transferability decisions to other contexts (Lincoln & Guba, 1985). Additionally, the case studies in this design are generalized to a particular set of results or a broader theory; in this instance, the study's primary guiding theory is institutional isomorphism (Yin, 1984). My task here was not to prove generalizability but rather to link findings back to organizational theory.

I simultaneously addressed the third and fourth claims, dependability and confirmability, using an inquiry audit. This is to say that I kept records leading from my data through my analysis to my findings, creating a tangible trail of the process by which the study's results were developed. Developing and maintaining this data base helped to strengthen my chain of evidence (Yin, 1984). Not only does this strategy enhance researcher accuracy, but it also provides a way for readers to trace the data trail backward to assess dependability and confirmability.

ROLE OF THE RESEARCHER

As a researcher, I adopted the paradigm of interpretivist, or constructivist,[11] in this study. Within Erickson's (1986) interpretivist paradigm, it is important to consider ontological, epistemological, and methodological assumptions. Erickson's ontological, epistemological, and methodological perspectives are circular in that the researcher is continually analyzing and reanalyzing data, evaluating and reevaluating one's assumptions, and examining and reexamining the research questions being asked. Ontological perspectives concerned with theories or perceptions of how things exist determine the questions asked in a study, which in turn influence the researcher's epistemological assumptions. Methodology, in turn, is established. This model guided the research design of this study.

Interpretivists are interested in what is being asked and assumed in the study. Using this interpretivist paradigm, I understand that multiple realities are imbedded in the social situations I am studying.

---

11. Qualitative researchers typically describe social constructivism and interpretivism as similar worldviews.

Consequently, using my conceptual framework as a loose guide, I identified themes that emerged from the ongoing data collection and analysis. Interpretivists perceive reality as a product of individual human beings, but in constructing meaning, they must remember that total understanding of all is not possible because of varying cultural realities.

Interpretivists' epistemological assumptions deal with how the researcher knows a thing, how something is counted as knowledge. The epistemological assumptions I embraced in this study are that knowledge and understanding of a thing is subject to individuals' own meanings and understandings. Thus, in my research work, I looked for meaning structures that were constructed rather than simply found or discovered. Said another way, the people told the stories of these schools' sagas in their own words during the interviews.

With regard to methodological assumptions, the interpretivist assumes that no one particular method can be trusted, as all methods are untrustworthy. Thus, the interpretivist assumes triangulation and multiple methods of data collection will be employed as part of the strategy. The assumption further states that there is no disconnection between the researcher and the instrument, since the researcher is the instrument. Further, the interpretivist observes actions and subsequent sequences of those actions in order to understand data and make meaning. In this project, I am concerned with observing, sorting, and identifying sequences of actions and decision-making in the colleges and universities of the ELCA.

My own personal beliefs, experiences, and perspectives are potential sources for researcher bias, especially in the qualitative Phase II portion of the study. As an alumnus of a Lutheran college, a former junior administrator at a Lutheran college, and a candidate for ordination in the Lutheran church, I have a vested interest in Lutheran higher education and the colleges and universities of the church. That I am identified by these roles in the context of the Lutheran higher education community will strengthen my credibility and association with members of the colleges and universities I seek to study. Accordingly, I presented myself candidly as a researcher studying Lutheran higher education, with specific attention to identity preservation and diminishment at ELCA colleges and universities.

Because my vocational goal is to serve in the future as a senior administrator at one of these institutions, I contend that holding a clear understanding of the identity issues related to these institutions, individually and as a collective body, provided me a useful frame for thinking about strategic planning, institutional change, and the role (and importance) of these institutions' Lutheran identity. I was careful not to place judgment on institutions' strategic planning and decision-making, especially regarding the extent to which the college or university embraces or rejects its Lutheran identity. This study was intended to explore schools' preservation or diminishment of their religiously-affiliated institutional identity; the study's goal was not to judge the value of these institutions' decisions to preserve or diminish their Lutheran identities. Triangulation and the participation of a critical peer reviewer, among other strategies already described, were thus vital in serving as a system of checks and balances for my potential bias as a researcher.

LIMITATIONS OF THE STUDY

Like any qualitative study, this one has its limitations. First, it is a descriptive and interpretive study, tracing the narratives of three schools; it is not a generalizable study. Despite my attempts to feature Lutheran colleges from different regions of the country, I do not claim universal representation in this study. This study is intended to offer insights into identity preservation and diminishment at colleges and universities of the ELCA.

Second, since confidentiality was not ensured in this study, respondents may have exhibited reluctance to respond with candor to the interview questions. Honest, critical answers from the respondents are necessary to depict an accurate representation of their school's Lutheran composition and ethos. That I sampled eight distinctly different institutional community perspectives—presidents, faculty members, provosts or deans, financial officers, and campus chaplains, among others—increased validity.[12] Furthermore, student voices are not present in this study. Rather, the three narratives are based upon administrative and faculty

---

12. Though not necessarily a limitation, the use of the pre-determined interview protocol is worth noting. As explained, the use of this standard protocol for each of the three schools was utilized as an effort to maintain congruency among the narratives. The case studies were based primarily upon the initial interviews conducted with the eight persons at each school. I did not intentionally seek alternative points of view, or dissenters, after the data was collected. Rather, this study was driven by the common set of questions asked of the same set of people at each school.

perspectives. Without doubt, including students would have provided an enriched perspective, but this inclusion would have likely resulted in a much different study. In the end, this study is deliberate about reflecting the perspectives of administrators and faculty members with regard to organizational identity.

Third, researcher bias is always a limitation to qualitative studies. I did, however, attempt to choose diverse sites, based upon a respected and widely-held typology, and I attempted to ask fair questions that would uncover relevant and meaningful data. Moreover, given the high volume of data generated in the study, it is possible that I overlooked important themes and insights related to my subject matter. At its best, I hope this study, a product of meticulous attention and conscientious research, yields useful revelations for the study of higher education.

PART 2

Case Studies

4

Concordia College

A Saga of Clarity, Calling, and Corncobs

I have always felt our mission statement was wildly audacious. Here we are: a wide spot in the prairies, and we claim we want to influence the affairs of the world. But Carl Bailey never used words he did not intend. And so maybe our influence will be small and limited in scope and geography, but we claim it nonetheless. Where there is no vision, the people perish.

Dr. Olin Storvik, Professor Emeritus
April 16, 2009 at Concordia College

INTRODUCTION

COLLEGES ARE ABOUT PEOPLE educating people. Concordia College was founded in 1891 in Moorhead, Minnesota, identified as an urgent priority by Lutheran immigrants who had arrived in America less than a decade earlier. Having settled in the Red River Valley of eastern North Dakota and western Minnesota, these Norwegian Lutherans, soon after their arrival, made provisions for educating their young men and women.

Comprised primarily of farmers, these settlers held education, along with faith and a strong work ethic, paramount in life.

Most had been educated in Norway's public school system before coming to America, and they understood that educating their children and grandchildren was vital to success in the new country. While Lutheran colleges were founded to prepare young men for ordained ministry, they were also intended to educate the laity for service in their church and communities, an expression of Martin Luther's doctrine of vocation. The conservative, pietistic Norwegian Lutheran tradition, which shaped Concordia for much of its life, continues to influence it even to the current day.

Other religiously affiliated colleges had arisen in the region. In eastern Minnesota and northeastern Iowa, Concordia eyed Lutheran competitors, St. Olaf College and Luther College. Closer to home in Moorhead was Hope Academy, another earlier Concordia competitor, founded by Swedish Lutherans. It was the students from Hope Academy who were responsible for Concordia College's nickname as the "Cobbers" (Engelhardt, 1991). Originally intended as a derisive term, the name "Cobbers" allegedly came from the Swedish students' mocking chants of Concordia's Norwegian students, calling them corncobs, perhaps because of the college's location among cornfields. The Concordia community eventually embraced the term, and today students, athletes, and alumni are known as the Concordia College Cobbers.

Hearing firsthand the compelling stories of Concordia from the people who lived and shaped the history of the college was an effective strategy for crafting an institutional identity history. As more and more of these Concordians shared their recollections, the stories began to take on the timbre and tone of a saga (Bolman & Deal, 2003; Clark, 1975; Mitroff & Kilmann, 1980; Pettigrew, 1979). Four themes, fashioned by critical events occurring within the college over the past forty-five years, emerged. *As noted in the methodological section, it is important to reiterate that these themes and critical events attempt to document patterns of how the institution has or has not preserved its Lutheran identity over the last forty-five years.*

The first theme was the remarkable singular influence of the college mission statement written by Concordia Professor Carl Bailey in the early 1960s. This statement, referenced by *every* participant during the interview process, is taught, memorized, studied, parsed, and used as a navigational tool for institutional strategy and decision-making. The second theme that emerged, marked by three successful administrations, was college presidential leadership. Almost universally, Concordians who were interviewed pointed to the strong leadership of Presidents Joseph Knutson, Paul Dovre, and Pamela Jolicoeur and their abilities to successfully exemplify and fulfill the institutional mission.

A third theme is the college's integration of faith and learning, evidenced most clearly by the establishment of the Dovre Center for Faith and Learning, as well as the institution's ongoing instruction and conversation with faculty and staff about the ideals and value of Lutheran higher education. Fourth, the college displayed a clear pattern of intentionally preserving its relationship with the church, its "Lutheranness." In its public and private documents, Concordia College consistently described itself as a "college of the church," most notably in the publication of its multi-series planning documents, entitled *A Blueprint for Concordia College*.

Founded in the late nineteenth century to serve the people of the Red River Valley, Concordia College today serves a global audience, enrolling students from some 37 states and 36 countries. In fact, Concordia's admissions publications' images and messages tout the college as global and relevant, abuzz with vibrant language villages, popular international majors, and a twelfth place national ranking of students who study abroad. Guided by a clear mission and a sense of calling and vocation, Concordia College invites its students to "light the world." Concordia faculty and administrators, past and present, shared in interviews that the college is still today an important educational and cultural resource for the people of the Red River Valley in both booming cities and quiet cornfields.

THE DEVELOPMENT OF AN ENDURING MISSION STATEMENT

In their popular bestseller, *Built to Last: Successful Habits of Visionary Companies*, James Collins and Jerry Porras (1994) extol the importance of an organization's purpose, often expressed in its core ideology. The authors conclude that, while no particular ideology is necessary for a visionary or successful organization, the extent to which the vision and purpose is lived out is of utmost importance, more than the content of the mission itself. Most significant, though, is that an organization *has* an expressed purpose, for it holds the potential to guide and inspire people within that organization. After visiting with members of the Concordia community and reviewing dozens of institutional documents, one can clearly recognize the remarkable attention, engagement, and deference the college pays its brief, economical, robust, profound twenty-eight-word mission statement. The statement is succinct: "The purpose of Concordia College is to influence the affairs of the world by sending into society thoughtful and informed men and women dedicated to the Christian life."

Olin Storvick, current Concordia College Classicalist in Residence and retired Professor of Classical Studies, offered a summation of the mission statement's institutional role. Storvick said: "I have always felt our mission statement was wildly audacious. Here we are: a wide spot in the prairies, and we claim we want to influence the affairs of the world. But (author) Carl Bailey never used words he did not intend. And so maybe our influence will be small and limited in scope and geography, but we claim it nonetheless. Where there is no vision, the people perish." This story of Concordia College could begin and end here with Storvick's remarks, for all institutional efforts do seem to point toward creating an educational environment where students are encouraged and empowered to learn, thrive, graduate, and go forth to influence the affairs of the world.

During a telephone conversation from his home near the Concordia campus, retired statement author Carl Bailey refused to accept sole authorship of the twenty-eight words. Bailey recalled how the preparation came about some fifty years ago during his work on the campus committee developing the new *A Blueprint for Concordia College* planning document. Bailey, who served Concordia as Dean of the College and Professor of Physics, had also worked as an atomic scientist during World War II at Los Alamos, New Mexico, playing a part in the Manhattan Project. At Concordia, Bailey was one of a half dozen members of an institutional planning group charged with developing a strategic plan for the college. It should be noted, however, that strategic plan was not the term used to describe the planning document, as this nomenclature did not appear widely in organizational vocabulary until the 1980s.

Part of that group's task was to develop a functional, compact mission statement. Leading that portion of the work as committee chairman was Bailey, who contends that the mission statement grew out of the collective work of the committee. Asked whether he had solely authored the statement, Bailey said that that rumor was "one of those pleasant fables." He refused to take credit as the singular author. However, others in the Concordia College community disagreed. Multiple interview participants praised Carl Bailey's work at writing the venerable mission statement, including the current and former presidents, faculty members, and other administrators. Despite his reluctance to accept credit, Bailey, "a man gifted in careful thinking and the capacity for writing clear prose" (Engelhardt, 1991:221), is forever closely linked to the authorship of the statement.

Whomever its precise author, the mission statement works. For nearly fifty years, its words have guided decision-making and imagination at Concordia College. Why is it so effective and appealing? Bailey argues that its virtues are clarity and brevity. "It is a cogent statement with a clear call, conveying a sense of duty and opportunity," says Bailey. "It suits what we people believe at Concordia College and how we should behave."

For Concordia College President Pamela Jolicoeur[1], the mission statement continues to guide the college everyday. She said, "I think it says a lot about the power of this one-sentence statement and about the Concordia community that it has lasted this long and that the vast majority of people on campus know it. That mission statement says it all." That the top administrator so strongly endorses the statement is a testament to its value and a reason for its longevity. In fact, the mission statement has enjoyed enduring support from Concordia's top administrators through the years.

Paul Dovre, who served as Concordia College president from 1975 until 1999 and then again in 2003 and 2004, described what the statement means to the college. He explained, "We think about it and exegete it all the time; people really care about what it means. It frees and unifies and directs us as a community. Students come to embrace the mission statement as it is modeled and expressed by their mentors and upper class peers." This presidential support dates back to the origin of the mission statement when President Joseph Knutson commissioned it during the development of the *Blueprint* planning series in 1960.

Passionate support for the statement also comes from Concordia's provost, Mark Krejci. Though a faithful Roman Catholic, Krejci articulated a clear understanding of both Lutheran higher education in general

---

1. Pam Jolicoeur died unexpectedly on June 9, 2010. Paul Dovre, who writes about Jolicoeur in this book's afterword , returned as Concordia's interim president. Dovre had previously served as Concordia's interim president in 2003 and 2004.

and the college mission specifically. In fact, during the nearly fifty interviews conducted for this study, Krejci offered one of the clearest, most ardent appeals for Lutheran colleges, Lutheran education, and preservation of this identity.

When asked to identify the purpose or goals of Concordia College, Krejci pointed to the mission statement, calling it "my words." After his first year at the college, Krejci knew the words by heart, for everything at Concordia begins with the mission statement. He explained, "As a community, we are always engaging and asking critical questions about our mission statement. It calls for our students to be responsibly engaged in the world, and this comes from the Lutheran understanding of vocation." The words call students to ask how they engage with the world, compelling them not only to learn, but to reflect critically about what they learn.

Two pastors, representing the Office of the Chaplain, also affirm the mission. While both Tim Megorden and Tessa Moon Leiseth do not share long histories at Concordia College as campus pastors, they both are alumni and spoke with deep fondness for the school. Both recognize the mission statement as the guiding ideal for Concordia's work. For Senior Campus Pastor Megorden, the words help the campus community to articulate its daily life and work. Associate Campus Pastor Leiseth observed in her short time at the college how the statement is embraced and lived out among members of the campus community. She described it as having something significant to offer, worth preserving, and offering the best of what God has commissioned Concordia to do.

Over the years, the faculty also embraced the mission statement. Dawn Duncan, Faculty Secretary and Professor of English and Global Studies, affirmed Concordia's mission to influence the affairs of the world by sending into society thoughtful and informed men and women dedicated to the Christian life. With keen attention to the college's core curriculum, Duncan added that the statement works well in supporting the primary academic mission of preparing students for service in the world. For this professor, the mission statement speaks directly to the interests of the faculty. In the abstract and the particular, the statement supports the faculty goals of instilling a love for learning, of developing foundational and transferable intellectual capacities, and of cultivating students' critically examined self-understandings.

Professor of Religion Ernie Simmons argued the potential of the mission statement to articulate and differentiate what Concordia College is about. Specifically, he identified a general challenge for all Lutheran colleges to offer a clear and confident counter-identity to the issue of fundamentalism. Lutheran colleges and universities are not Bible colleges, and coherent mission statements can help these institutions articulate this distinction. Likewise, Simmons suggests that Concordia's statement, while succinct, is also broad enough to respond to the growing issue of pluralism and demographics at Lutheran colleges and universities. How do decision-makers and teachers at these schools respond to the needs of this changing student population? Simmons believes that Concordia's statement is relevant enough to help guide this task. Moreover, Olin Storvick, who described so clearly the potential of the mission statement, also said that it is "relevant, flexible, and calls us to something. It still works."

During a data collection visit to the campus of Concordia College in April 2009, this researcher observed the mission statement in action. In one of the student dining areas, called the Maize, two Concordia students were overheard remarking about the historic floods that were threatening the Fargo and Moorhead communities. The college had dispatched students, faculty, and staff into the surrounding communities to help with sandbagging and flood relief, an effort that had been ongoing for almost two weeks. One of the students in the lunch line, having obviously participated in the community relief efforts, said to her friend, "Influencing the affairs of the world, one sandbag at a time." She was wearing a T-shirt bearing the Concordia mission statement and the image of a sandbag barrier. This was not an isolated observation. Over and over again during the college visit, interview participants and random campus passers-by cited the mission statement, word-for-word, with a kind of respect and affection. It was remarkable.

Perhaps the ubiquity of the mission statement on this campus is part of its merit and appeal. It seems that the words are written on the minds, if not hearts, of all Concordia folk. So often, as the literature has suggested, mission statements are regarded by the organization as obligatory, at best published for constituents' consumption, or at weakest, shelved and forgotten. Retired Concordia Professor and Historian Carroll Engelhardt chronicled the first one hundred years of the college in *On Firm Foundation Grounded: The First Century of Concordia College*. In his historical account and in a personal interview, Engelhardt noted the pervasiveness of the statement on campus. "Every Cobber knows it. That mission statement has served the college very well in all sorts of ways."

It is likely impossible to exaggerate the significance of the mission statement in guiding Concordia College over the last forty-five years. The development of this mission statement by Carl Bailey in the early 1960s is among the most influential turning points because the words, in a pragmatic way, link the original purpose of the institution with the vocation of the college today. The statement is not simply a string of words affixed to the preface of planning documents. Rather, the mission statement is dynamic and alive, demonstrating a sturdiness that has withstood decades of critical review and organizational change.

STRONG PRESIDENTIAL LEADERSHIP ACROSS THREE ADMINISTRATIONS

Stories become sagas when the involved characters shift toward the heroic and mythic, legitimized and shaped by public opinion. Sagas embody what we believe about ourselves and our organizations. As Mitroff and Kilmann (1980) described, sagas and epic myths engage rich narratives of an organization's history and portray its leaders in heroic terms, often creating a corporate myth that establishes organizational tradition and identity. While the forty-five-year identity history of Concordia College often resembles that of a saga, this is most obvious in the theme of presidential leadership and the emphasis on a well-defined institutional mission.[2] Almost without exception, interview participants mentioned the outstanding leadership of the college's presidents dating back over the past half century: Joseph Knutson (1951–1975), Paul Dovre (1975–1999 and 2003–2004), and Pamela Jolicoeur (2004–present).[3]

If the previous critical event was the development of the Concordia College mission statement, a foundational focus of the Knutson, Dovre,

2. Details about the saga are included in chapter 3. The organizational saga is "a collective understanding of a unique accomplishment based on historical exploits of a formal organization, offering strong normative bonds within and outside the organization" (Clark, 1972:178). The saga is a story that at some time has had a particular set of believers.

3. A brief presidency, described by several interviewees as generally unsuccessful, occurred between the Dovre and Jolicoeur Administrations. Two participants attributed this president's challenges to his inability to put into practice the college mission statement. President Jolicoeur suggested that this president's challenges might have been attributed to his task of immediately following the transformative administration of Paul Dovre.

and Jolicoeur Administrations was vigilant and perpetual support of that mission statement. Most of the stories shared about each president began with warm reminiscences of the leaders' personalities and traits. Other recollections pointed more specifically at the administration transitions. However, all participants spoke of the considerable leadership qualities that Knutson and Dovre demonstrated and that Jolicoeur currently demonstrates. Remarkably, in a time when college presidencies last approximately five years, the Knutson, Dovre, and Jolicoeur Administrations have lasted for a combined fifty-eight years. Although long-term administrations can pose threats to a college's ability to adapt to a dynamic environment, consistency can also provide stability and constancy of message and mission.

Pam Jolicoeur offered her perspective on her predecessors, Knutson and Dovre, noting that the smooth presidential transitions and consistency were significant critical events in the last forty-five years of Concordia's history. Pointing to Knutson and Dovre specifically, Jolicoeur suggests that no modern president, herself included, holds sway on campus the way previous presidents had. Appointed president in 1951, Joseph Knutson reinforced the college's pietistic Norwegian tradition, which posed a challenge during the rebellious and turbulent 1960s. Among his other duties, he understood his role to be that of campus spiritual leader and for the first ten years of his presidency, fulfilled that role without the aid of a chaplain. Carl Lee was called as Concordia's first campus pastor in 1961. Jolicoeur called Knutson, an ordained Lutheran pastor, a "fiery prairie preacher." She added, "I only know about him from the memories and legends that live on in Concordia lore. What he brought to the job was not an academic background but rather his dynamic forcefulness, expressed often in his preaching and folksy charm. He made it clear that, in accepting the call, his chief concern was 'always to keep Christ and His church preeminent in the policy and life of Concordia College.'"

Jolicoeur also expressed admiration that Knutson presided over a period of transition from a financially poor institution to one that was on a very firm foundation. Olin Storvick agreed, citing Knutson's leadership. During his administration, Knutson appointed Bill Smaby, a respected local banker, to handle the college's finances. Knutson's leadership and Smaby's steady control of fiscal affairs changed the perception of Concordia, especially locally and regionally. Not only did the team increase pecuniary strength and financing options, but it restored confidence in the college. Carl Bailey, the Dean of the College, was the third variable in that formula of early success in the Knutson Administration. Storvick explained, "Prexy Joe—as many affectionately called him—and Carl Bailey had a great working relationship: Bailey was the academic, and Knutson ran the college and was the community's spiritual leader."

The Knutson Administration was characterized by growth and faithfulness to the institution's religious roots. During his twenty-four-year tenure, Knutson oversaw marvelous growth of the physical plant, including sixteen buildings, more than half of the twenty-eight major campus structures (Engelhardt, 1991). Similarly, endowment increased $1.5 million, the operating budget increased from $800,000 in 1951 to $9 million in 1975, and enrollment increased from 890 in 1951 to 2,482 students in 1974 (Engelhardt, 1991). Simultaneously, the Knutson Administration also maintained a close relationship with its Christian tradition, the Lutheran church, and the ideals of liberal education.

Shaping and nurturing the faith community was important to Knutson, which yielded a wider and vibrant worshipping population. Storvick said that if the faith community is to flourish, it must start with the president. The president sets the tone; if he or she does not, then no one else has legitimate authority for advocacy. Engelhardt concurred, noting that the presidents have always played the most important role in maintaining that institutional religious character. The identity question was always at the forefront of the institutional conversation, mainly because of Knutson and Dovre's enthusiasm for the issue. Engelhardt recalled the prominence of Lutheran identity messages and symbols at every fall faculty and staff workshop and at every important public college event.

Campus Pastor Megorden emphasized Knutson's conservatism and accent on the pietistic religious tradition. Contrasting the Concordia College of today, Megorden explained, "He steered the college away from drinking, condoms, smoking, card-playing; this piety stretched into the Dovre years." Although today's Concordia appears less socially conservative and pietistic than during the Knutson years, interview participants generally agreed that the campus climate is decidedly more traditionalist than some of the other Lutheran colleges and universities,[4] though this is anecdotal.

4. Specifically, the Concordia College campus climate is compared most directly with the other two institutions examined in this study, Lenoir-Rhyne University and Gettysburg College.

Following Knutson as president was Paul Dovre, who returned to Concordia after earning his Ph.D. in speech communication from Northwestern University in 1963. A Concordia alumnus, Dovre served in several roles at the college, including vice president for academic affairs, before being elected president in 1974. From most accounts, the Dovre Administration continued the policies of growth, steady fiscal responsibility, and attention to the Lutheran tradition that the previous administration had championed. However, interviewees noted two differences. First, Dovre was, and is, an academician whereas Knutson was not. Second, Knutson was an ordained Lutheran pastor, whereas Dovre was a layperson. This is not to say that Dovre did not adhere to Concordia's Lutheran Christian values, but rather continued in the Knutson tradition of shaping the presidency as an important campus spiritual leader.

In the foreword of a compilation of Dovre's (2009) homilies, Jolicoeur suggests that Dovre was able to achieve successfully the role of campus spiritual leader through his expert preaching and rhetorical skills. Jolicoeur writes, "[The homilies and speeches] drew on real experiences in the college community—from celebrations to sudden deaths—or his own experience growing up on the prairie as he modeled how the examined life was lived and how the dialogue of faith and reason enriched one's spiritual life" (Dovre, 2009:viii). These speeches demonstrate Dovre's considerable oratory skills, his deep understanding of Lutheran higher education, and his steadfast commitment to the integration of faith and learning.

As Provost Krejci noted, "Not only was he an exceptional leader, he was the first non-rostered[5] ELCA member. He was a lay person but clearly understood what it means to be a Lutheran and a Lutheran college. He lived the mission of Concordia in a new way." Part of that "new way" Krejci described was raising the academic profile of Concordia. President Jolicoeur affirmed this notion.

Paul Dovre, in addition to understanding and advocating the value of Lutheran higher education, was an extraordinary leader who is remembered for his strong managerial style, steadiness, and clear vision. Dovre crafted what it means to be a Lutheran college, work that has not only guided Concordia College but also other colleges and universities of the ELCA. His scholarship and clarion voice on the subject is well-known

---

5. Non-clergy.

and highly regarded, especially within the Lutheran higher education community. Dovre brought a well-articulated faith statement and ramped up the academic excellence of the college. Megorden recalled, observing as an alumnus external to the campus community in Dovre's early days as president, how Dovre tied together faith and life very well, careful to slowly introduce the secular to Concordia. Retired Professor of English Barbara Olive offered a keen insight into his leadership style:

> He demonstrated that he was a good spiritual leader by consider-ing sympathy with Lutheran higher education and the liberal arts when hiring new faculty (the former was not required but taken into account).[6] He encouraged existing faculty to refresh their own learning about Lutheran theology, of vocation in particular, and to consider research that examines faith-related issues. He also encouraged dialogue about all such issues among faculty, as a way to build and maintain community. All were invited to take part, no matter the faith tradition or degree of faith.

In 2005, after a brief presidency generally judged to be unsuccess-ful, the Board and Presidential Search Committee sought for Concordia College a leader more aligned with the visions of Joe Knutson and Paul Dovre. At first glance, the choice to tap Pamela Jolicoeur to carry on the Concordia mission might seem to have been another misstep. The candi-date was a sociologist, a female (all previous presidents had been male), and a former Roman Catholic who had lived most of her life in California, far away from the culture of the Red River Valley in the Northern Plains. However, a closer look at Jolicoeur reveals an accomplished scholar, a professor and provost at California Lutheran University, an active Lu-theran lay leader, and a passionate advocate of Lutheran higher education and colleges of the church.

The provost, faculty secretary, and senior campus pastor all noted, independently of one another, that the institutional decision to appoint Jolicoeur as its tenth president was wise and calculated in perpetuating the ideals and vision of the successful Knutson and Dovre Administra-tions. Moreover, her selection recommitted the college to the ideals of its mission statement and to the preservation of its Lutheran identity, while maintaining and strengthening academics. In her inaugural address, Joli-coeur outlined her understanding of the Lutheran approach to education,

---

6. The issue of faculty hiring is addressed in depth later in the chapter.

a vision shaped by Gustavus Adolphus College Professor Darryl Jodock, among others. In this composite, Jolicoeur cited a preparation for vocation, academic excellence in the liberal arts tradition, academic freedom, and the engagement and critique of a diverse set of ideas.

But Jolicoeur is not without new ideas. While she does share a similar vision of her predecessors, Jolicoeur asks new questions. For Jolicoeur, no questions are off limits for the academic community. She reaches out to Concordia constituents—alumni, parents, donors, synods, board members, prospective students—in an effective and engaging style. Krejci noted that Jolicoeur asks good questions, like what it means to be a Lutheran college. One of her favorites, he noted and she affirmed, is "Where is the public Lutheran intellectual?" Abundant in other church traditions, namely in the Roman Catholic community, public intellectuals among Lutherans are far rarer, according to Jolicoeur. She envisions a goal in which Lutheran colleges and universities develop these public intellectuals—widely known, influential public scholars—in a more intentional way than has been done in the past.

Faculty Secretary Duncan noted another related turning point in the identity history: the transition from Dovre to a brief unsuccessful president. This misstep was a significant lesson for Concordia's leaders as it underscored the importance of presidents who clearly understand and affirm the college's mission, while working within a dynamic academic, fiscal, and demographic milieu to respond to changing environmental variables. Jolicoeur, whose "Lutheran credentials" had been proven and prized, was carefully selected to come to Moorhead to continue in the similar visions of Knutson and Dovre. Critics might deem this approach to be insular or even incestuous. However, given the centrality of the vibrant institutional mission, successful Concordia presidents must advocate and—in essence, have faith in—those twenty-eight words. Together, mission and leadership have proven important ingredients in the continuing Concordia saga.

Community members spoke of Concordia College's tradition of capable presidents. Joseph Knutson is remembered for maintaining growth and envisioning a more prosperous institution; Paul Dovre is remembered for enhancing quality and creating a more prestigious college. Both are remembered for their unwavering commitment to Concordia's calling as a college of the church. Pamela Jolicoeur, in candid conversations, exudes self-awareness of her own important role in continuing the preservation of Concordia's Lutheran identity and a confidence to fulfill her role.

In her inaugural address, Jolicoeur spoke of reaching beyond the confines of the Northern Plains to connect Concordia students to a global diversity while simultaneously fulfilling the venerable institutional mission. What is more, she argued that Concordia College "can become known for the unique way [it] expresses faithfulness to mission, for the quality of the educational experience, and for the impact it has on students' lives." The presidencies of Knutson, Dovre, and Jolicoeur mark important critical events in the recent history of Concordia.

INTEGRATION OF FAITH AND LEARNING THROUGH INSTRUCTION AND CONVERSATION

Preservation of institutional identity does not happen by chance or without work. To this point, specific critical events have emerged that illustrate Concordia College's strategic institutional effort to preserve its Lutheran identity. Integration of faith and learning is a starting point for the college's plan to faithfully live out its mission as a college of the church. And it accomplishes this primarily by intentional and prolonged instruction on what it means to be a Lutheran college, in specific, and a religiously-affiliated college, in general. Careful document review and multiple interviews with campus community members indicate that integration of faith and learning is accomplished through ongoing inclusive conversation about identity.

The primary critical event within this theme is the institutional decision to provide intentional and continued education for its faculty and staff on what it means to be a Lutheran college. Expressed within this decision are several specific significant events: (1) the establishment of the Dovre Center for Faith and Learning; (2) the development of a faculty and staff orientation program that includes instruction on Lutheran higher education; (3) the development of campus programming that perpetuates this conversation, including retreats and travel programs; and (4) the growing prominence and popularity of the topic of vocation. Except for the establishment of the Dovre Center, the other events are not pinpointed to a specific time but rather are ongoing work of the college community. Therefore, these themes and events will be addressed aggregately in this section.

To begin, when asked to describe the faith community at Concordia, President Jolicoeur responded, "First, we *are* a faith community." Not only does the college boast its commitment to engaging issues of religious tradition, the campus community demonstrates its faith-based character in word and deed. An "extraordinarily high number of faculty," according to Jolicoeur, are engaged with the Christian and Lutheran life on the campus. These people, along with staff and administrators, are frequently asked to speak at chapel, persons who might not ordinarily be actively engaged in the campus faith environment. Besides, such wide engagement allows for different expressions of faith to be shared with the campus community, especially students.

On the integration of faith and learning, nearly all interviewees articulated thoughtful responses about what it means to be a Lutheran college. This point should not be overlooked. That members of its community can speak cogently about Lutheran higher education is a vital part of an institution's self-understanding as a college of the church. By attempting a general description of Lutheran higher education, Concordia participants demonstrated how difficult such a task is. No simple formulaic answer exists, though there are characteristic marks of the Lutheran approach to higher education. Detailed explanations of these models and markings are found in the literature review. Concordia alumnus and Professor of Religion Per Anderson claimed that no particular essence can be retrieved to demonstrate what it means to be a Lutheran college, unlike some religious traditions that see higher education as a means of precipitating its own denominational gains. He added, "A considerable part of Lutheran higher education is a focus on critical reasoning. As a faculty member at a college of the Lutheran church, I have never felt any constraint on academic freedom; faculty here understands that academic freedom and Lutheran higher education are not at odds with one another."

Paul Dovre, who has written and spoken extensively on the subject, describes a Lutheran college as representing a tradition, responding to a call to vocation, and nurturing a community that conveys that call to its students. He adds that a Lutheran college takes seriously different faith perspectives but ultimately privileges the Lutheran tradition; this occurs within a dynamic academic community marked by rigor and openness. From the parish to the academy, Lutherans have traditionally been fervent about connecting faith and learning. Luther's concept of vocation is a vital part of this nexus: Christians are called to live out their baptisms through their vocations, shaped and prepared in many cases by education.

Eight of the eleven interview participants, including Dovre, named the concept of vocation as central to their own definitions of Lutheran higher education. Pastors Megorden and Leiseth share a vision of Concordia's affirmation of vocation. For Megorden, the expression of the institution's Lutheran identity starts with its understanding of vocation, and it is endorsed by the way the president speaks of vocation publicly. Similarly, Leiseth sees vocation as a core belief that shapes the work of Lutheran colleges. She said, "Vocation is a calling for everyone. This [concept] intersects beautifully with the purpose of the journey of higher education: to better learn about who we are and how we find our place in the world." Over and over in Concordia's institutional documents, including strategic plans and admissions publications, vocation is acknowledged and even celebrated.

Professor of Religion Ernie Simmons, who also directs Concordia's Dovre Center, insists that Lutheran colleges must talk about vocation. What does the relationship of education and vocation mean for public life? It means that we can offer a transcendent critique which can more effectively engage today's college students.[7] It means colleges seek to pursue the common good, for there is a public dimension of vocation and students' service and engagement in the world. Along with vocation, Simmons asserts that the dialectical relationship of faith and learning is also a distinctive marker of Lutheran higher education. This relationship connects the practical, or academic freedom, with the existential, or Christian freedom. Faith is not imposed at Lutheran colleges, but it is not separated either. Simmons said, "All questions are on the table at ELCA colleges." These questions spark the dialogue between faith and learning and encourage the exploration of vocation.

The Lilly Endowment's work on advocating vocation at American colleges and universities has fueled greater interest and broadened the conversation on the topic. Called "Programs for the Theological Exploration of Vocation," the initiative is intended to support efforts of church-related liberal arts colleges and universities to establish programs that

---

7. Simmons discusses this transcendent critique in his book, *Lutheran Higher Education: An Introduction*, as well as in a report prepared for the Lutheran World Federation Global Consultation, which he delivered in March 2009. Simmons argues that today's youth consider popular culture to *be* culture. Consequently, questions posed to students about Lutheran theology must be conditioned and in dialogue with popular culture.

assist students in exploring faith and vocation. A second aim, no less important, is to provide support for faculty and staff to mentor and serve as resources for students about vocation. During the college experience, faculty and staff serving within the church-related liberal arts setting are deeply influential at helping mentor students along their discernment paths. Included in this larger dialogue is a refreshed, reconstructed notion of Lutheran higher education centered on vocation.

At Concordia, instruction for faculty and staff about issues related to Lutheran higher education comes from strategic ongoing conversation. Part of that dialogue is sparked by the college's perpetual engagement with the mission statement. Another significant influence results from the administration's commitment to emphasizing the discussion of what it means to be a Lutheran college. And yet another factor perpetuating this conversation is the institution's established programs and resources for discussing topics related to church colleges and Lutheran theology. Through the years, Concordia has provided forums for faculty and staff to learn about and discuss what it means to function as a Lutheran college. The most significant development in the effort to inform Concordia's campus community is the establishment of the Dovre Center for Faith and Learning.

Founded in 1999 by Paul Dovre and his wife, Mardeth, the Dovre Center is dedicated to helping integrate faith and learning on Concordia's campus. While other ELCA colleges and universities have begun to establish centers for similar purposes, the Dovre Center was one of the first. The Center serves as a resource for faculty and staff and is guided by four goals: (1) to keep questions of faith and learning alive on campus; (2) to assist faculty in linking faith issues with their scholarship, teaching, and the college's identity; (3) to develop faculty community; and (4) to encourage new initiatives for relating faith and learning to students.

ELCA colleges and universities interested in issues of faith and learning often urge students to reflect critically on issues of faith. This ongoing, open reflection is the Dovre Center's central focus. The college views the Center as a means of perpetuating a public discussion on matters of faith, especially in a broader culture where such conversation is often unwelcome. Center Director Ernie Simmons explains, "Christian colleges assist this meaning-seeking, identity-forming process by cultivating an environment in which faith and learning can by kept in dynamic relationship, and where scholarly study and teaching can be understood as spiritual activity." Part of the purpose of the center is to offer resources that encourage new scholarship, research, and publications related to Lutheran higher education. Dovre Center programs, grants, and resources include, among others:

- *Faculty study grants, research teams, and faculty-administrator discussions*: grant programs that support research, conference attendance, publication, and mentoring

- *Faculty mentoring*: monthly dinner discussion program addressing the integration of faith and work on campus

- *Faculty publications*: program assisting faculty and staff with publication of articles addressing faith and learning issues

- *Advanced faculty and administrator study seminar and spiritual retreats*: additional, in-depth mentoring and discussion program for members of the campus community

- *Lutheran Heritage Seminar*: travel program for campus community led by Ernest Simmons to Luther and Reformation sites in Germany

- *Lutheran Academy*: annual two-week faculty seminar at Harvard University aimed to generate research and publications related to Lutheran higher education

- *Conferences*: support for faculty and staff to attend conferences, including the annual "Vocation of a Lutheran College Conference"

Today the Dovre Center for Faith and Learning serves as Concordia College's hub for coordinating instruction and resources for issues related to Lutheran higher education. As discussed previously, the Knutson Administration was keenly interested in ensuring that Concordia would live out its mission as a Lutheran college. Since the dawn of the Dovre Administration in the mid-1970s, however, three specific strategies were implemented to educate faculty and staff about the Lutheran approach to higher education. According to Dovre, the first was the launch of an annual summer workshop for faculty and staff on Lutheran higher education. Concomitantly, over the years many faculty and staff have participated in the Lutheran Heritage Seminar, led by Simmons. Second, the college experimented with a new component in the hiring process, which invited each finalist to contemplate and respond to three questions, one of which was related to the mission statement.[8] This significant effort proved to be helpful in creating a faculty sympathetic to and knowledgeable of Lutheran educational ideals. Third, the college initiated a faculty-wide study of the mission and Lutheran identity under the leadership of a Commission on Faith and Learning. Incidentally, one of the results of this work was the creation of the Dovre Center for Faith and Learning.

In August 1995, this Commission on Faith and Learning published a comprehensive report entitled *Faith and Learning in the Concordia Community: A Report to the Faculty.* Its expressed purpose was to serve as a resource to the faculty in carrying forward the mission of the college. The report, building upon the mission statement and *A Blueprint for Concordia College* planning documents published since the early 1960s, identified the reiteration of the recurring theme: the integration of faith and learning. Prepared by a steering committee of faculty and administrators, the report was intended to serve as a teaching resource.

The first of its three sections traces a clear, succinct composite of the Lutheran tradition, its theology, and its possibilities for linking to the classroom. The second section features ten essays from Lutheran and non-Lutheran faculty members, describing their own perspectives and experiences with integrating faith and learning in and out of the classroom. The third section presents the value and challenges of reflective education and linking faith and learning in the classroom. The entire report, which was presented to the campus community and actively engaged as a resource, was intended to spark conversation and encourage dialogue about the integration of faith and learning at Concordia College. Its publication and subsequent use is another example of the institution's commitment to reflecting critically on the topic of faith and learning.

The report was received by an interested Lutheran and non-Lutheran campus community. Today, more than sixty percent of the Concordia College faculty is Lutheran, a high percentage among the ELCA colleges and universities. As will be discussed in the next section, this composition is not by accident. However, this is not to say that the campus community is a single-faith homogeneous body. Non-Lutherans, non-Christians, and non-believers are also among the faculty. In fact, three of the interview participants in this study identified themselves from faith traditions other than Lutheran. It is important to note that these three—Provost Krejci,

---

8. These three questions will be addressed in detail in Theme 4.

Faculty Secretary Duncan, and Professor Emeritus Engelhardt—offered impassioned and well-informed responses about the value of the Lutheran approach to higher education. Duncan, who had previously served only at secular universities, gave a particularly insightful and illuminating response, which serves as a persuasive testimonial for the merits of Lutheran colleges:

> There were three compelling aspects to Concordia that first attracted me: a global consciousness, a focus on language, and a commitment to open dialogue about faith and learning. Once I arrived on campus, the aspect that made Concordia more appealing than other places that I interviewed was the sense of a truly collegial community. I wanted to work where I would enjoy the people with whom I work, as I do my colleagues. Concordia is a faith-based institution in the Lutheran tradition. As a non-Lutheran, I especially appreciated the commitment to questioning and critical thinking as part of living the life of faith. I am free to both practice my faith as a Christian from another tradition and to engage in dialogue with students, staff, and faculty about issues of faith as a natural part of our learning and living together. Having only ever attended and taught at secular universities before coming to Concordia, I can honestly say that at this Lutheran college we are freer to engage with any issue, to turn it a variety of ways as we critically think about the issue and multiple perspectives, to explicitly dialogue about the role of faith in literature, history, sociology, and science. We consider the challenges and imagine how to meet them from the context of a Lutheran identity.

The reason this theme is so important in tracing Concordia's identity history is because, in order for a college to embrace and preserve its Lutheran organizational identity, members of the campus community must first understand what it means to be a Lutheran college. The nearly forty interviews conducted for this study revealed that only about half could clearly articulate the basic tenets of Lutheran higher education. The institutional commitment to deepening the campus' understanding of these issues has been demonstrated over the last forty-five years in its systematic instructional resources and programs. To be clear, Concordia College has demonstrated a long pattern of intentionally providing instruction—and in the very least, the resources for an informed conversation—for its entire campus community. That Concordia College affirms and supports this conversation is paramount to its identity preservation as a college of the Lutheran church.

FAITHFULLY LIVING AS A COLLEGE OF THE CHURCH

The third and fourth themes share similar characteristics, distinguished by related critical events. While the institution made an intentional policy decision to integrate systematically faith and learning, it has foundationally operated as a college of the Lutheran church. In fact, at its core, Concordia College understands itself to be an institution of the church and subsequently strives to realize its mission as such. A long-standing pattern of decision-making illustrates points along the way in which Concordia has shown itself to live faithfully as a college of the church. Two critical events, however, are noteworthy: the development of *A Blueprint for Concordia College* planning documents and the introduction of the "three questions" to the institutional hiring process. In a very real sense, the other themes and their associated critical events already addressed are also applicable to this theme, for the decision to faithfully function as a church-related Lutheran college involves clear mission, resolute leadership, and thoughtful strategic planning.

Evidence of Concordia's commitment to its religious tradition seems ubiquitous in its public messages and published images. Strolling across the Concordia campus, one is immediately struck by the imposing Centennial Campaign Bell Tower at the center of campus. Rising some 100 feet above the campus, the tower is visible across the Red River in neighboring Fargo, North Dakota. Engraved on the base of the bell tower are these words: "Dedicated to the glory of God and all who have built and continue to sustain Concordia College." Atop the tower is affixed a cross, the highest point on campus.

In fact, all across the campus—in the library, classroom buildings, theatre, art gallery, administrative offices, student center—are displays of public art featuring Christian, if not Lutheran, themes and images. Examples are a bronze bust of Martin Luther and a lovely tiled scene featuring the Concordia College motto, *soli deo gloria*,[9] both prominently displayed in the library lobby. Even in the highly foot-trafficked lobby of the gymnasium and small basketball arena, seen by a large number

---

9. "For the glory of God alone."

of external visitors, an elaborate hand-painted collage depicts scenes of Concordia's history, including images from its Norwegian Lutheran tradition. The campus chapel is centrally located in the new multi-million dollar Knutson Student Center, which also houses the student services offices, dining halls, meeting rooms, a bookstore, and a commons area. The configuration of the new student center, as well as the central location of the building in relation to other campus buildings, makes the chapel and the goings-on inside part of the daily campus activity. Not only does the chapel enjoy daily use, but it is located at the physical and symbolic heart of the campus.

Whereas these physical signs send strong public messages about how Concordia values its religious tradition, similar profound messages can be found in the college's publications. Of all of the official institutional publications a school prepares, among the most important for a tuition-driven college like Concordia are the admissions materials. Not only are they carefully designed to capture the college's essence and briefly retell its narrative in a clever and appealing style, these publications must also be truthful and genuine in the eyes of a smart, discriminating audience.

The current admissions materials are comprised of a six-piece series, entitled "Light the World." The well-designed and carefully written booklets manage to be polished and cosmopolitan while also telling engaging and earnest stories about Concordia and its students. Filled with contrasting images of cutting-edge science opportunities and self-less community service options, the flagship viewbook emphasizes the practical. The materials also acknowledge the provincial perceptions of the Northern Plains region, while also showcasing the Fargo-Moorhead "Twin College Towns" as a thriving, growing, and appealing medium-sized city. Simultaneously, the materials underscore a decidedly global perspective, juxtaposing Concordia as a mere spot on the map with a complex and ever-changing world, full of opportunity for bright, well-prepared students.

The six booklets each serve a specific purpose: a flagship viewbook, a general search piece, a "World Fluency" study abroad piece, an academic programs piece called "Great Programs," a "Destination Fargo-Moorhead (Twin College Towns)" piece, and a piece for parents of prospective students. Each of the booklets focuses on usable, pragmatic information that speaks directly to the concerns and interests of today's prospective students. Like most other similar college publications, the Concordia materials include success rates of its students, a litany of its academic majors, a general profile of its students, and so on.

However, the "Light the World" series unabashedly speaks of Concordia's relationship with the Lutheran church. Every booklet includes both the mission statement ("to influence the affairs of the world by sending into society thoughtful and informed men and women dedicated to the Christian life") and the official institutional profile ("Concordia is a private, coeducational, four-year liberal arts college of the Evangelical Lutheran Church in America"). Using bold and unambiguous language, Concordia College describes itself to prospective students as a college of the Lutheran church.

Similarly, the college communicates this faith tradition with its other constituencies, too. The current institutional planning document, called *Strategic Plan: 2005–2010*, and its predecessors are all imprinted with similar faith-related vocabulary and images. Incidentally, the current planning document is preceded by a multi-series plan, called the *Blueprint* series. The inaugural document, *A Blueprint for Concordia College*, was unveiled in November 1962, and the college prepared completely overhauled versions for the 1970s (*Blueprint II* published in January 1974), the 1980s (*Blueprint III* published in March 1983), and the 1990s (*Blueprint IV* published in April 1991). Two supplemental documents were published during the *Blueprint* years: *An Agenda for Concordia's Academic Life* in August 1984 and *Faith and Learning in the Concordia Community*, addressed in Theme 3, in August 1995. For unspecified reasons, campus administrators decided that the newest planning document would not carry the name of the *Blueprint* series. In any event, all of these institutional planning documents identify and uphold the college's faith tradition as central to the Concordia identity.

Document analysis for this study engaged the current strategic plan. However, development of the *Blueprint* series emerged as a crucial critical event in Concordia's identity history since the 1960s. While previous documents had boldly declared Concordia's identity as a college of the church, the current strategic plan seems to go a step further. At its center, this new plan predicts that its "set of initiatives have been crafted that will ensure Concordia national recognition as an exemplar among church-related liberal arts colleges for faithfulness to mission, the quality of the educational experience, and impact on students' lives." Not only is the college striving to preserve its identity as a college of the Lutheran church, but it is striving to be a national leader among church-related colleges.

President Jolicoeur affirmed this. "To be a Lutheran college means to unabashedly claim the Lutheran tradition. Some of our (ELCA) colleges are skittish about that. We are unabashedly claiming our Lutheran identity." One of the three primary strategic foci of the new plan is faithfulness to mission, and inside of that focus are two initiatives and goals that speak directly to the religious identity of the college: living its mission as a Lutheran college and developing leaders for the church and society.

These ambitious goals are lifted up beside other fundamental aims, which include educational distinctiveness, enhanced profile, and fiscal balance. Although the language may not be exactly the same, the intent in the current plan is reflective of a near-fifty year pattern of maintaining a strong church-related identity. For instance, *Blueprint II* contained a chapter called "The Religious Milieu," emphasizing these fundamental characteristics as necessary values for the college.[10]

This "religious milieu" is described over and over by the interview participants as Concordia's vibrant faith community. The *Blueprint* series helped to ensure that the college would sustain this attention to its faith community. The primary reason the development of the *Blueprint* series is identified as a critical event in the identity history of Concordia is because these documents guided the college to embrace and sustain its Lutheran identity. Its directive was effective in maintaining a strong faith community on the campus, as the interview participants strongly affirmed.

Interestingly, their responses revealed a theme of diversity in faith thriving within a decidedly Lutheran environment. For instance, Faculty Secretary Duncan, a non-Lutheran, described the college's faith community as strong, active, engaging, embracing non-Lutherans who wish to serve and worship within the campus community. She added, "It is an open community that embraces those outside the tradition yet unashamedly and joyfully worships together, dialogues with all, and acts out its mission of service-leadership based on knowledge and critical thinking." This openness in attitude is reflective of the college's mission, as well as the faith community in the world. Krejci pointed to the institutional decision not to exclusively serve Lutherans as an important outcome of the

10. To achieve congruency in dates with the other two colleges investigated in this study, I have employed *Blueprint II* as the historic planning document for analysis.

planning process. "If we are only serving Lutherans," he observed, "then we are not living out what it means to be a Lutheran college."

Storvick agreed: "We're a better institution because we are not all Lutheran." Concordia College is a Lutheran institution by intent, but it does not require uniformity in the style of its sister body, the Lutheran Church Missouri Synod (LCMS). Storvick recalled in its continued engagement with the *Blueprint* series during the latter four decades of the twentieth century, Concordia insisted upon asking the central question, "Who are we and what are we trying to do?"

Professor Olive, another life-long Lutheran like Storvick, also described a relative diversity of faith perspectives that actually strengthened the faith community. She recalled that faculty from many faith traditions and degrees of belief, including atheists, have been willing to engage in the Lutheran and/or faith conversation on campus. For the faith and learning conversation to occur, Olive explained, "We don't all have to be Lutherans, Christians, or even religious, but we all must be part of the dialogue."

Ernie Simmons contended that Concordia's intentional church-relatedness has continuously shaped the narrative of the college. This is demonstrated, in part, by the membership of the board and the active Lutherans engaged in the campus community here, including the faculty and the student body. "Concordia is also a regional, not a national, college. The decision to be this has determined who Concordia serves and what it is," Simmons said.

Engelhardt and Dovre agree that the faith community is strong and vibrant, but they also believe that it has shifted over the years. First, Engelhardt noted that Norwegian-American Lutherans, the immigrants who founded Concordia, comprised most of the student body during the college's first seventy-five years. Over the last forty-five years, the predominance of that ethnic community has faded. Engelhardt argued that, as Concordia became less sociologically and ethnically Lutheran, the college attempted to become more theologically Lutheran. Engelhardt's assertion is supported by the *Blueprints'* calls for Concordia "to live out its vocation of a Lutheran college." As demonstrated in the literature review, this directive is based upon a theological argument. President Dovre similarly recognized the vitality present in the spiritual life of the college. He also noted that, while the college composition is less Lutheran today in faculty and students compared with the 1960s, Concordia's affirmation of its Lutheran identity is as strong as ever.

Perhaps Engelhardt and Dovre's assertions suggest that some Lutheran colleges have learned to express their Lutheran identity in different ways in recent years. Specifically, instead of colleges relying on their ethnic Lutheran ties, these institutions are indeed thoughtfully articulating their Lutheran tradition on theological grounds. The focus on vocation is an obvious example. Dovre called this a shift in Lutheran expression from ethos to logos. Briefly, this is to say that the new emphasis on logos is a persuasion of what the college stands for, compared with ethos, the college's "way of life." Dovre added, "Having the right people on campus who care about the tradition creates the ethos, and those people then cultivate the logos that has integrity with the tradition." This suggests the notion of critical mass, leading to the development of the "three questions."

Just as the *Blueprint* series called for a paradox of sorts—both faith diversity of faculty *and* a critical mass of Lutheran faculty—the development of the "three questions," as they were called by interviewees, ensured that the faculty hired by the college would serve Concordia with a clear understanding of the seriousness and centrality of the mission statement. To be sure, the inclusion of these three questions as an important part of the hiring process was and continues to be a delicate development. It appears, at times, to flirt with the boundaries of discriminatory hiring practices. However, as was carefully described in face-to-face conversations with Concordia leaders, the three questions are merely a tool for assuring that the mission statement is understood and respected by its professors. These questions, in essence, are a litmus test, in the best sense of the term. Ultimately, the questions ask, "Will you fit into this college community?"

The three questions asked of all potential faculty are:[11] (1) What motivates you to teach at a liberal arts college? (2) How is your scholarly life? (3) How will you contribute to the mission of the college? The most vital of the three questions, however, concerns the mission. Will this

---

11. The complete essay questions follow: (1) What motivates you to teach at a liberal arts college? What positive qualities do you have to offer students as a teacher and mentor? (2) Describe the research interests you might wish to pursue at Concordia College. Are your interests feasible at an undergraduate liberal arts college? Are there ways for undergraduate students to become involved in your research? (3) One criterion for teaching at Concordia is support of the mission of a Lutheran liberal arts college. Included with these questions is a description of the mission of the college. From your perspective, how do you believe you would contribute to the college's mission?

prospective faculty member live out the venerable mission statement of Concordia College without rancor or reservation?

Though these questions were introduced after the 1960s, it was during this decade that the Concordia faculty expanded and improved academically, with nearly forty percent having earned doctorates by 1970. However, four years before, President Knutson had posed a pressing question to a group of fellow Lutheran college presidents, demonstrating his concern about the potential for diminishment of identity. He asked, "How long shall we remain colleges of the church if our faculties become less and less committedly Christian?" (Engelhardt, 1991:260). Arguing for the necessity of religiously-centered faculty members, Knutson perhaps at this moment planted seeds for the eventual introduction of the three questions.

Provost Krejci likes the questioning process. Speaking candidly, he shared that some 80 percent of the faculty are "on board" with the Lutheran ideals of higher education, endorse the mission statement, and are active in campus dialogue about faith and learning issues. An answer to the third question that resembles, "I do not have a problem with your mission statement," is problematic in the hiring process. On the other hand, Krejci recalled a Muslim faculty member who chose to come to Concordia because, as that professor said, "You are serious about faith and religion here." These three questions can help uncover such important perspectives. There is no discriminatory or punitive spirit about the questions; rather they are intended to help match candidates with the college's mission and the campus community.

Simmons, Storvick, and Engelhardt all agreed independently of one another on the importance of recruiting faculty who have a Lutheran understanding of vocation and have a willingness to engage thoughtfully in discussing and perpetuating an understanding of what it means to be a Lutheran liberal arts college. For Barbara Olive, the inclusion of the questions in the hiring process first created a bit of uneasiness. "I was uncomfortable (with the questions) at first, but I later realized the questions were helpful. They match values of potential faculty members with what is important at Concordia." The questions, in part, serve as a means of building a faculty sympathetic to and interested this kind of education.

This discussion of the three questions sparked comments about critical mass.[12] Specifically, must a college of any faith tradition build a faculty containing a critical mass of supporters in order to successfully perpetuate and demonstrate its sponsoring faith tradition? No interview participant specifically quantified an appropriate and effective critical mass. In his book, Bob Benne defined critical mass as "strong enough to define, shape, and maintain the public identity and mission of the college consonant with the sponsoring tradition" (2001:50). Surprisingly, there was minor disagreement among some participants on whether critical mass is even necessary. Duncan held that a critical mass of Lutherans is not necessary, as long as the faculty can support the mission philosophically and actively. She did add, however, that Concordia would likely attract like-minded Lutherans anyway, because of its nature.

Pastor Leiseth also debunked the critical mass requirement. She bases her judgment on the experience of her husband, a Lutheran, who served successfully as a professor at a northeastern Jesuit university. In the interview process, he found compatibility between his teaching philosophy and the institution. During his orientation as a new faculty member at the Jesuit institution, he was continually instructed on the vision and purpose of Jesuit higher education. Though Lutheran, Leiseth's husband, she argued, successfully taught and served at a Jesuit university. In Leiseth's estimation, a Lutheran critical mass need not exist, though the college must continually teach the mission and institutional identity of the college so that all can clearly understand and subsequently share the institutional vision.

Professor Olive said that it is not enough in and of itself to have critical mass unless the people part of the critical mass are interested in issues of faith and faith communities. The three questions might help guide potential faculty to self select, to decide if the centrality of the Concordia mission deters their service at the college. She recalled an episode in which a devout Mormon faculty member self-selected to leave Concordia, as the professor's faith tradition ultimately was irreconcilable to the Lutheran tradition.

Even among the faithful, there is, of course, disagreement. Dovre, among others, concluded that critical mass is necessary, though that

---

12. The notion of critical mass, referring to a "significant" number of organizational members who endorse a specific idea, is addressed at several points in this study. It often refers to a critical mass of Lutherans.

group of committed individuals does not have to be exclusively Lutheran. Certainly other committed Christians can have a strong and salutary influence. In any event, whatever the means of building a faith-centered faculty—and in the case of Concordia College, the introduction of the three questions was critical—strong institutional religious identity is closely connected with a campus community committed to that sponsoring faith tradition.

This fourth theme, the institutional decision to faithfully function as a college of the church, encompasses the entire identity and purpose of Concordia College. It bears repeating that preservation of organizational identity is not by accident. Both the launch of the *Blueprint* series that so aggressively called the college to clear mission and the introduction of the bold three questions in the hiring process are significant critical events that have helped sustain the college's intention to live as a religiously-affiliated college.

SUMMARY

The saga of Concordia College over the past forty-five years has been shaped by an enduring mission statement, visionary presidents, a systematic strategy to integrate faith and learning, and an institutional decision to function as a college of the church.[13] Presidents, chaplains, faculty, and staff all have roles to play—as they are willing and able—to develop

---

13. A fifth theme is worth mentioning, albeit in a footnote. It could be classified as a strategy for academic rigor in the liberal arts. Concordia College, not unlike nearly every other institution of higher education, professes a commitment to academic excellence. However, the primary expressed reason for Concordia's aim to achieve academic excellence and rigor is worth noting, as it is distinctive. While this attention to academics certainly fulfilled a goal of raising the profile of the institution, it also demonstrated its commitment to Lutheran higher educational values and the bedrock principles of liberal education. By definition outlined in the literature review, Lutheran colleges and universities are committed to providing an education steeped in the tradition of the liberal arts. Concordia College imagines its strategic focus to be academic excellence as a function of fulfilling its mission, providing the best liberal arts education that it can, engaging students with the world, and delivering the Concordia experience to its students. Concordia College understands that academic excellence, scholastic rigor, and a curriculum firmly rooted in the liberal arts is a faithful expression of its Lutheran identity. Provost Krejci explained, "Mixed with the mission then is the notion of excellence. It is about pursuing God's gifts to the fullest." Again and again at Concordia College, the institutional goals and strategies are discussed and demonstrated in the context of fulfilling its mission.

and participate in the faith and learning conversation. Carol Engelhardt chronicled the college's first one hundred years and reflected, in a dialogue in April 2009, on the issue of the Concordia identity. Concordia College, Engelhardt contends, has been a leader in promoting Lutheran identity, saying, "I think it has profited from its fidelity and its leadership of that issue. I think other ELCA colleges have looked to Concordia as a 'model' in this question. I am sure that many are unwilling or unable to follow what Concordia has done. More important is whether or not they are willing to engage seriously the question of Lutheran identity."

With regard to its ethos and logos as a Lutheran college, how has Concordia College changed from 1965 to today? For Concordia, with regard to institutional Lutheran identity, there is little marked difference between the 1965 and the 2009 campus community. What is remarkable is how the college has maintained its commitment and course of following its identity. The Concordia saga is a story of continuity and like-minded administrators. In an environment of secularization, discussed in chapter 7, Concordia College worked to maintain its own vocation as a college of the church. And none of this happened by accident.

5

Lenoir-Rhyne University
A Saga of a Southern Fair Star

Fair star of Caroline, our college glorious, our college loved by all to thee we sing. May she forever shine clear and bright victorious, to her our song of loyalty we bring.
Fling wide the red and black, O sing aloud her praises!
This is the song we sing, Lenoir-Rhyne to thee.

John C. Seegers, Jr.
"Fair Star of Caroline"

INTRODUCTION

Southern Lutherans are an unusual crowd. Their theology is nuanced and distinctive, perhaps because of their very geography. For the most part, they are descended from the German Lutherans that settled the American East Coast in 1648,[1] predominantly in the Delaware Valley region near Philadelphia (Gritsch, 1994). It was in the eighteenth century, however,

---

1. Lutherans, primarily from Germany and Sweden actually arrived in America in the 1600s, settling primarily in current-day New York City. The Swedes, however, did not begin heavy immigration until the mid-1800s. In the 1700s, however, Lutherans settled in Pennsylvania and later moved into Ohio and the Mid-Atlantic and Southeastern states.

between 1725 and 1775 that the immigration of Lutherans to America sharply increased. These immigrants settled primarily in Pennsylvania, Maryland, Virginia, and North Carolina. Austrian Lutherans settled South Carolina and Georgia in the 1730s. It was not until the nineteenth century that the Norwegian, Swedish, Danish, and Finnish Lutherans would come to America, settling this time in the Midwest. Between 1820 and 1875, nearly 200,000 Norwegian Lutherans immigrated; by 1870, nearly 100,000 Swedish Lutherans had come to America, though some had immigrated and settled years before along the East Coast (Nelson, 1975).

From its beginnings, American Lutheranism was marked by ethnic differences of the immigrating groups. It is widely held that these various ethnicities—German, Swedish, Norwegian, and Danish, to name a few—have impeded the Lutheran church's ability to unite into a large national church. Along with these ethnic differences, which include a spectrum of cultural expressions, is the wide interpretation of Lutheran theology. Generally speaking, two primary Lutheran groups settled in America: the Germans on the East Coast who comprised the Lutheran Church in America (LCA) and the Scandinavians in the Mid-West who comprised the American Lutheran Church (ALC).[2]

Theologically, the two bodies were basically congruent, but there were differences in issues related to polity, liturgics, and ethos. For instance, East Coast LCA Lutherans emphasized the interrelatedness of congregations and the national church and valued standardization of practice guided by church polity; Midwestern ALC Lutherans were more congregationally-based and tended to follow a "low church" liturgical expression (Trexler, 2003).

Ecclesial differences also appeared along regional lines, demonstrated by the suggested distinctiveness of the Southern Lutheran parishioner. The specific expression of a parish's Lutheran faith depends, in part, upon the extent to which the Southern Lutherans have been inoculated against the fiery legalism of the ubiquitous Southern Baptist churches that dot the landscape of the South. Stated another way, is the ethos of one's Lutheran faith community as strong an influence as the Southern Baptist and Evangelical cultures so prevalent in the South? Do these Lutherans articulate their own religious convictions—justification by grace through

2. The LCA and the ALC merged on January 1, 1988, to form the Evangelical Lutheran Church in America (ELCA).

faith—in contrast to the religion of their Southern Baptist and Evangelical neighbors, a faith marked by talk of backsliding, meritorious conduct, and earning one's salvation? Perhaps this point is a bit over-emphasized here, or maybe it is not emphasized enough. If these Southern Lutherans are indeed distinctive from other American Lutherans, as well as other Southern Christians, then it only follows that their related colleges and universities would also be different, distinctive.

Situated in the Bible Belt in Hickory, North Carolina, is Lenoir-Rhyne University, founded in 1891 by four Lutheran pastors. The only Lutheran college located in North Carolina and one of only three in the Southeast,[3] Lenoir-Rhyne is akin to an outpost of Lutheranism among Baptists, Evangelicals,[4] and the other faith traditions that heavily populate the South. Perhaps in their desire to differentiate themselves from theologically legalistic Southern Baptist and Evangelical theology, Southern Lutherans have over-emphasized their German tradition of de-emphasizing personal religious piety. This chapter, which traces the Lenoir-Rhyne narrative, demonstrates how the institution developed throughout its history a distinct voice among Lutheran colleges and universities across the country and among its rival Southern schools.

All colleges and universities are fashioned by their geography; Lenoir-Rhyne University is no different. Its location in the South has shaped its outlook, theology, mission, and identity. So the Lenoir-Rhyne saga is characterized by geography and identity, described and guided in this chapter by four major themes and a series of related critical events of the past half century. The first theme that reveals patterns of how Lenoir-Rhyne has treated its Lutheran identity is found in the complex definition of this university itself, an often elusive identity that has changed with time. What is a southern fair star? Understanding the answer is the starting point for tracing the Lenoir-Rhyne saga. The second theme is the university's persistent financial challenges. While literature shows that small, private colleges and universities frequently face financial struggle, Lenoir-Rhyne seems to have had more than its share of fiscal turmoil throughout the years. The university's response to these challenges is noteworthy.

Third, Lenoir-Rhyne's Lutheran identity has been shaped over the past forty-five years by steady leadership. Leaders, including presidents,

3. Roanoke College is located in Salem, Virginia; Newberry College is located in Newberry, South Carolina.

4. "Evangelical" is defined in detail in the glossary found in chapter 1.

faculty, and chaplains, have navigated the institution over the course of years. While their leadership may not be readily characterized as transformational, their presidencies have done something perhaps more essential and amazing: saved the school from irretrievable drift and complete collapse. A fourth theme that has influenced the Lutheran identity of Lenoir-Rhyne University is a phenomenon this author calls the Fanning Factor. Essentially, this idea underscores the power of diverse voices and theological outlooks in supporting the university's common identity as a college of the church.

Richard Solberg (1985) called the Lutheran church in the South a story of church in diaspora. The same can be said of southern Lutheran colleges and universities. In a visit to the lovely Carolina campus, presidents, faculty, staff, and alumni all shared their recollections of Lenoir-Rhyne through the years, recalling the institution's turbulent episodes, its steadfast leaders, its devoted community of learning, and its identity as a local, Lutheran college of liberal learning. Is the Lenoir-Rhyne saga one that showcases a Lutheran identity gleaming "clear and bright victorious," as the alma mater suggests, or is the light of this southern fair star fading?

DEFINING AND BECOMING A SOUTHERN FAIR STAR

In 1917, College Librarian John Seegers, Jr. wrote the Lenoir-Rhyne alma mater, "Fair Star of Caroline." Fair Star, this term of endearment, is charming but ambiguous. What does it mean? Though a lyrical and beautiful name, what is the Fair Star of Caroline? It is argued in this chapter that Lenoir-Rhyne has not always seemed fully aware, or at least expressed confidence in, its institutional identity, especially with regard to mission and purpose. Too often, it seems that Lenoir-Rhyne has defined its institutional identity ambiguously and imprecisely, perhaps in a defensive mode reacting to its frequent financial woes.

Like its nickname, Fair Star, Lenoir-Rhyne's institutional identity is quite attractive, but it lacks precision. Through its history, though, Lenoir-Rhyne has remained remarkably engaged with and connected to its *Lutheran* identity. Defining what Lenoir-Rhyne is—and what it is not—is where this chapter must begin, for this ultimately informs how the institution has addressed its Lutheran identity throughout the timeline of its history. Briefly stated, three ideas help to outline a composite of Lenoir-Rhyne University: Lutheran identity, local ties, and liberal learning.

First, Lenoir-Rhyne has maintained a close relationship with the Lutheran church through its 118-year history. Even today, an institutional commission issued a major study in 2006, finding that one of Lenoir-Rhyne's most valuable assets and marketable strengths is its healthy connection to the church. This same commission also recommended that the college officially shift from the status of college to university, a move also taken by other "transformational institutions."

The Board of Trustees voted in August 2008 to adopt officially university status for Lenoir-Rhyne. While the Commission for Lenoir-Rhyne identified several characteristic themes for the institution, discussed throughout this chapter, perhaps the most surprising revelation was the importance of the school's religious affiliation to the college brand. In the many focus groups conducted for the commission's study, Lenoir-Rhyne's church relationship emerged as a common response. This religious affiliation continues to shape and guide the university's future, evidenced in the most recent strategic plan.

One hundred eighteen years earlier, the college that would eventually become Lenoir-Rhyne University was founded as Highland Academy in Catawba County with a relatively high number of Lutherans.[5] Although the school was situated geographically in the North Carolina Lutheran Synod, it was chartered by the Tennessee Lutheran Synod and founded by four Lutheran pastors from that synod: Robert Yoder, Andrew Crouse, William Cline, and Jason Moser. The effort to launch a new school was a response to the establishment of North Carolina College by the North Carolina Synod, Roanoke College by Virginia Lutherans, and Newberry College by South Carolina Lutherans (Norris & Boatmon, 1990). In fact, between 1865 and 1890, some 20 Lutheran institutions of higher education were founded, but most failed because of insufficient resources, likely perpetuated by the Civil War (Solberg, 1985). Of these, only Roanoke College and Newberry College, both founded prior to the war, survived.

In September 1891, Highland College opened in Hickory, North Carolina, and its name was changed in January 1892 to Lenoir College in honor of Colonel Walter Lenoir, a wealthy local judge who provided a land grant for the establishment of the college. Guided by its four founders,

5. German Lutherans settled heavily in the North Carolina Piedmont, especially in Catawba County and the immediate surrounding region.

Lenoir College enrolled more than 60 students, male and female, and was intended to be adopted by the Tennessee Synod, which it was in 1899 (Solberg, 1985). After a period of both cooperation and resistance, the North Carolina and Tennessee Synods merged in 1921 and fully backed a single Lutheran college. In 1923, the college became Lenoir-Rhyne, named after local benefactor Daniel Rhyne.

Unlike Gettysburg College, Lenoir-Rhyne's sister school founded in 1832 by Simon Schmucker, Lenoir-Rhyne's charter called for the school to teach "Christianity in its purest form." Larry Yoder—who served the college as a chaplain, professor, Center for Theology director, and faculty assembly chair and is also a descendent of one of the college's four founders—said, "The original [college] charter of 1891 indicated that Lenoir-Rhyne would be a school where Scripture and the Confessions would be taught, even if the Synod did not.

The four founders of the College were members of the Tennessee Synod, the founding synod of the college." Historically speaking, Lenoir-Rhyne was always a Lutheran college, from the beginning. What is more, its Lutheran outlook was decidedly conservative, doctrinally speaking. This is to say that the college would closely follow the Lutheran Confessions, unlike some Lutheran schools, including Gettysburg College which favored a more ecumenical American Protestantism. In fact, the school would employ the Bible and Luther's Catechism as standard textbooks (Solberg, 1985). From its founding, Lenoir-Rhyne set out to proclaim a clarion Lutheran identity.

Members of the campus community also agree that Lenoir-Rhyne's geographical birthmark as a Southern Lutheran college has shaped its identity. Larry Yoder noted the college's distinctive ethos in contrast to the Lutheran ethos of sister institution Concordia College. The German Lutherans that founded Lenoir-Rhyne had settled in America some 150 years before founding the college, while Concordia's Norwegian Lutherans, with "their American piety," arrived much later and almost immediately established schools. Lenoir-Rhyne alumnus and Campus Pastor Andrew Weisner, who described himself as an Evangelical Lutheran, explained Lenoir-Rhyne's distinctiveness this way:

> Is there Lutheran distinctiveness? We are church-related. What Luther stresses in the creed shows up in Lutheran higher education: we respect all of Creation, and thus all is open for us to explore and critique. We honor God when we do these things. L-R has had a

second article focus, too, which is Jesus the Son.[6] That Christian focus—the Jesus focus—emerges for three reasons. First, the Tennessee Synod that founded L-R was very Christo-centric, and that has stayed with the college. Second, Lenoir-Rhyne is in the South, the Bible Belt. Third, L-R primarily attracts Southern students.

Retired Professor of Philosophy Richard Von Dohlen,[7] a Baptist who showed perpetual interest in and engagement with the Lutheran higher education conversation during his long career at Lenoir-Rhyne, offered his humorous and incisive perspective: "German Lutherans, as I view them, are loath to wear their piety on sleeves. This may be especially Southern German Lutherans who feel a need to distinguish themselves from Baptists. This doesn't mean that [Southern German Lutherans] don't possess piety. They just don't want anybody to know."

Hearing firsthand stories from members of the campus community, both current and past, provided invaluable insight into understanding the Lenoir-Rhyne story. During an April 2009 visit to the campus and subsequent telephone calls and email correspondence, members of the campus community, including the president, provost, chaplain, professors, and other long-time staff, shared their own perspectives on the university. The first substantial question posed to each of the interviewees was complex: what does it mean to be a Lutheran college? The answers were revealing, and in most cases, rather well-informed. Perhaps the briefest yet most insightful response to this question came from retired Professor of Theology Rufus Moretz, who reported succinctly:

> In my view, a Lutheran college is one whose existence is rooted in the Reformation. Those sixteenth century roots were nurtured in a university setting. Such roots in a modern Lutheran institution of higher education lead to the presumption that the truth will make us free. That means that truth is to be pursued wherever it

6. Weisner is referring to the three articles of the Apostles' Creed, the catholic statement of belief for creedal Christians, which outlines each part of the Holy Trinity. The first article addresses God the Father; the second article focuses on God the Son made manifest in the person of Jesus Christ; and the third article focuses on God the Holy Spirit.

7. Richard Von Dohlen even wrote of his personal and professional experience as a person of faith (a Baptist) actively engaged in the Lenoir-Rhyne community. Witty and full of humor and insight, the essay is called "Strangers in Luther Land: The Calling to Be and not to Be One of Us," and addresses the ambiguity of being part of a Lutheran college faith community.

leads, even if the results are unexpected and appear unwelcome. The search, however, is tempered by the belief that ultimate truth is bound to the Gospel, the good news of what God has done in the person of Christ.

Other campus community members offered their own outlooks. Lenoir-Rhyne President Wayne Powell, an alumnus of Texas Lutheran University and Past Chair of the ELCA Council of College and University Presidents, noted the differences between Midwestern and Southern Lutheran colleges. He explained that Lutheran colleges in the upper Midwest are ones that have a heritage in Lutheran traditions and are still today almost completely Lutheran in student body and theology.

In the Southeast, on the other hand, a Lutheran college is one that has a heritage founded in the Lutheran church but today serves a very broad and diverse group of students. The southeastern Lutheran schools still take a "Lutheran" approach to higher education by ensuring that spirituality is part of all that happens, but by being open to people of all faiths. Powell added a disadvantage, suggesting that, "Because Lutherans are small in number and very few people really know what they are, in the Southeast we're are often misunderstood or ignored. We simply don't have a niche." Powell's own perception of Lutheran higher education in the South would shape his own pragmatic vision for directing Lenoir-Rhyne's faith-relatedness.

Provost Larry Hall explained that the university mission is "to provide an educational experience for students and to cultivate growth with classes and the co-curriculum. The question we must ask ourselves is, 'How have we promoted growth?'" The faith community is an important part of the campus experience, a community in which Baptists, not Lutherans, are the majority. A Baptist himself, the provost added that, no matter the faith tradition, "students like it [at Lenoir-Rhyne] because they know their faith will be honored." Another non-Lutheran, Professor of History Carolyn Huff, also affirmed the value of Lenoir-Rhyne's relationship with the Lutheran church. She said, "Lenoir-Rhyne has always, and I believe still does, value its historic affiliation as a college of the Lutheran church. This is reflected in our active campus ministry and in the place of the Christian faith in the core curriculum."

Joe Smith, an alumnus, professor, and the current faculty assembly chair, insisted that a Lutheran college must be open and accepting of a variety of ideas, a community of learning where people are encouraged in their faith. He said, "It's also about vocation, but we don't talk about that enough here. I do think about it, and it does happen here." Smith compared the college educational experience to a laboratory setting, a place for trial and error both curricularly and socially. In a world full of new problems and challenges, college experiences offered at Lutheran universities can help prepare students for critical thinking and problem-solving. Smith said, "What did Luther teach? Justification by grace through faith; this is not a strict path. [Luther would] probably like that we want our students to be global citizens without parameters. We think faith can be 'done' in different ways."

Pastor Weisner, a visible presence on campus, is called to ministry as an ordained Lutheran pastor, but he is fully aware that his ministry at Lenoir-Rhyne encompasses a much wider population than Lutheran students, faculty, and staff. He regards the openness of Lutheran theology as a catalyst for this broad ministry. "At L-R," Weisner explained, "you get to be who and what you are. We Lutherans don't pin down too firmly; that would be the law.[8] Here we have evangelical freedom."

Weisner went on to underscore that, even among the diversity of religious beliefs at the university, the annual National Survey of Student Engagement (NSSE) survey shows that Lenoir-Rhyne students have consistently ranked spirituality as an important part of their lives. This statistic is reinforced by the finding of the 2007 Commission for Lenoir-Rhyne. The pastor referenced the mission statement and its "focus on the whole person," which was printed upon a worn card he pulled from the pocket of his black clerical collar. Weisner added, "We don't force people into a mold here. It's easy to be Christian here, and it's also easy to find temptations. But we don't try to stamp those temptations out here. After all, Lenoir-Rhyne is in the world, engaged."

Professor of Theology Larry Yoder, who served as the college chaplain[9] from 1977 to 1982, noted that the student ethos is more secular than religious today, compared to thirty years ago when he served as chaplain. He added, however, that if Lutheran colleges are true to their heritage, there is a *simul* dimension, a "both/and" construct. That is to say that

8. By the law, Weisner is referring to the Lutheran tension of Law and Gospel, one of the basic tenets of the Lutheran faith. The Law condemns; the Gospel sets free.

9. Upon his arrival in 1994, President Ryan LaHurd changed the name from College Chaplain to College Pastor to describe more accurately the wider ministry this person performs for the campus community, a decision that Weisner strongly affirmed.

both learning and wisdom, both worship and work, are lifted up in the Lutheran perspective. Yoder explained the mission of the college in his own words: "To undertake higher education from the point of view of the arts and sciences for the foundation of learning informed by the Lutheran perspective of the Two Kingdoms, *sola gratia* [Lutheran theology], and the development of the students thereto."

Alumnus Bill Mauney, Dean of the College of Professional and Mathematical Studies and the Moretz Professor of Economics, also referenced the mission statement, which he retrieved from his desk during a conversation in his office. He read aloud, in part, the university mission statement:

> In pursuit of the development of the whole person, Lenoir-Rhyne University seeks to liberate mind and spirit, clarify personal faith, foster physical wholeness, build a sense of community, and promote responsible leadership for service in the world. As an institution of the North Carolina Synod of the Evangelical Lutheran Church in America, the university holds the conviction that wholeness of person, true vocation, and the most useful service to God and the world are best discerned from the perspective of Christian faith. As a community of learning, the university provides programs of undergraduate, graduate, and continuing study committed to the liberal arts and sciences as a foundation for a wide variety of careers and as guidance for a meaningful life.

Mauney asserted that, for Lenoir-Rhyne, the best way to discern an education is through the perspective of the Christian faith, the central focus of Lutheran higher education.

Mauney also observed that denominational loyalty in America is waning, citing a recent article he read that claimed people have a greater loyalty to their toothpaste than their religious denomination. Despite this threat to denominational allegiance, Mauney insisted that the Lutheran ethos at Lenoir-Rhyne is strong. This is evidenced in the college choir, the baccalaureate services, the opening prayers at faculty assembly meetings, in the college's public liturgy, and in the long-range plan of the institution. Mauney said, "What it means to be a Lutheran has changed institutionally but not theologically. We at L-R must reflect that. At Lenoir-Rhyne we are not here to further a denomination. To be a Lutheran is to be an ecumenist."

Three other members of the campus community underscored Lenoir-Rhyne's close ties to its Lutheran identity. Professor of History Carolyn Huff pointed to the Lutheran affiliation reflected in the university's core curriculum, particularly in its requirements for two courses in the Christian faith. David Ratke, Professor of Theology and ordained Lutheran pastor, explained that being a Lutheran college means "thinking hard about how [the university's] primary activity, education, reflects the values and principles of Lutheran Christianity, a sacramental view of creation, the Doctrine of the Two Kingdoms, and the theology of the cross."

Alumna Rachel Nichols, Vice President for Enrollment Management, commented on the protocols and best practices of her team's efforts. She said, "Following that Lutheran example, we adhere to a notion of grace in our work, free from judgment. By this I mean that we work with all students from many different backgrounds, meeting people where they are." Nichols has even invited a Lutheran pastor to participate in her staff's annual planning retreat, the purpose being to discuss the role of grace and Lutheran theology in the admissions decision-making process.

Related to the issue of identity, the notion of academic freedom and the Lutheran tradition also emerged during the interviews. That church-related colleges and universities, Lutheran institutions anyway, suppress academic freedom is a common misunderstanding. Perhaps this suppression does occur at some fundamentalist institutions, but not at Lutheran colleges, if they are true to their mission and theology. Provost Hall suggested that public universities are denied the ability to talk about spirituality and a very important part of human existence, adding, "While fundamentalist schools stifle the relationship between faith and learning and push a specific doctrine, L-R does not. There is paradox in Lutheran theology, and paradox is good." Similarly, Bill Mauney reasoned: "Public institutions think they have academic freedom, but we *really have it*. We are free to investigate our faith and question it, or not, if we choose. The publics don't have this option. Luther was both a priest and a professor, and that fact influences who we are as a Lutheran college. [Luther's] nailing those ninety-five debate questions onto the church door is the ultimate statement of academic freedom."

A commitment to preserving the institution's relationship with the church is clearly articulated in the strategic plan presented in 1969, *Strategy for the Seventies*, and the current plan, *University Rising: The Strategic Plan 2008–2013*. In the description of the institutional characteristics, the first plan proclaimed that Lenoir-Rhyne's church relationship is "fundamental to the college's purpose and undergirds both its concern for relating life and learning to Jesus Christ and its commitment to strive for academic excellence in its program." The current planning document names as one of its primary themes a commitment to faith development. Lutheran identity, then and now, has been a foundational factor in defining the Fair Star.

Local ties describe the second component of the university's definition. Lenoir-Rhyne is infused with a populist spirit.[10] This is to say that the university understands itself to be a college of the "common person," serving local and regional families and many first generation students. While Lenoir-Rhyne's home, Hickory, is not a classic college town,[11] the university and the city enjoy a long-standing warm and collegial town-gown relationship. This good relationship is evidenced in several ways, particularly in the community's involvement with the college and the extent to which the university serves the educational needs of the local communities and region. Offering the perspective of a college admissions professional, Rachel Nichols insisted that Lenoir-Rhyne's association with Hickory is critical, saying that the university "enjoys an ongoing and outstanding relationship with Hickory."

In addition to the institution's steadfast religious affiliation, the 2007 Commission for Lenoir-Rhyne also found that the university benefits from the strong relationship with the local community. Specific to these community partnerships and relationships, the Commission reported the following advantages:

- the (university) is a true asset to the community and the community can be a true asset to the (university)

- the architectural beauty and location of the campus

- a cultural asset to the community and region

- faculty and staff are engaged in community service

10. I do not mean to use populist in the political sense, but rather as an expression of Lenoir-Rhyne's commitment to the common person.

11. Hickory was long-regarded as a center for textile and furniture manufacturing. With the changing economy, Hickory has moved away from these industries toward more technology-based industries like fiber-optic cable manufacturing. In recent years, even that industry has been distressed in the Hickory region.

- the university is an anchor in the community through cultural programs, physical activities, aesthetic presentation, and sports

The capital and potential of this healthy town-gown relationship is subsequently reflected in *University Rising: The Strategic Plan 2008–2013*. Echoing its new marketing slogan, "Rise Up," Lenoir-Rhyne leaders identified the fourth point of the plan to be "Service to the Community," in which Hickory and the surrounding area play a vital role. The specific goal states, "The University will be the intellectual, cultural, and artistic center of the Hickory Metro."[12] An objective related to this goal includes the expansion and enhancement of relevant intellectual, cultural, and artistic forums in the community.

The community has also played a significant role in institutional governance and fundraising efforts at Lenoir-Rhyne. Institutional bylaws deemed that a high number of the Board of Trustees would be comprised of Lutherans. Because Lutherans were abundant in Hickory, Catawba County, and the surrounding area, this criterion was easily met. It should be noted that Board members were tapped from outside the immediate region, too. What is more, the bylaws specified that one fourth of the Board be Lutheran clergy. Many of these seats were filled by local, if not regional or synodical representatives. The North Carolina Lutheran Synod, which also enjoys a close relationship with Lenoir-Rhyne, also maintained a voice on the Board of Trustees.

For much of its history, the college looked to local leaders, primarily wealthy and influential Hickory families, to serve as trustees. Through the years, some have been alumni; others have been classified as friends of the college. In both cases, local Hickory and Catawba County leaders have served on the leadership boards[13] of the institution. Most of the trustees and visitors have been business leaders, philanthropists, physicians, bankers, and attorneys.

While their leadership and service is greatly valued by the university, at times the level of engagement of the Board of Trustees, in particular, has been questionable, especially during times of financial crisis. Thus, this high level of involvement by the same families and individuals in

12. The United States Census Bureau defines the greater Hickory region as the Hickory-Metro. The 2000 census recorded a Hickory-Metro population of 341,851, and it estimated in 2007 that that population had risen to 360,471.

13. The university leadership boards are the Board of Trustees, the Board of Visitors (originally called the Development Board), and the Alumni Association Board.

the institution's board governance is not without disadvantage. On the other hand, these same families and many other loyal alumni and friends have provided firm financial support of Lenoir-Rhyne throughout its history. In fact, Catawba County and Hickory residents boasted the highest regional participation among donors of 1991's Centennial Renewal Campaign.[14]

Finally, Lenoir-Rhyne is well-connected to North Carolina. Although the university serves students from seventeen states and five countries, seventy-eight percent of the student body was drawn from North Carolina for the 2009–2010 academic year.[15] That number has increased sharply in recent years. While the university certainly values this constituency it serves, the college might seek a greater number of out-of-state students. In 2009, twenty freshmen were from Hickory alone, not counting Catawba County or the greater Hickory Metro region.

According to Vice President Nichols, "enrollment in the Hickory area has increased." In brief, Lenoir-Rhyne maintains a global focus in its curriculum, but it serves primarily a local, regional, and state population. It is a university supported generously by the citizens of Hickory and Catawba County, alumni and friends alike. And it is an institution of the church, evidenced by an important relationship with the North Carolina Synod. Pastor Weisner said, "There is a strong relationship between the college and the synod, and President Powell has made it clear: 'We want the synod involved here.'"

The third factor in defining the university is related to its commitment to liberal learning. To be sure, Lenoir-Rhyne is not and never has been a liberal arts college. This is not to say, however, that the institution does not value liberal learning and that its core curriculum includes a solid, well-developed liberal arts program. In fact, since its founding in 1891, Lenoir-Rhyne's foundational curriculum has been deeply rooted in the liberal arts tradition.

Simultaneously, the institution has always graduated male and female students who studied professional courses of study, especially education, business, clergy, and nursing. Even after a series of elective

14. According to campaign documents (General Chairman's Statement) the Catawba County goal was five times higher than the other major regions targeted in the campaign, which ultimately surpassed its goal by some fifteen percent.

15. Nichols reported that Lenoir-Rhyne experience a surprising 33% increase of overall enrollment for Fall 2009, an impressive accomplishment in the weak economy.

courses was introduced in 1894, the college curriculum followed a classical liberal arts program (Norris & Boatmon, 1990). By 1930, the college had graduated 321 teachers, 112 ministers, 49 businessmen, 17 lawyers, 15 physicians, 9 farmers, 7 government officials, 4 bankers, and 61 other miscellaneous alumni (Norris & Boatmon, 1990). The vast majority of these alumni matriculated after study in a professional or pre-professional program, though at the core of their educational experience was a liberal arts foundation.

Because of the high number of graduates in the professional programs, Carnegie classification criteria would define Lenoir-Rhyne as something other than a liberal arts college (Breneman, 1994). Currently, it is more accurately described as a comprehensive university with, as its mission statement details, "programs . . . committed to the liberal arts and sciences as a foundation for a wide variety of careers and as guidance for a meaningful life." To name Lenoir-Rhyne merely a liberal arts college would not only be imprecise, but it would deny an important institutional tradition and mission of providing preparation in the professional and pre-professional programs.

The Commission for Lenoir-Rhyne named one of its four characteristic themes to be the university's liberal arts foundation, which encompasses a curriculum founded in the liberal arts, a mission to educate the whole person, and a marriage of the liberal arts and professional programs. Another of the four themes is tangentially related to teaching and the liberal arts tradition: small class size, close faculty-student relationships, the faculty's focus on teaching, and academic rigor. In the university's new vision statement, influenced by the Commission's findings and presented in the 2008 strategic plan, institutional decision-makers are positioning Lenoir-Rhyne as "a national liberal arts university of choice."

Sorting, identifying, and defining the complexities of a university's identity is not an easy task. The characteristics, though intrinsic to the institution, are also dynamic and malleable. To sketch an honest, accurate composite of Lenoir-Rhyne University, one must include its Lutheran identity, its local ties, and its commitment to liberal learning. Upon these three bedrock ideas was built what librarian John Seegers called the Fair Star of Caroline.

THE PERSISTENCE OF FINANCIAL CHALLENGES

Political shifts, state and federal policy modifications, demographic changes, economic trends, and rising costs have all influenced the higher education financial environment since World War II, especially at small, private colleges and universities (Breneman, 1994). At the same time, Breneman (2008) also contends that these same colleges and universities have responded well to such challenges during this same period of time, writing, "[they] are indeed remarkably adaptable and able to adjust to shifting economic, demographic, technological, and political environments." Lenoir-Rhyne, not immune to a sometimes challenging financial climate, is a small, tuition-driven university lacking a large institutional endowment. Persistent financial struggles, particularly one in the early 1990s, is a second theme that has shaped the university's identity over the last forty-five years.

This theme is an unpleasant, unflattering one to include in a college story, but it was cited over and over by the interview participants. This struggle is part of the institutional saga. The financial challenges of the university—and particularly the crisis of the early 1990s—affected the institution's identity in very interesting ways. In a broad sense, the university's financial struggles made subsequent institutional planning all the more important. Most essential to this chapter, however, is the singular fact that during these financial downturns, Lenoir-Rhyne could have forsaken its Lutheran identity in favor of quick remedies that may very well have diminished its relationship to the church. Lenoir-Rhyne did not seek this path.

It is also worth noting that the persistence of financial turmoil often resulted in restraint on presidential power and accomplishment. This is to say that the agendas of some Lenoir-Rhyne chiefs who have been dealt presidencies following financially-beleaguered administrations have found their own agendas waylaid by issues of institutional survival. Bold presidential initiatives frequently fade when organizational survival is at stake. The best example is the administration of Ryan LaHurd, which followed the dismal financial crisis of the early 1990s over which John Trainer presided. Much of the eight-year LaHurd Administration was devoted to institutional recovery and morale rebuilding.

While this chapter focuses primarily on the crisis of the early 1990s, other notable periods of financial turbulence have affected the institution.

The first decades of the college's existence were characterized by financial stress, depending upon the support of the Tennessee Synod, as well as tuition revenue. With the merger of the Tennessee and North Carolina Synods in 1921 and the shuttering of North Carolina College, the combined resources of the two synods were available to support Lenoir College (Solberg, 1985). This support, however, was not enough. In 1922, local industrialist Daniel Efird Rhyne contributed $300,000 as part of an $850,000 capital campaign with the stipulation that the college name be changed to Daniel Rhyne College (Solberg, 1985; Norris & Boatmon, 1990). Later, Rhyne agreed to a compromise on the naming, and in April 1923, the Board of Trustees approved the new name to be Lenoir-Rhyne College. To say that Rhyne's gift saved the college from collapse is not an overstatement.

From 1920 through the mid-1930s, the college endowment experienced sharp growth and retraction, fluctuating from $210,000 in 1920 to $570,000 in 1928 and then back to $280,000 in 1934, of which $64,000 was generated income (Norris & Boatmon, 1990). In an October 2009 telephone conversation with him from his home in Blowing Rock, North Carolina, Norris pointed to a financial crisis that emerged at the turn of the twentieth century. Norris specified that the challenge began as a "leadership crisis," when a significant number of administrators and faculty resigned, citing excessive work and low pay. This small period of turbulence, like others, was part of the persistent fiscal challenges the institution faced throughout its history.

Several interviewees pointed to the Great Recession that occurred in September 2008 as a potential new challenge for Lenoir-Rhyne. Anticipating financial insecurity due to the poor economy, Joe Smith said, "I suspect something big is happening now. There's so much unknown. We have to find new ways to engage the student experience." Like Smith, Rachel Nichols suggested that the current economy could "pose challenges." Nichols, however, is confident that a strengthened financial strategy, led by an experienced administrative team, can serve as a vital tool in meeting this new challenge. However, Lenoir-Rhyne's entering freshman classes in 2008 and 2009 were among the best in years.

Without a doubt, the greatest institutional financial challenge of the past five decades, and perhaps in the university's history, is the crisis of the early 1990s. This crisis was cited repeatedly as a critical event in the institution's recent history. Though the details of the crisis were never fully disclosed in a formal manner, the basic problem was mismanagement of college funds. The financial crisis coincided with the Centennial Renewal Celebration, an elaborate 100-year anniversary milestone and related $26 million comprehensive fundraising campaign.

In the midst of this celebration, however, news of financial problems began to surface. Briefly stated, college administrators spent the gift income prior to receipt of the gifts, resulting in significant revenue shortfalls. In the end, it was determined that the crisis was a result of poor administrative decision-making rather than criminal activity. The combination of lax presidential leadership, negligent financial accounting practices, board disengagement, and inept fiscal decision-making led to a dire financial situation that crippled the school and damaged morale for at least the next decade.

Ryan LaHurd arrived as the college's tenth president in 1994, after the disclosure of the financial debacle. In a telephone conversation in August 2009, LaHurd described the event as "financial mismanagement that brought down [the former president] and, in my opinion, significantly tarnished the college's reputation and was responsible for a deep loss of trust." Professor of Biology Marsha Fanning also identified the 1990 financial crisis as a critical event. Her own observation of the event was that the former chief financial officer made poor fiscal choices that resulted in "ill effects" and misperceptions, including allegations of mismanagement of funds. Fanning said, "The College was spending pledges before the money was in hand. We were in the red several years following the crisis, and then SACS comes along and points out this poor financial management. Years of poor faculty and staff morale followed."

The early 1990s was a time of both soaring success and desperate turmoil. On the good side, the college had experienced success in its comprehensive fundraising effort, the most ambitious in the history of the school. *U.S. News & World Report* had named Lenoir-Rhyne the eighth best liberal arts institution in the South.[16] Admissions classes were at healthy numbers, and faculty morale was upbeat, suggesting a hopeful and successful decade that would usher the college into the twenty-first century. The celebration energized the campus community, local communities, and alumni population and did result in a sharp increase in endowment gifts. Clarence Pugh, the former Vice President of Development

16. In recent years, Lenoir-Rhyne has not been classified as a liberal arts college by the *U.S. News and World Report* annual college ranking.

who helped oversee part of the campaign, reported that the Centennial Renewal Campaign generated a $2 million endowment for the specific purpose of providing financial aid to North Carolina Lutherans. History Professor Carolyn Huff described the centennial celebration "as a high-point in my nearly 40 years at L-R."

Juxtaposed with this success were fear, uncertainty, and rancor stirred by the financial situation. What is more, the Southern Association of Colleges and Schools (SACS) re-accreditation officials arrived at this same time for their regular ten-year evaluation. Citing the severe financial situation, SACS placed Lenoir-Rhyne on probation. Whispers about the unknown only exacerbated the bitter climate. Recalling the period, Joe Smith said:

> It should have launched [Lenoir-Rhyne] into a much higher level of success. The campaign was once an asset but has since been viewed as an anchor. The only positive, tangible results of that campaign were the renovation of the football stadium and the scholarships. The failure to deliver on the promised capital projects and other campaign objectives was a blow to the college. The community, especially the faculty, was deflated and bitter. The college has never really recovered.

Vice President Nichols remembered the early 1990s to be "quite unpleasant," and in her judgment, the problems were tied to weak leadership. She is encouraged, however, by the close attention the institution now pays to fiduciary matters as a result of the early 1990s crisis. She said, "Those here now at the college value the strength and integrity of the leaders and the stability of the institution. The current CFO maintains fully open financial disclosures to avoid another similar crisis."

"It is no secret that Lenoir-Rhyne has faced its share of financial difficulties through the years," lamented Dean Bill Mauney. A 1965 Lenoir-Rhyne alumnus and active Lutheran in North Carolina Synod activities and a long-time Professor of Economics, Mauney offered a particularly poignant perspective on the crisis and the institutional response to the crisis. In his comments, he emphasized the potential for growth and planning to sprout from such distress. Moreover, such challenge even forces sharper attention and more deliberate planning. It was obvious during the interview that Mauney had given serious thought to the institution's financial ups and downs. He said:

When financial challenge happens, we must ask what is important
to the institution. It forces us to plan. The big crisis in the early
1990s resulted from bad financial decisions that left big holes in
budgets. This crisis occurred just before the ten-year SACS ac-
creditation process, and so that process only highlighted the financial weaknesses. The morale of the campus was stressed. No,
no one was happy. However, many people, when they saw that we
must deal with these problems, rallied around the mission of the
college. We were celebrating the centennial during this time; it was
a real paradox.

When an organization must spend excessive time, energy, and resources on addressing issues related to financial struggle, it often does so
at the expense of other important institutional business. By all accounts
recorded during interviews at Lenoir-Rhyne, the university did not make
trade-offs with regard to its Lutheran identity, a sign of commitment to
that ecclesial relationship. In the face of ruin, the institution remained
steadfast as a college of the church, even when a different strategy might
have yielded more tuition-paying students.

Multiple interview respondents noted that, when faced with the
choice of diminishing the focus on Lutheran identity, the university chose
not to make this trade-off. Both President Wayne Powell and Larry Yoder responded that no trade-offs had been made at the expense of the
institutional Lutheran identity. Mauney echoed their opinions, insisting
that financial issues have not affected the Lutheran identity. "Following
best practices for accounting is not a sign of 'Lutheranness,'" he added.
"It is actually the opposite with the admissions office. We seek out and
attract Lutheran students from other states. This funnel started with the
Lutheran connection, especially in Florida."

Nichols reiterated this admissions strategy. She explained how new-
ly-adopted data-driven enrollment management strategies now guide
the Lenoir-Rhyne admissions effort, unlike in the past. Research and
the findings of the Commission for Lenoir-Rhyne recommend that the
university's relationship to the church should be preserved, a notion that
holds very broad appeal to various Lenoir-Rhyne constituencies. Thus,
there is enrollment potential in the preservation of the institution's religious affiliation.

Provost Hall suggested that the winning formula for a successful
small university could very likely include a strong affiliation with the

sponsoring faith tradition. This "winning formula" he posed includes an institution with a smallish student body of 3,000 to 6,000 students,[17] a focus on students (a non-research university), an emphasis on small class size, a liberal arts core with pre-professional offerings, engaged and experiential learning, and integration of all of these components.

Hall argued that religious identity can be an important environment in which this educational experience happens, especially at Lenoir-Rhyne. Citing the recommendation by the Commission for Lenoir-Rhyne that the Lutheran identity should be preserved, Hall said, "Now why would we eliminate the Lutheran identity? Everything answers to that mission. This growth can occur and this extension into new forms and delivery of education can occur without impacting our Lutheran identity."

As Clarence Pugh indicated, the Centennial Renewal Campaign, as well as subsequent development initiatives, focused on Lutheran students in particular. For example, fundraising priorities have included scholarship endowments for Lutheran students, financial support for the Center for Theology, start-up costs for a sacred music major, and plans for a new campus chapel. Not only have these efforts generated funds and interest in topics related to college-church relations, but they have maintained strong ties between Lenoir-Rhyne and the North Carolina Synod.

Mauney pointed out that the crisis also led the university to have serious conversations with the North Carolina Synod. He remarked, "What are our long-term commitments? What do we mean to each other? It has never been the case at Lenoir Rhyne that the Synod has been unsupportive." The conversations and questions have led to identifying formally what the college-synod relationship might mean. Mauney cited several examples of the college-synod relationship, including the engagement and support of the bishop on the Lenoir-Rhyne Board of Trustees, the fact that the annual Synod Assembly is held at the university, and the numerous student aid programs made possible by the synod.

Both strategic planning documents, *Strategy for the Seventies* and *University Rising*, include a substantial focus on financial matters. The former plan called for efforts to strengthen the academic program, improve student services, double the endowment, increase faculty salaries, augment the staff, and expand the campus physical plant. "A crucial factor in the realization of these goals for Lenoir-Rhyne," the plan stated, "will

---

17. Hall did not indicate that Lenoir-Rhyne would seek to grow its student body to these sizes.

clearly be finances." In the years that followed, even with careful planning, the institution was able to accomplish most of these goals but was unable to avoid financial hardship. The first financial goal in *University Rising* keenly seeks to manage and develop institutional budgets responsibly and effectively. Other goals are strikingly similar to the previous plan: increasing endowment, enhancing faculty and staff salaries, and updating the physical plant. Has the institution learned from past lessons? Can the new ambitious plan fulfill its promise?

The persistence of financial challenges continues to influence the identity of Lenoir-Rhyne University. These times of hardship have sharpened the institution's capacity for planning and its resolve to preserve its relationship with the Lutheran church. In his February 1995 inaugural address, President Ryan LaHurd said of the then-college community, "We can make no future which we have not first imagined." Perhaps this notion is the ultimate Lenoir-Rhyne paradox: grand plans often have been tempered by harsh financial realities. Holding onto those pieces of institutional DNA that define and sustain—the identity as a small college of the church committed to education in the liberal arts—was perhaps the best and only remedy for crisis at Lenoir-Rhyne. The theme of financial challenge is tied closely to the next theme addressed in this chapter, leadership. Presidents who governed during these difficult times have often focused on institutional repair, leaving little room for transformational leadership. As a consequence to the reality of financial struggle, steady leadership is all the more critical.

STEADY LEADERSHIP

Peter Northouse (2007), leadership expert and Western Michigan University Professor of Communication, differentiates between two common forms of leadership, assigned and emergent. Assigned leadership is demonstrated by a person serving in a particular position within an organization, while emergent leadership occurs when other individuals in the organization recognize and accept a particular person's behavior regardless of his or her distinction as the group's official leader. Northouse writes, "This type of leadership is not assigned by position; rather, it emerges over a period of time through communication . . . which include being verbally involved, being informed, seeking others' opinions, initiating new ideas, and being firm but not rigid" (Fisher, 1974; Northouse, 2007:5–6).

Effective leaders at Lenoir-Rhyne over the past five decades have been both assigned and emergent, especially in the process of influencing Lutheran identity. While a university is a complex organization, based upon hierarchy and assigned leadership roles, the opportunities for emergent leadership to flourish are also abundant. At Lenoir-Rhyne, four general leader-types most influenced the university's relationship with the church: presidents, chaplains, the religion department faculty, and the governing board. Each had both positive and negative influence on how much or how little the institution paid to that ecclesial relationship since 1965.

Seven presidents have served Lenoir-Rhyne since 1965: Voigt Cromer (1949–1968),[18] Raymond Bost (1968–1976), Albert Anderson (1976–1982), Albert Allran, interim (1983–1984),[19] John Trainer (1984–1994), Ryan LaHurd (1994–2002), and Wayne Powell, the current president who assumed office in 2003. While the president is most definitely the assigned leader of the organization, his leadership can also be characterized as emergent. With regard to the issue of Lutheran identity, as with other institutional issues, the president holds great power and responsibility in setting the tone and direction. Powell insisted that the president must set the agenda by "intentionally building the partnerships with the church and by showing through words and deeds that he or she is a spiritual person."

Provost Hall agreed. "The president has the responsibility to set the tone and demonstrate by example, said Hall. "Then people see that these things are important to the institution. At this point, it is really a cultivation of ideas." Joe Smith argued that the president should keep the concept of being a faith-based religious school in front of the college community.

18. Voigt Cromer, an ordained Lutheran pastor who had served as the college's president since 1949, was in poor health in the final years of his presidency. Though the Cromer Administration is remembered for tremendous growth of the college's physical plant and observation of close ties with the Lutheran church, Cromer's name was not mentioned in any of the interviews. This is due primarily to the parameters of the study's time horizon.

19. Perhaps because he served an interim presidency, albeit a relatively long nineteen month post, only one respondent, Larry Yoder, referenced his administration in the interviews. Robert Spuller and Norman Fintel also served brief interim presidencies at Lenoir-Rhyne.

"President Powell," he added, "speaks publicly and very openly of the strong commitment of L-R as an ELCA college." Mauney simply said that the president is the leader, setting the agenda. This goal-setting, however, does not occur exclusively by the president in a vacuum, but rather the setting of this agenda comes with the help of all of the campus community. "The president is the captain of the ship and the only person at Lenoir-Rhyne who is required to be an ELCA Lutheran," Mauney declared.[20]

David Ratke, Professor of Religion, offered his take on the faith identity of the school. According to Ratke, the president, faculty, and chaplain all have important roles to play in the conversation, seeking to bring the church into dialogue with the world. But the president is foundational. Ratke asserted, "The president, I've come to believe ever more, really sets the tone. The president needs to signal to the faculty, students, alumni, and other constituencies that religion matters in what the university does, even if it finds itself compromising at times." Weisner pointed out the two ways that President Powell and former President LaHurd expressed their own support of the institution's Lutheran identity. He explained, "I am extremely thankful for Powell's public statements about Lenoir-Rhyne's identity as a college of the church, though he does not regularly attend chapel. Ryan LaHurd, who did not speak so publicly about the college's Lutheran identity, certainly led by example. He hardly ever missed chapel, and his Lutheran faith was deeply important to him."

Over and over again in the interviews, participants remarked about the consistency, the steadiness, of Lenoir-Rhyne presidents, chaplains, and faculty in perpetuating the institutional religious identity. Even as respondents singled out turbulent financial times that by their own description were due to poor leadership, the interview respondents refrained from indicting particular individuals.[21] One interesting and unexpected critical event cited by four respondents was the institution's decision to appoint its first non-clergy president in 1976. This president, Albert Anderson of North Dakota, was a philosopher educated at Lenoir-Rhyne's sister school, Concordia College. Wayne Powell described the significance of this decision with regard to Lutheran identity, saying, "In doing so, L-R

20. Mauney clarified that the college pastor of Lenoir-Rhyne must also be Lutheran. However, one previous L-R chaplain, Don Just, was not a member of the ELCA but rather a member of the Lutheran Church-Missouri Synod.

21. The one exception to this was the naming of the former chief financial officer who was in charge during the financial challenges of the early 1990s.

made a statement about its own faith in its mission, that that mission was not predicated upon titles or vocations of the president but on the commitments and beliefs in principles and mission."

Larry Yoder described Anderson as "the best president at articulating Lutheran higher education." Yoder suggested that Anderson's preparation as a philosopher helped him to articulate clearly and persuasively these ideals. Weisner also cited Anderson's election as a critical event in the college's history. "Appointing a faithful layman as president," Weisner said, "demonstrated that this position can be a layperson's vocation."

Rufus Moretz also cited the decision by the Board of Trustees to elect a non-clergy president, but unlike his colleagues, Moretz suggested that the decision may have contributed to the diminishment of the institution's Lutheran identity. For Powell, the university's persistent decision-making to hire a president who, when faced with a choice, chose to remain a college of the church demonstrates a pattern of critical events that have shaped the organizational identity through the years. Incidentally, Marsha Fanning named Powell as "the most intentional [president] about Lutheran higher education."

Four interview respondents recalled the Raymond Bost Administration and its commitment to the Lutheran tradition. Professor Richard Von Dohlen remembered Bost as a president whose focus was expansion of the faculty guided by the plan to recruit faculty with a commitment to the Christian, and specifically Lutheran, character of the institution. Interviewees more commonly pointed to the Bost Administration's effort to revise the curriculum, which was connected to his plan to expand the faculty. In *Strategy for the Seventies*, Bost charged the campus community to strengthen the quality of the existing academic program, one that would remain rooted in the liberal arts with additional professional offerings. Bost commissioned the assembly of an advisory committee, called CEPAC, to lead this effort.

The Committee on Educational Program and Academic Calendar (CEPAC) was concerned with evaluating the curriculum and calendar, investigating the introduction of interdisciplinary studies, and considering the addition of learning based upon "first hand experiences" (community research, work-study, and study-abroad). Nevertheless, the revision of the core curriculum was a central goal. Carolyn Huff identified the changes in curriculum, particularly the adoption of the CEPAC core, as a critical institutional event. Huff said, "The [CEPAC core] modified our academic focus but never changed it from the traditional emphasis on being a liberal arts college, now university, of the church."

Fanning recalled Bost's goal for CEPAC to be strengthening the educational quality of the academic program, while introducing a distribution of core requirements over a student's four-year career, and to ensure that the learning be contemporary and relevant. Fanning said, "Part of this effort was President Bost's desire to increase the quality of the faculty. There was a big push to hire more Ph.D.s. That's how I was hired." Though generally supportive of Bost's CEPAC strategy, Moretz offered a response that suggests the curriculum changes had both positive and negative effects. Moretz explained:

> The institution adopted a new core curriculum. In some respects it was similar to its predecessor. It continued a large block of liberal arts requirements, including courses in religion and philosophy. Although required courses in Old and New Testament and in Christian ethics were abandoned, more general courses that treated Bible, theology, and ethics replaced the more specific courses of the previous core curriculum. More importantly, the atmosphere of change allowed the passage of a proposal from the religion faculty for a true major in religious studies. Previously there had been a so-called religious education major that required a hodgepodge of courses in religion and history plus a completely different major.

Although more traditional Christian and biblical classes were replaced or their content diluted, the curricular changes introduced by CEPAC did lead to the establishment of a respectable religion department, one that would certainly positively influence and further reinforce the school's Lutheran identity.

Perhaps more than any other academic office during the past 40 years, the Lenoir-Rhyne Department of Religion has consistently demonstrated solidarity, excellence, and a powerful voice for the college's relationship with the ELCA. This group of professors also expresses clearly the concept of emergent leadership, showing how their work can inspire and influence the college community. President Powell asserted that faculty members are so varied in their own beliefs, but that they each should have an undeniable appreciation of the value of a faith-based educational community; the religion department exemplifies Powell's expectation.

A retired member of the religion department, Richard Von Dohlen counted Michael McDaniel as "perhaps the most articulate and energetic spokesman for the Lutheran identity of the college. He combined scholarship, passion and a generous spirit as few could." The Rev. Michael McDaniel joined Lenoir-Rhyne as a religion professor in 1971 but left in 1981 after being elected Bishop of the North Carolina Synod. He returned to the college after his service as bishop, where he retired. McDaniel's voice was confident, pastoral, and conservative, and his stature brought much credit and esteem to both the college and the religion department.

McDaniel's critics argued that his views were too conservative and that his influence at the college created a parochial understanding of the Lenoir-Rhyne faith community. Ryan LaHurd also recognized McDaniel's influence on the institutional identity, noting McDaniel's "conservative and sometimes exclusionist definition of what it means to be a Lutheran." LaHurd added, "Yoder and McDaniel set the boundaries of the discussion about L-R's Lutheran identity both on and off campus."

Larry Yoder described the religion department success as "a pattern of deliberate continuity over the 40-year time period." Despite the fewer number of Lutheran students on campus in recent years, the university's self-understanding as a Lutheran college has not diminished. According to Yoder, this is due to the people who are here and have been here—namely Ratke, Weisner, Pugh, McDaniel, Moretz, and me—who advocate Lutheran identity." The religion department created a rich climate for encouraging the identity dialogue and what it means to be a Lutheran college.

During his thirty two year tenure as first the chaplain and later as a religion professor, Larry Yoder has played a remarkably significant role in setting the college-church conversation at Lenoir-Rhyne. In a very real way, Yoder has shaped Lenoir-Rhyne's Lutheran identity, or at least driven that conversation, more than any other single person over the past thirty-two years. Von Dohlen said, "Larry Yoder has been and continues to be the chief spokesman for the tradition. He combines scholarship, articulate expression of the basic mission of the school, and great administrative gifts." Like McDaniel, Yoder is not without his critics, some charging him with articulating too narrow a view of the Lutheran tradition. Indeed, the president sets institutional priorities, as has been the case at Lenoir-Rhyne over the years. But others in the campus community emerge as leaders who lift up the president's banner to discuss central issues like ecclesial relationship. Agree or disagree with his outlook, one cannot mistake Yoder's emergent leadership on this topic.

In an April 2009 interview on the front porch of Russell House, the home of the Lenoir-Rhyne Department of Religion, Yoder offered an account of how the religion department developed its pattern of influence and continuity. He said in no uncertain terms:

> In 1972, Michael McDaniel came to Lenoir-Rhyne. He was a force, along with Rufus Moretz, Emmanuel Gitlin, Joe Glass, and later joined by Dick von Dohlen, creating a formidable department of religion and a sense of centrality for the campus' religious identity. Yoder as chaplain fit well into that paradigm and helped give it strength. Then the transition from McDaniel to Yoder in 1977, an imposing person in presence and intellect, confirmed that no other discipline, no other department on campus, could disparage. This presence gave the religion department a voice to speak credibly about Lenoir-Rhyne's Lutheran identity. It was a force to be reckoned with.

This is to say that no other academic department doubted the strength and intellect of the religion department, and thus, its advocacy of the Lutheran message. Yoder also described the role of other key figures, tangentially related to the religion department. Yoder added:

> From 1977 to 1994, I sat on the President's Cabinet. When I arrived in 1977 as the college chaplain, I served on the President's Cabinet under Al Anderson. When Al Allran took over in the interim between Anderson and Trainer, and Don Just became chaplain, Allran asked me to continue serving on the cabinet because he said, "I want your savvy here." Upon Al's departure, John Trainer kept me, continuing into his administration that began in 1984. During that long time period, the cabinet was populated by administrators that included [Development Vice President Clarence] Pugh, [Chaplain Don] Just, and [Professor of Religion Larry] Yoder, three figures who represented strong Lutheran voices. These were three strong Lutheran voices, two with earned Ph.D.s that served on the President's Cabinet for twenty years. Thus, this presence held steady the Lutheran compass and moorings during this long period. I should add that Michael McDaniel served as the bishop during a number of these years. All of this made possible a strong, credible, undeniable platform for the College's Lutheran message. In 1994, with the LaHurd Administration, Pugh, Just, and Yoder left the Cabinet.

Yoder was careful to explain that this was not a punitive move by LaHurd but one due to attrition. Don Just left the college, and Clarence Pugh assumed another role at the college. Yoder went on to say that this was not a reflection of LaHurd's commitment to the institution's Lutheran identity.

Chaplains represent a third group that has demonstrated steady leadership over the years. It should be no surprise that their leadership has also influenced the institutional Lutheran identity over the years. Clarence Pugh argued that the hiring of a full-time Lutheran chaplain gave more emphasis to the college's ecclesial relationship. The influence of Yoder and Just as chaplains has been argued in previous paragraphs.[22] To be more precise, Yoder's significant impact occurred in his years as Professor of Religion and Director of the Center for Theology. With regard to the chaplain's influence on Lenoir-Rhyne's Lutheran identity, interview respondents most frequently named Andrew Weisner as a driving force. President Powell summarized the basic role of the Lenoir-Rhyne chaplain, or college pastor, when he said that he or she "must reach out to all people regardless of faith and be there to guide in spiritual exploration." Energetic and compassionate, Weisner embodies this expectation.

From Yoder to Just to Weisner, all of the chaplains have been Confessional Lutherans, keeping in tradition with the earliest theological perspective the college espoused. Weisner's style is markedly different than that of his predecessor, Don Just. Chaplain Just's ministry style was characterized by intellectualism, quiet introspection, and conservatism. Weisner, on the other hand, brought to Lenoir-Rhyne a warm and charismatic outreach, an effervescent personality, and a deep pastoral presence. Multiple interview participants commented on Weisner's distinctive pastoral style.

Weisner also brought a diverse pastoral identity: his lively preaching style seemed to be influenced by Southern preachers, while his liturgical expression seemed shaped by the high-church practices of Roman Catholic and Eastern Orthodox Christians. In his first months at Lenoir-Rhyne, Pastor Weisner would appear in the Cromer Student Center in full ecclesial vestments, swinging his smoking thurible and broadcasting sweet-smelling incense across the plaza and quad. In addition to the weekly

22. Two chaplains preceded Larry Yoder's arrival in 1977. Robert Walker, the first official chaplain of the college, served from 1961–1965, and Louis Rogers served from 1966–1976. During the interview process, one comment was offered about these two chaplains: Marsha Fanning said simply, "Chaplain Rogers was a presence."

traditional chapel service he leads, Weisner presides at a daily Celebration of the Holy Eucharist, complete with candles and incense.

Weisner, also a Lenoir-Rhyne alumnus, reminisced about his first visit to campus. He described walking into the Rhyne Building, the university's lovely Gothic classroom structure, and seeing in its quiet lobby an oil mural, entitled *Jesus and the Rich Young Ruler*. Said Weisner, "That made an impression on me. I thought to myself, 'This is the kind of place I want to be part of. This is where I want to study.'" He was moved by that remembrance. Years later, he shepherds this same campus community, describing his role as offering a friendly voice and serving as a counselor.

When asked who most shapes the faith community at the university, Weisner responded, "God. I don't have anything to do with this. I pray for them. There is something bigger than me here." Weisner's college ministry is student-focused and contemporary but still in keeping with his own theologically traditional and ceremonially liturgical expression of faith. The campus pastor also recollected that he still prays, by name, for all members of the campus community each week, a tradition he has maintained since his arrival at Lenoir-Rhyne.

To be sure, Weisner's style is distinctive, and his assertive, charismatic pastoral style was a departure from previous chaplains. Upon his arrival, the campus took note of Weisner's caring, compassion, and enthusiasm, but was he a college pastor that would appeal to the entire campus community? Ryan LaHurd, who appointed Weisner as campus pastor months after his own arrival in 1994, recalled this significance of Weisner to the campus community. LaHurd said, "With him as with McDaniel and Yoder, I think the college gained or lost prestige and appeal with various groups and attracted or 'repelled' certain kinds of students, thus shaping the image and the Lutheran identity discussion."

Marsha Fanning indicated that Weisner "has grown into his position." She said, "I think at first his time here was marked by pageantry. He has become a character and an asset. His flexibility helps him relate to students." Joe Smith put it this way: "I believe the faith community is strong at L-R because of Andrew Weisner. I can't think of a better shepherd. His theology and message is not thrust upon students, but he's always around campus. He doesn't proselytize; he is just there for the campus."

Finally, the Board of Trustees and other governing boards have provided a source of steady leadership over the forty-five-year time horizon, shaping decisions that have ultimately preserved the religious identity of the institution. Some critics contend that the Board of Trustees has sometimes been disengaged and even negligent in matters of institutional management, including relaxing requirements for Lutheran member-ship on the Board. In contrast, others argue that this governing board has made decisions over the past forty-five years that have preserved the Lutheran identity of Lenoir-Rhyne. Most of these interviewees' percep-tions were related to Board membership and presidential criteria policies.

Three interview respondents commented that Board leadership had generally preserved the university's Lutheran identity. Smith said that the Board of Trustees clearly demonstrates a commitment to the college-church relationship, saying, "This is who we are." In Smith's judgment, the college's Lutheran identity has never really been in jeopardy because of the commitment of the Trustees. Huff agreed with Smith, stating simply, "The Board values this [Lutheran] identity."

Mauney cited the work of another leadership board, the Board of Visitors, which was established in 1968 as the Development Board. Ac-cording to Mauney, "this board was intended to allow non-Lutherans who cared about L-R to be involved." Essentially, the establishment of the Development Board allowed for an injection of new energy and diverse, non-Lutheran voices, while maintaining the "Lutheran integrity" of the Board of Trustees.

Others viewed membership decisions made by the Board of Trust-ees as threats to the college's Lutheran identity. Pugh cited the decision to lower the percentage requirement of Lutheran clergy on the Board of Trustees as a negative effect on the Lutheran identity. Jeff Norris echoed Pugh's sentiment, but he also identified as a threat the decision to open the position of Chairman of the Board of Trustees to a non-Lutheran. Last, Moretz critiqued the decision by the board to allow a gradual influx of non-Lutherans. He explained, "While this change was made for good reasons, I believe it has contributed to some diminishment of the institu-tion's Lutheran identity." Moretz added that, since a majority of the mem-bers of the Board of Trustees are Lutherans, he is reasonably sure that there is the intention to maintain a Lutheran identity for the institution.

In their own ways, the leaders evoked by the interviewed members of the campus community have helped preserve the bond between Lenoir-Rhyne University and the Lutheran church. The chaplains shepherded the campus community, and the religion department built a reputation of re-spect and excellence. The presidents each embossed their own mark: Bost strengthened the curriculum and sought a faith-centered faculty; Anderson articulated the ideals of Lutheran higher education; Trainer raised the college profile; LaHurd led recovery and healing after great institutional struggle; and Powell, building on LaHurd's success, has initiated bold (and risky) moves that position Lenoir-Rhyne for transformational change.

THE FANNING FACTOR

It is widely held that having a critical mass of organizational members that affirms a college's religious identity is imperative to the vitality of the institution's expression of that religious identity (Burtchaell, 1998; Benne, 2001). Using Robert Benne's (2001) typology for sorting and describing church-related colleges, Lenoir-Rhyne University fulfills the criteria for the intentionally pluralistic college, as demonstrated in Phase I of this study. Closer examination of the Lenoir-Rhyne saga, however, reveals a more complex situation. Along Benne's typology spectrum, Lenoir-Rhyne University is situated somewhere between the critical-mass point and the intentionally pluralistic point. Given its geographic location which lacks a large Lutheran population, among other factors, Lenoir-Rhyne does not have—and likely never will have—a critical mass of Lutheran faculty and staff. What happens, then, when a college expresses an institutional mission to live out its identity as a college of the church, yet does not hold a critical mass from its sponsoring tradition among its campus community?

This fourth theme, the Fanning Factor, is at heart a critical mass issue, shaped by a series of cumulative critical events: the hiring of faculty and staff who generally affirm the church-relatedness of Lenoir-Rhyne, as well as the sustained dialogue about institutional Lutheran identity. First, a definition of critical mass is necessary, and Benne's definition, though rigorous, works well. Benne (2001) writes:

> Critical-mass colleges and universities do not insist that all members of the community be believers in their tradition or even believers in the Christian tradition, though they do insist that a critical mass of adherents from their tradition inhabit all the constituencies of the educational enterprise—board, administration, faculty, and student body. However, they define "critical mass" in different ways. For some it is three-fourths or more; for others it may be a bare majority, while for a few it may be a strong minority. But at any rate, the critical mass must be strong enough to define,

shape, and maintain the public identity and mission of the college consonant with the sponsoring tradition.

This section of chapter 5 suggests that strategic placement of the "right people,"[23] Lutheran or non-Lutheran faculty and staff who support the institution's relationship with the church, can help support the institution's mission to express its identity as a college of the church. Said another way, if a school cannot achieve a critical mass of Lutheran faculty and staff, then the school must depend upon strategically placing the few it does have in key positions, attracting others who will support its mission, hiring those who will affirm and live out the mission, and inspiring those already part of the campus community.

In some cases, the university must also rely on non-Lutheran faculty and staff to help maintain the institution's church-relatedness. In order to fulfill the criteria for Benne's definition, these strategically placed faculty members, even if non-Lutheran—must not only fulfill the religious ideals of the institution, but they must work to fulfill the specific ideals of the *sponsoring religious tradition*. This occurs at Lenoir-Rhyne University, a phenomenon this author calls the Fanning Factor.

Lenoir-Rhyne has traditionally boasted a caring, committed faculty and staff. The Commission for Lenoir-Rhyne reported as its first thematic finding "special attention given to students," shaped by close student-teacher relationships and teaching-centered faculty. In turn, *University Rising* identified specific goals and objectives to strengthen this traditional institutional strength. Related to this strength is the pervasive ethos of a vibrant faith community. While Lenoir-Rhyne does not record the number of practicing Lutherans among the faculty and staff, interview participants did comment on their own general perceptions of the university faith community. To be clear, Lutheran faculty and staff are by no means a majority at Lenoir-Rhyne; in fact, the Lutherans among the student body total only sixteen percent.[24]

Remarkably, though, the Lenoir-Rhyne campus appears to maintain an identity as a dynamic, lively Lutheran school. Why? Is demonstrating an institutional identity as a Lutheran college distinctively different from demonstrating a robust campus faith community? The answers lie with the people of Lenoir-Rhyne, for it is a community populated with faculty

23. Andrew Weisner used this term in his interview.

24. This is according to 2008 data.

and staff mentors who live out their faith, Lutheran and non-Lutheran, in their daily vocations. While a number of these faculty and staff are Lutheran, many are not. Professor of Biology Marsha Fanning, who was interviewed for this study, is an apt example for this engaged community of non-Lutheran faculty and staff who, despite following another Christian faith tradition, affirm, support, and engage in the conversation about Lenoir-Rhyne's Lutheran identity. She, and other non-Lutherans like her, enlivens the institution's church-related identity.

Who is Marsha Fanning? Fanning, a gentle, warm, and energetic woman, was enthusiastic about sharing her reflections on her time at the university. The interview with Fanning took place in a small laboratory in the Minges Science Building during the site visit to Lenoir-Rhyne. Because she has been on the faculty for 36 years as a biology professor, Fanning possessed a valuable insight into the campus ethos. She explained that she came to Lenoir-Rhyne in 1973, after graduating from Columbia College, a Methodist institution. Fanning, however, is Baptist, active in one of the large local Baptist churches near the Lenoir-Rhyne campus. Fanning emphasized that she does not subscribe to the fundamentalism of the Southern Baptist Convention but instead favors a more moderate Baptist outlook.

She said, "I mainly applied to small, church-related institutions in the Southeast. I was offered two jobs and chose to come to Lenoir-Rhyne. It was funny; L-R was offering $8 more per year. Really." That Lenoir-Rhyne was a college committed to the relationship with its sponsoring church body was attractive to Fanning. The church-relatedness and the liberal arts tradition are both, in fact, important factors in Fanning's teaching vocation. When asked to describe the mission statement of Lenoir-Rhyne, Fanning responded, "To educate the whole person. That's from the mission statement. We maintain the liberal arts as the foundation for lifelong vocation. Vocation encompasses both career and the approach to life and its purpose." Fanning added that she had had a role in revising the mission statement at one point during the 1990s.

Fanning said that she did not know much about Lutheranism when she arrived at Lenoir-Rhyne, but over the years she has become involved in the religious conversation on campus. She noted the many "different styles of expressing faith at L-R." Fanning became involved with the Baptist Student Union (BSU) at the college, serving as a faculty advisor and mentor to countless students through the years. The Baptist population is in fact the largest of all faith traditions represented at Lenoir-Rhyne. Fanning noted, "I have noted that, over the years, many of the members of BSU are conservative Baptists, more conservative than me. There is still some of that conservatism today, and other students are not interested in [faith issues] at all."

Over the years, Fanning has enthusiastically engaged in the ongoing campus conversation about Lutheran higher education and about what it means to be a Lutheran college. In addition to being encouraged by the administration to be part of the campus dialogue, Fanning expressed an interest in the topic of church-relatedness and was interested in seeing Lenoir-Rhyne live out its mission as a college of the church, even if the sponsoring faith tradition was different from her own. Despite the ongoing institutional forums and retreats focused on Lutheran higher education, Fanning admitted that defining a Lutheran college is difficult, especially at a place like Lenoir-Rhyne, in which Lutheran students and Lutheran faculty and staff are the minority.

With regard to faith engagement at the institution, Fanning takes her lead from the president, who sets the tone for the faith community. "The president models how we should engage our faith," said Fanning. The faculty has a role, too, but it is primarily by the example they set. She added, "My role in this regard is what I do, not what I say." Fanning indicated a self-selection of faculty and staff that choose to come to Lenoir-Rhyne, for potential candidates are well aware of the institution's mission as a college of the church. She asserted, "Most people who work here acknowledge the importance of faith in their lives. We have both conservative and liberal faculty members." Fanning models her faith for her students and colleagues without forcing her beliefs on others. She attends chapel occasionally, relates faith issues to her discipline when applicable, mentors BSU students, and perhaps most importantly, interprets her work as a teacher, mentor, and scholar through the lens of vocation.

To be sure, other campus personalities like Marsha Fanning could adequately represent the phenomenon of meaningful faculty and staff engagement with the institutional faith identity. In fact, various interview participants suggested a series of possibilities, though certainly not an exhaustive list of the engaged non-Lutherans at Lenoir-Rhyne: Richard Von Dohlen, Carolyn Huff, Linda Johanson, Linda Reece, Sarah Wallace, Dan Kiser, and Charles Wells. The faith community, as the interview respondents demonstrated, is diverse and dynamic, though there is some disagreement on how it is manifested on campus.

Lenoir-Rhyne publicly proclaims a strong tie to its religious tradition and the presence of a robust faith community, but the Lutheran population is a minority, surpassed by or generally comparable to Baptist and Roman Catholic populations on campus. While other Protestant traditions are also well-represented, Lenoir-Rhyne reported no Jewish or Muslim students in 2008 (Council of ELCA-Related College & University Presidents Annual Meeting). What is this campus community like, especially since it is influenced by many non-Lutherans? Interviewees provided rich, albeit sometimes incongruent, descriptions of the Lenoir-Rhyne faith community.

President Powell described the faith community as "varied," ranging from very fundamentalist Christian to completely atheistic, in both the faculty and student body. He added, "There is, however, a general appreciation of our commitment to faith. We openly espouse Lutheranism as an avenue for all to explore. I think we are undeniably Christian, but to most we are not very Lutheran." Powell suggested that the gradual turnover of faculty and staff from those with Lenoir-Rhyne and Lutheran connections to a campus community without a Lutheran background is a threat to preserving the institutional Lutheran identity. Moreover, Powell noted the trend in wider diversity of backgrounds and beliefs at Lenoir-Rhyne, an example of permanent demographic shift.

Provost Hall described the university faith community as "very strong," noting Lenoir-Rhyne's intentional integration of faith and learning across the campus. Hall said, "Some schools provide church programs outside the classroom but do not integrate the two. Faith is integrated into students' lives." Pastor Weisner, Hall added, played an important role in helping articulate some of the faith-related goals outlined in the new strategic plan. Hall added, "Even faculty who do not share the Lutheran faith—or any faith, for that matter—understands the importance of the [Lutheran] heritage. To prospective faculty members, we ask the important question: 'How would you live out the mission and values of the university?'"

Smith characterized the faith community as "strong . . . due to the variety of faiths on campus. We have atheists on the faculty, but there are no complaints. The faculty knows who we are as a college." Smith acknowledged that the composition of the faculty, with regard to faith orientation, is changing, but he predicted that the university would continue to attract people interested in issues of faith and learning, Lutheran or non-Lutheran, because of the stated institutional mission. Carolyn Huff added, "I know that many of the faculty and staff are persons of sincere faith, and I believe that is true of many of our students as well. In fact, many choose L-R for that reason."

Pastor Weisner echoed Smith's sentiment, calling the community "strong." Added Weisner, "When I visit our religious groups, I see engagement." Seven religiously-affiliated groups are under the Office of the College Pastor: Intervarsity, FCA (Fellowship of Christian Athletes), LSM (Lutheran Student Movement), BSU (Baptist Student Union), Newman Society (Roman Catholics), Campus Crusade, and Young Life. These groups, in some cases, are staffed part-time or full-time, but all are under the guidance and spiritual direction of the Office of the Campus Pastor.

Weisner noted that some 250 students are engaged in these activities on a regular basis through service and leadership during the school year, approximately 17 percent of the full-time student body. Yoder, a former chaplain, estimated the student involvement to be at the same level suggested by Weisner, expressed primarily in chapel attendance and group involvement. Faculty and staff, Yoder explained, also are part of the faith community in chapel, in religious groups, and in campus dialogue. Yoder said, "There are only a few faculty on campus who are not publicly practicing Christians. None, to my knowledge, are hostile. The repartee at the table does have religious overtones."

David Ratke characterized the weekly worshipping faith community as "overwhelmingly white and overwhelmingly Lutheran and Roman Catholic in its orientation." He went on to say that Evangelical Christians and "low church" Protestants, are likely to find an unfamiliar worship experience at Lenoir-Rhyne. On the other hand, Mauney said, "I would say that our students are not as attracted to liturgical trappings as much as they are engaged in ministries that they see as speaking to their lives."

Mauney offered the example of a Lenoir-Rhyne nursing professor, a non-Lutheran, who takes students each year to Mexico for service-learning. These engaged learning trips are popular among students, but they also demonstrate clearly how students, faculty, and staff—people of God—can live out their professional lives in service to one another, a reflection of the theology of vocation. Dean Mauney insisted that this shift in how students understand faith and its application reflects the change in the student body. "Students want learning to be experiential," Mauney said. Finally, Richard Von Dohlen summarized the faith community this way: "I think that it is healthy. It has been and always will be somewhat precarious. There is always a group who are in favor of the Lutheran identity of the college or university, as long as it doesn't interfere with their regular academic and teaching work. Others are not particularly committed but like the atmosphere. Still others are deeply committed but do not have the ability to be articulate representatives of the tradition."

For a college of the Lutheran church, the Lenoir-Rhyne faith community is expressed diversely and celebrated differently according to particular members of the campus community. Some faculty members participate in this community; others do not. Engaged in this faith community or not, what is the expectation of a faculty depends on what this means," Hall responded. "Faculty should first be role models. Values should be considered member at this specific religiously-affiliated school with regard to issues of faith? "It but not necessarily promoted. Faculty must approach all intellectual inquiry with humility, but proselytizing in the classroom is not good." To be sure, proselytizing is not expected of faculty at Lutheran colleges and universities, nor is this practice particularly prevalent in the Lutheran ethos anyway. Hall noted the three criteria employed for the Lenoir-Rhyne faculty tenure review process: teaching and mentoring, research development, and service.

Smith, like Fanning, pointed to the impact of institutionally-sponsored seminars and forums on the topic of Lutheran higher education. Smith found these intentional conversations helpful to him as he formulated his own vocation of teaching and mentoring. Being a Lutheran college is the intent of Lenoir-Rhyne; according to Smith, the challenge is to inspire the faculty to support this mission. Weisner argued that, even if faculty members do not subscribe to Christianity or Lutheranism, they should still be willing to bring up this perspective in their disciplines, as they are able.

Both Von Dohlen and Huff agreed, especially as the faculty serve as examples of good work, faithfulness, and service to their students. About the role of faculty at Lenoir-Rhyne, Huff added, "Inasmuch as those proclaimed ideals are the search for truth and knowledge and wholeness of the individual, including the spiritual nature, there is no incompatibility." Ratke, however, observed that, in recent ongoing discussions about the university's core curriculum, some faculty members have been either ignorant of Lenoir-Rhyne's Lutheran heritage or altogether dismissive of it.

At the university's periodic forums on Lutheran higher education and institutional identity, the issue of critical mass is often visited and revisited. As previously noted, the literature shows that a college community must have a critical mass, especially of faculty, to support a serious institutional effort of maintaining a meaningful relationship with the sponsoring church body. But if Lenoir-Rhyne does not have a critical mass of Lutheran faculty, can it preserve an institutional Lutheran identity even if its mission envisions this? Interviewees offered a variety of responses on the issue, but all of them pointed to the indispensible nature of critical mass—though expressed differently—for maintaining a strong religious identity.

About maintaining a critical mass of Lutheran faculty, Fanning answered, "[Critical mass] helps. I'm glad it's not all Lutherans at Lenoir-Rhyne. In fact, that might be 'unLutheran.'" While Powell saw a large Lutheran faculty essential in the traditional sense, he also noted the flexibility of Lutheranism, arguing that the Lutheran identity could be enhanced regardless of the denomination of the faculty. Hall argued that maintaining a critical mass was not necessary for achieving a Lutheran identity, though he contended that a strong Lutheran identity would likely attract other faculty, staff, and students interested in supporting the Lutheran mission.

Yoder asserted that having critical mass is "absolutely essential, and by critical mass is meant both a respectable percentage, on the one hand, and on the other strong leadership of persons whose respect is unquestioned and whose identity is Lutheran." Yoder went on to say that faculty must know the perspective, even if all do not believe it. Moreover, a few of these faculty members must be genuine leaders who are willing to share, understand, abide, and live the Lutheran perspective. Moretz said, "I believe maintaining a critical mass of Lutheran faculty is crucial to sustaining a robust Lutheran identity. At the same time, I also believe that diversity is essential to the search for truth."

Huff, who is not a Lutheran, embodies this diversity that Moretz values. "Although I am not Lutheran," Huff responded, "I am glad that there are strong faculty and staff of the Lutheran faith and also a willingness to recognize that those of us of other faiths have contributions to make as well." Ratke tends to hold a fairly rigorous standard, as well as a clear understanding, of the place of Lutheran higher education in colleges and universities.

However, on the point of critical mass, Ratke suggested that non-Lutheran faculty and staff can also be effective in engaging in the campus's Lutheran dialogue. He said, "We've had some really articulate people for Lutheran identity who are not Lutheran. Moreover, some Lutherans have been so very ineffective in such conversations. I'd say that some critical mass is important, but this by itself is far from enough. Intentional and conscientious conversations convened, or at least encouraged, by the president are absolutely necessary." Ratke is joined by other members of the campus community in endorsing the necessity of intentional institutional dialogue.

Lenoir-Rhyne, throughout its history, has employed a steadfast, committed faculty, comprised of Lutherans and non-Lutherans alike. While Evangelical colleges and universities often have a religiously homogeneous faculty and staff, the mainline Protestant schools, Lutheran included, are less likely to demonstrate this homogeneity (Dovre, 2002). Mauney suggested, "There has been too much focus here on that question [of critical mass]. It's really misleading. Look at [Professor of Music] Dan Kiser and his engagement and support of the mission. And he's Baptist, I believe. Another example is [retired Professor of Religion] Dick Von Dohlen. He's Baptist and very supportive of the college's mission."

Indeed, Von Dohlen is an excellent example of non-Lutherans who are interested in, engaged in, and supportive of the Lutheran conversation, as well as the Lutheran identity of Lenoir-Rhyne. Von Dohlen stated, "Numbers are not, however, what always counts. Articulate representatives are very important." Weisner provided an answer most harmonious with this author's argument: "Critical mass is perhaps necessary, though I don't know the number. If strategically and critically placed, the right 10 percent can make the difference." If this theory holds, then the role of the non-Lutherans becomes crucial.

A significant reason for faculty and staff engagement in the Lutheran higher education conversation at Lenoir-Rhyne is the university's intentional and systematic opportunity for this dialogue to occur. Whether this conversation occurs during faculty assembly, new employee orientation, summer retreats, fall convocations, or informally at the lunch table, faculty and staff must be encouraged and instructed about the value and promise that Lutheran higher education can hold for the educational experience. In order for the Fanning Factor phenomenon to continue, this systematic instruction and conversation must also continue.

SUMMARY

A central part of the new strategic plan, *University Rising*, is a comprehensive campaign that will raise funds for several capital projects, including the construction of a chapel and a science building. The image created by this strategic initiative—the proposed construction of a chapel and a science building—is profound and illustrative, an excellent symbol for Lutheran higher education and the healthy, robust dialogue between faith and reason. Reflecting indispensable attention to the dialectic of faith and learning, Lenoir-Rhyne is a university of the Lutheran church. The institution professes to celebrate this identity and strategizes to live out its mission as a college of the church.

How has Lenoir-Rhyne changed as a college of the church from 1965 to 2009? After interviewing thirteen people, making observations during the campus visit, and reviewing numerous documents, it is clear that Lenoir-Rhyne is intentionally seeking to preserve its Lutheran identity. The ethos and logos in the 1960s, 1970s, and 1980s were characterized by a dynamic faith community, high-profile and influential Lutheran voices on campus, and a mission statement that proclaimed a commitment to faith and learning in the Lutheran tradition.

Despite the 1990s being marked by financial turmoil and low morale for the campus community, the decade was also a time of remarkable faithfulness to its ecclesial tradition. Today, Lenoir-Rhyne publicly proclaims a commitment to its Lutheran tradition, in particular, and to a dynamic community of faith, in general. Evidenced by the report of the Commission for Lenoir-Rhyne, the 2008 strategic plan, and the numerous interviewee perspectives, the institution's religious identity is a valuable and marketable asset.

The saga of Lenoir-Rhyne University over the past forty-five years has been shaped by its identity as a local, Lutheran school rooted in the liberal arts; by the persistence of financial struggles that did not unravel its ties with the Lutheran church; by a continuation of steady leadership; and by a faith-centered yet diverse faculty and staff, an idea called the Fanning Factor. Lenoir-Rhyne's story is complex, and today, this new university faces a crossroads with regard to its Lutheran identity. In 2009, the university set out on a renewed commitment to academic excellence, faculty scholarship and mentoring, faith development, service to neighbor, and institutional stability.

What part will the Lutheran identity continue to play in Lenoir-Rhyne's future? The board and president have wagered high stakes in imagining the university's future as a college of the church. Today, Lenoir-Rhyne leaders are taking big institutional risks, including changing from college to university status, attempting to reposition the institution as a nationally recognized university of choice, and implementing new admissions strategies. Perhaps the biggest risk of all is the institution's expressed commitment to maintain close ties to its religious tradition in a changing twenty-first century environment.

6

Gettysburg College
A Saga of Old Battlefields and Distant Lutherans

Strict morality is required of every student; and, whilst true piety is studiously promoted, *everything sectarian is absolutely avoided.* Students from a distance, unless placed by their parents under the particular charge of some citizens of this town, are also responsible to the teachers for their conduct out of school; and on the Lord's day, they are required to attend the public worship of such one of the several churches as their parents may prefer.

The Rev. Samuel Simon Schmucker, Professor
From a Prospectus of Gettysburg Gymnasium, 1830

INTRODUCTION

SURROUNDING THE CAMPUS OF Gettysburg College, within the shot of a musket, lie long-silent, storied Civil War battlefields. During the first three days of July 1863, the infamous Battle of Gettysburg marked one of the bloodiest episodes of the American Civil War. Enormous casualties beset both sides, including over 23,000 Union and 28,000 Confederate soldiers.[1] Pennsylvania Hall, still in use today at the heart of the Gettysburg College campus, became a make-shift hospital for the Union and Confederate wounded during the bloody battle.

Short months later, a Gettysburg attorney proposed the idea of dedicating a portion of the battlefield as a National Soldiers' Cemetery. Though not intended to be the chief speaker at the dedication ceremony, President Abraham Lincoln was invited to speak at the November 19, 1863, event. Just down the street from the campus, Lincoln delivered his renowned address, a statement on war and American democracy, and was accorded a sustained ovation, after which he left Gettysburg for the eighty-mile trip to Washington. Each year, the Gettysburg College community marches to Cemetery Hill to hear an annual recitation of the Address.

Years later, in the early twentieth century, the life of another U.S. President intersected with Gettysburg College. President Dwight Eisenhower, who lived on the perimeters of campus, trained on the Gettysburg Battlefield before his ascent to military command during World War II. Upon the completion of his presidency, Eisenhower retired to Gettysburg, even serving on the Gettysburg College Board of Trustees and writing his memoirs in Eisenhower House, which is today the college admissions office. In addition, Eisenhower's former home houses the College's Eisenhower Institute, a non-partisan organization dedicated to promoting public service and civic engagement.

In a very real sense, the Gettysburg College saga is forever entwined with the American story, particularly with events tangential to a national war and two American presidents. While the Civil War and Presidents Abraham Lincoln and Dwight D. Eisenhower share with Gettysburg College noteworthy places in history, the college also plays a significant role in the history of American Lutheranism. Founded as Pennsylvania College of Gettysburg in 1832 by Samuel Simon Schmucker, Gettysburg was the first Lutheran college founded in America.[2] Schmucker himself, manifestly linked with Gettysburg College, was a significant driving force in early American Lutheranism, serving as pastor, professor, theologian,

1. More than 3,000 Union troops and at least 4,000 Confederates were killed on the battlefield alone.

2. In another connection to American history, Gettysburg College was built upon land donated by Congressman Thaddeus Stevens, staunch abolitionist and author of the 14th Amendment, which guaranteed civil rights.

anti-slavery abolitionist, leader of the General Synod, and early Lutheran Church leader.

Schmucker, allied with fellow Lutheran pastors Philip Krauth and Benjamin Kurtz, called for the establishment of a Lutheran seminary. Affirmed by the General Synod in November 1825, Gettysburg Seminary was founded the following year. The primary purpose of the seminary was the preparation of Lutheran pastors. Shortly after, however, Schmucker noted that seminary candidates were inadequately prepared for higher academic study.

Though consisting of a three-year curriculum, seminary study was often abbreviated when churches called seminary students to the pastorate before the conclusion of coursework (Nelson, 1975). To aid in preparing seminarians, Schmucker called for the establishment of a college. In 1832, the institution that would come to be called Gettysburg College was founded as a classical school based upon the European model. It is important to note, however, that Schmucker envisioned this school to be "un-sectarian," a point that has significantly shaped the college to this day.

Rich history, then, is the saga of Gettysburg College. It is this history that frames the themes and concomitant critical events of the forty-five-year identity history outlined in this chapter. Four themes, characterized by critical events, reveal patterns of Gettysburg College's handling of its Lutheran identity. The first theme, which actually predates the forty-five-year time horizon of the study, is Schmucker's original vision for a non-sectarian[3] college, evidenced in the original organization's charter. Second, the appointment of transformational leaders shaped the course of the institution over the past half-century. These leaders include presidents and chaplains alike.

A third critical event is the establishment of the Center for Public Service in the early 1990s. Not only have public service and social justice issues been important to the college historically, the launch of this new center marked a separation from its traditional connection to the Office of the Chaplain. A final theme that has shaped the Lutheran identity of Gettysburg College is the institutional decision to become a nationally recognized, top-ranked liberal arts college. This final theme sparks the intriguing question of whether Gettysburg can be both an elite national school and a college of the Lutheran church.

---

3. Schmucker uses the term "un-sectarian."

Founded in 1832 as the first Lutheran college in North America, Gettysburg College is steeped in the history of both America and American Lutheranism. Indelibly connected to Lincoln's famous address and to the quiet battlefields that surround its trees and classrooms, Gettysburg College boasts a rich saga of auspicious beginnings, transformational leaders, and seminal turning points in Americana. Today, Gettysburg College continues its rise to prominence as one of the premier liberal arts colleges in the country. Amidst this institutional blossoming, is the college seeking to preserve an authentic relationship with the Lutheran tradition, or is this ecclesial relationship merely an historical artifact?

SCHMUCKER'S VISION FOR A NON-SECTARIAN COLLEGE

Although Lutheran in its orientation, Gettysburg College was founded by Samuel Schmucker to be "un-sectarian in its instructions." This is a critical starting point, one that cannot be overemphasized. Whether this original declaration programmed the school's purpose from the beginning or whether it provided an exit strategy for more recent decision-makers who sought to loosen Gettysburg College's Lutheran ties, Schmucker's vision must be noted. In outlining his plan for the college, Schmucker created a paradox: he insisted the school be under Lutheran control while simultaneously being un-sectarian. The extent to which Gettysburg College was, from its beginning, an institution strongly affixed to the Lutheran church is a primary focus of this chapter, as well as the Gettysburg story itself.

Educated at the University of Pennsylvania and Princeton Seminary, Samuel Simon Schmucker was an influential Lutheran pastor and theologian who strived to create a solid footing for American Lutheranism, as well as a particular Lutheran systematic theology (Gritsch, 1994). He also wanted schools intended to educate Lutheran students. Less than a decade before the founding of Gettysburg College, Schmucker had helped to establish Gettysburg Seminary, along with a classical school that became known as Gettysburg Gymnasium.

Intended to prepare students for study at the seminary, the experience was to consist of study at the gymnasium followed by seminary study and was built upon the classical liberal arts tradition, including courses in classical languages, mathematics, geography, astronomy, history, philosophy, and so on (Burtchaell, 1998). Not only did Schmucker advocate the pedagogy of the curriculum, this European model was particularly important to Schmucker's strategy to appeal to the German population in Pennsylvania and surrounding areas, especially as he attempted to generate interest among potential students and potential financiers. A great number of these German immigrants were Lutheran. By 1830, Schmucker was making the argument for the establishment of a Lutheran college.

From all accounts, Samuel Schmucker was a different kind of Lutheran. To the point, he was an American Lutheran, a new breed created during the immigration of Lutherans to the United States. Schmucker was focused on finding a compromise between the Lutheran Confessions and American Protestantism, but assimilation was not without challenge. Although Schmucker used the Augsburg Confession, the doctrine of the Lutheran Church, as an outline for his theology, he later proposed radical reform to the Confessions.

This compromise, as it were, sparked controversy among synods, conservative and liberal Lutherans alike. Schmucker's own theology seemed to mold Lutheran doctrine toward a more generic American Protestantism, essentially deemphasizing a distinctive Lutheran theological identity. This point is debatable. Nevertheless, Schmucker was instrumental in founding both Gettysburg College and Gettysburg Seminary as he thought Lutheran students needed their own institutions of higher education (Birkner, 2006).

In 1832, Pennsylvania College of Gettysburg was founded as a German and Lutheran institution, though many of its benefactors were neither German nor Lutheran (Burtchaell, 1998). Savvy and pragmatic, Schmucker understood that he must initially articulate a broader scope for the college's mission to appeal to potential financiers uninterested in the institution's Lutheran connection. In his request to Pennsylvania legislators, for example, Schmucker argued that the new college would serve a larger audience than just Lutherans, especially given that taxpayers were not eager to support endeavors they interpreted as non-beneficial to them (Burtchaell, 1998). In fact, the original charter did not reference the Lutheran church, the Board of Trustees offered the first presidency of the college to a non-Lutheran, and trustees' language publicly communicated that the college was "the property of all denominations" (Glatfelter, 1987). Paradoxically, Gettysburg College was, as Schmucker described, "prevailingly under Lutheran influence and control." So from its earliest days, the tension of Gettysburg College's Lutheran identity was entwined with issues of financing, donorship, doctrine, leadership, and mission.

Schmucker's original un-sectarian vision continues to influence current members of the Gettysburg College community. Among these eight faculty, staff, and administrators, three general outlooks can be identified. Generally speaking, Campus Pastor Joseph Donnella and Professor of Biology Sherman Hendrix lamented the challenges of sustaining a Lutheran identity at Gettysburg College. On the other end of the spectrum are Economics Professor Char Weise, History Professor Michael Birkner, and Provost Jay White, who expressed little to no interest in nurturing a Lutheran identity at the college; in fact, they argued that this component of Gettysburg's composition does and should continue to play a very limited role.

Somewhere in between these two outlooks are President Janet Riggs, Associate Vice-President of Enrollment and Educational Services Salvatore Ciolino, and former Campus Pastor Karl Mattson. Together, this group generally adopted a more reserved, contemplative view of the college's Lutheran identity, speaking of it with a measure of dispassion, objectivity, or both. The wide range of participants' perspectives underscores Schmucker's original organizational vision.

Perhaps more than the other three themes, this statement about the college's purpose has shaped Gettysburg Lutheran identity. During a March 2009 campus visit, these eight leaders shared thoughts on the school's Lutheran identity, as well as its engagement as a faith community. President Janet Morgan Riggs, who is a longtime Gettysburg faculty member and alumna, explained, "We are proud and respectful of our Lutheran heritage. It is here, but it is not the centerpiece. Our chaplain is Lutheran, and we're satisfied with that. We continue to have a Lutheran voice on our Board of Trustees. The [Lutheran identity] is not strong here, but what we have is worth preserving." Similarly, economist and faculty leader[4] Char Weise offered an interesting metaphor, calling the college's Lutheran identity its family history. "The [Lutheran identity] is an historical importance," he explained, "but where do we go from here?"

Former Chaplain Karl Mattson also emphasized the historical nature of the college's Lutheran identity. When asked to describe what it means to be a Lutheran college, Mattson answered, "It means history. It's

4. Char Weise's formal title is Convener of Chairs and the Coordinators Council of the Faculty, in addition to Associate Professor of Economics.

about history and the connection that these schools have with the Lutheran church. You cannot understand Gettysburg College without the context of its Lutheran history." He went on to portray the Lutheran composition of Gettysburg to be "chiefly historical in nature," indicating that the chaplain no longer has a seat on the President's Cabinet and is instead administered by the student affairs office. Mattson added, "Gettysburg has a mushy mission with no clarity. One thing that is ever-present at Gettysburg is the battlefield. It's part of who we are, or rather an image people recall when they think of Gettysburg College."

In fact, participant after participant described the college's Lutheran identity, unprompted by the interviewer, as primarily an historical component. History Professor Michael Birkner, who authored a 2006 pictorial history of Gettysburg College, also relies on the term "heritage" to describe the institution's Lutheran identity. Just as most of the other participants had done, Birkner also cited Schmucker's un-sectarian vision, adding, "The majority of the [Gettysburg] faculty is apathetic or uninterested in Lutheran identity." Given the high frequency that Schmucker's charter was cited during the campus interviews, it can be concluded that the non-sectarian spirit of the college is enduring even today, at least among the key participants interviewed. In fact, the responses of the eight people interviewed at Gettysburg College summarize a college community that functions as a non-sectarian college that offers religious programming for students who wish to participate.

A common thought was repeated by the interviewees, namely that Gettysburg College was a different Lutheran college model from its founding and that the organization never demonstrated a particularly strong Lutheran identity. Ciolino explained, "At Gettysburg, it was different from the start. Gettysburg was non-sectarian to begin with. And there was no Lutheran course required of students in recent times. So, employees and students may have changed, but Gettysburg has not. Gettysburg was a different model to begin with. Making a strong connection with its Lutheran identity would be attempting to bring the institution back to something it never was." Mattson agreed that the Gettysburg relationship to the church is different, saying, "There's no reality of [preserving a critical mass of faculty] here now. Instead of focusing on this question, the point should be to reform the relationship between the church and college, asking what it means to be a Lutheran college."

The language Schmucker used in the college charter did not call for a robust Lutheran identity but rather a church-relatedness. In fact, the original passage did not mention the term Lutheran at all. Consequently, no widespread systematic programming by the college offered instruction to faculty and staff about the values and markings of Lutheran higher education. As a result, the majority of the interview participants at Gettysburg could not clearly articulate a clear understanding of what it means to be a Lutheran college. Rather than articulating the characteristics of a Lutheran college, Mattson, offered a good point, suggesting that determining the ideals of Lutheran higher education is a difficult task. This assessment is supported by other interviewees, agreeing with Mattson that formulating a precise definition is not easy.

Mattson went on to say that nothing distinctive exists, in his estimation, to make colleges Lutheran. Rather, the president, faculty, and students do play an important role in the identity. To the point, "You have to have some Lutherans to be Lutheran," said Mattson. It is worth noting that, since the 1960s, Gettysburg's percentage of Lutheran students has steadily decreased. Mattson noted that the Lutheran student population was 40% when he began his ministry as chaplain in 1977. Today, an estimated six percent of the Gettysburg faculty are practicing Lutherans; students who self-identified themselves as Lutherans currently comprise five percent of the student body.[5]

That several key interview participants failed to articulate a clear understanding of Lutheran higher education is revelatory in the task of exploring identity preservation and diminishment at Gettysburg College. Yes, naming the hallmarks of a Lutheran college is a challenge. But as the literature revealed, basic theological tenets mark Lutheran higher education. In the participants' defense, Gettysburg College has not in the last several decades produced a regular program of discussion on the topic of Lutheran identity for its campus community, a vital practice for instruction. But then functioning as a college of the Lutheran church is not, nor ever has been, an expressed purpose of Gettysburg College.

All eight interviewees expressed in their own words the mission of the college. Overwhelmingly, their responses closely matched the current

5. The percentage of Lutheran faculty is no longer recorded by any of the ELCA colleges and universities, nor is it tracked by the national church office. Three different participants, independent of one another, estimated the Lutheran faculty percentage, based upon specific faculty they identified.

Gettysburg mission statement, which does not include proclamation of a Lutheran identity: "Gettysburg College, a national, residential, undergraduate college committed to a liberal education, prepares students to be active leaders and participants in a changing world." Supporting the mission statement are six institutional core values. Although each of them aligns with the values and characteristics of a Lutheran college, the core values do not include any reference to a Lutheran relationship.

The fourth core value, however, does reference spiritual exploration. It states: "The free and open marketplace of ideas and the exploration of the ethical and spiritual dimension of those ideas, both indispensible to helping students learn to determine which have lasting value." The mission of Gettysburg College is succinctly stated, and its success at achieving premier status as a liberal arts college is evident.

What does it mean to be a Lutheran college? Participants' answers varied. While some knew the basic vocabulary of Lutheran higher education, other participants rejected the notion that Gettysburg College's Lutheran identity was anything more than an historic relationship. President Riggs offered an interesting and illuminating perspective, important because of the widely regarded notion that the president sets the institutional tone of mission and identity.

Riggs sat for the interview just weeks after being appointed Gettysburg's fourteenth president. During the conversation, Riggs' general demeanor was contemplative, reflective, and candid. The college's goal to live out its mission as a highly regarded liberal arts college clearly guides Riggs, who explained, "Gettysburg offers a residential, undergraduate liberal arts education. We prepare students for active participation and leadership in a changing world. Gettysburg is focused on providing a superb academic experience and in preparing students for lives of citizenship, integrity, and lifelong learning."

Interestingly, Riggs avoided using familiar "Lutheran language," words and phrases that commonly appear in the literature on the subject of Lutheran higher education. Instead, she seemed to talk *around* the hallmarks of the subject. However, near the end of the interview, Riggs discussed the idea of vocation, a foundational word in talking about Lutheran learning. Her explanation of the Gettysburg mission is quite similar to the notion of vocation, though she did not explicitly connect this learning to vocation and baptism. Almost like a revelation during the interview, Riggs offered an explanation of how Gettysburg College shapes students' lives for meaningful work.

On vocation, Riggs said, "I think it is important to help students think about how they are going to take their excellent academic experience and put it to good use in their communities and in their professions." An active Lutheran herself, Riggs seemed generally sympathetic to the ideals of Lutheran higher education. That Gettysburg College has not been particularly focused on its Lutheran identity in recent decades seems to be an ongoing challenge that Riggs will have to address, especially if she envisions the identity playing a larger role in the college's future.

Two interview participants, Provost White and Professor Weise, candidly admitted their own unawareness of what it means to be a Lutheran college. White noted that he is a non-Lutheran Protestant; Weise is a Roman Catholic. White described the mission of the college as a task to take individuals and send them out to be great souls, though he said he did not know what being a Lutheran college was about. He added that Gettysburg "feels not very Lutheran, a secular institution." Weise's assessment was more critical, hinting that the college should not emphasize its Lutheran identity, as Gettysburg seeks to serve a more diverse audience in its quest to be a top-ranked liberal arts institution.

Ironically, to be a Lutheran college is to educate students—diverse and homogeneous alike—in the liberal arts tradition. When asked what it means to be a Lutheran college, Weise answered, "Not much. It's really a formal arrangement with not many practical implications. When I think of Lutherans, I think of Garrison Keillor. And don't forget: Gettysburg didn't start with a very strong Lutheran identity."

Even faculty and staff who are familiar with the Lutheran tradition require periodic critical conversation and reflection about Lutheran higher education issues if any Lutheran ethos and logos is to be cultivated. That White, Weise, and most of the Gettysburg faculty are not Lutherans nor have a good understanding of Lutheran theology jeopardizes any chance to build and sustain a robust Lutheran identity, especially if institutional instruction and dialogue on the subject are not occurring regularly and systematically. Such an intentional institutional conversation would seem to have been adverse to and conflicting with Schmucker's original vision.

Perhaps the most revealing comments about Gettysburg's current Lutheran identity came from Pastor Joseph Donnella, the college chaplain. An African American himself, Donnella served the prestigious

HBCU Howard University in Washington, DC, prior to his call to Gettysburg College. He recalled how Howard University demonstrated a more palpable faith community than Gettysburg. By this, Donnella meant that religious life participation at Howard happened with all facets of the community visibly participating in university events. Of his current school, he said, "Gettysburg *really is* a liberal arts college. That's what it wants to be. There is often an overt hostility toward [my Lutheran chaplaincy] by some, but not all, of the faculty and students here."

In Donnella's presence, one is struck with his gentle, pastoral, pensive nature. It is easy to imagine his calming and hospitable presence for members of the campus community, Lutheran or not. The posture of hospitality certainly influenced Donnella's theological understanding, as well as his ministry at Gettysburg College. Hospitality, Donnella explained, is how we receive one another and the stranger in our midst. He said, "The founders of Gettysburg College wanted to create a college that would be open to all who desired higher learning. This school was never conceptualized as a place for Lutherans only."

In explaining the definition of a Lutheran college, Donnella contextualized the question to the Gettysburg experience and accordingly answered the question by outlining what these colleges are not. Specifically, Donnella noted upon his arrival at the college that many people at Gettysburg equate being a Lutheran college with being a narrow Bible college. During his ministry at the school, he has worked to dispel this myth and to underscore that this was never the understanding of Gettysburg's founders, nor of Lutheran higher education. Donnella shared a story about his arrival at Gettysburg College in 1997:

> People come to Gettysburg [College] with stereotypes of clergy and religious life. It's not easy being the chaplain here. I'll give you an example. When I arrived in 1997, I wrote a letter to the faculty introducing myself as the new chaplain for the college and as a Lutheran pastor. Part of that letter was an explanation of what I believe it means to be a Lutheran college. The collective response by a significant number of faculty was, "How dare you try to make this college a provincial sectarian Lutheran institution!" It was really hostile. And I should add that not everyone shared this response, but a considerable number did. I believe that this response belies the great misunderstanding the public has about what it means for a college or university to be church-related. Gettysburg College was established as a non-sectarian, not a non-denominational,

institution. In the nineteenth century, 'non-denominational' as nomenclature did not exist, and the charter for Gettysburg speaks of the Lutheran heritage as something to be valued while the college was to be open to all.

Despite this chilly reception of the chaplain, the campus does maintain certain rituals related to the college's church-relatedness. Two particular customs were noted by most of the interviewees: the preservation of the Lutheran chaplaincy and the presence of prayer at faculty meetings and official college events. At the risk of diminishing their sacredness and substance among the Gettysburg community, these rituals seem to be mostly symbolic and cursory. That six of the eight interview participants named these rituals, unprompted by the interviewer, suggests several possible points. It could mean that these campus practices are truly sacred and valued events embraced by the campus community, specifically those interviewed for the study.[6]

Second, the consensus by the respondents could indicate a shallow understanding of Lutheran higher education. This is to say that a college's church-relatedness could be reduced to occasional prayer and the employment of an ordained pastor. As the literature suggests, functioning as a Lutheran college is more than this. Another explanation could be that, for Gettysburg College, appointed institutional prayer and the presence of a Lutheran chaplain is indeed a suitable expression of Lutheran identity, as the college interprets this identity.

It is not that Gettysburg began with a weak Lutheran identity. To the contrary, the institution was quite closely connected to the Lutheran tradition and to one of the most important early American Lutheran leaders. That identity, however, could be described as tentative and apprehensive. Ironically, this timidity resulted from the very Lutheran leader who established the college. First, in establishing Gettysburg, Schmucker had to appeal to a wider audience, some who were non-Lutheran and not interested in the Lutheran tradition, to garner financial and legislative support. Second, Schmucker's own theology, though decidedly Lutheran, seemed to dilute the Lutheran identity over time in the move toward a more Americanized Lutheranism.

---

6. No participant either endorsed or denounced these customs. Rather, interviewees noted the practice of campus prayer and the presence of the Lutheran chaplain as a fact.

One cannot help but wonder how Schmucker's paradoxical vision for the college affects these campus leaders today. In a sense, Schmucker was clear that his institution would be un-sectarian; at the same time, Gettysburg did function as a vibrant and dynamic college of the Lutheran church during a large portion of its existence. In fact, not until the 1960s did Gettysburg College begin to show significant signs of Lutheran identity diminishment. What role did college leaders have on these developments? The next section addresses this point.

TRANSFORMATIONAL LEADERS

A discussion of the transformational leaders of Gettysburg College must begin with Samuel Schmucker. For the reasons outlined in the previous section, Schmucker's original vision has shaped and continues to shape the college he founded. To be sure, other administrators and personalities throughout the college's history could be identified as influential, but the interview participants consistently named several modern leaders as transformational. In particular, interviewees pointed to two presidents and two chaplains as leaders who most shaped the institution's Lutheran identity over the past five decades.

Presidents Charles Glassick and Gordon Haaland led the college from 1977 to 2004; John Vannorsdall and then Karl Mattson shaped campus ministry from 1962 to 1991. Because of their powerful voices and sway, these names were repeated over and over during the campus interviews. The following three sections addressed in this chapter are inter-related because of the role these key transformational leaders played in sparking the third and fourth themes.

To begin, Gettysburg College still maintained a relatively healthy Lutheran presence into the early 1970s, though signs of diminishment were emerging in the 1960s. Most illustrative were the changing demographics of the campus population. There was a marked decrease of Lutherans during the 1960s and a simultaneous increase of Roman Catholics. At the same time, institutional hiring was on the rise, but much of this new faculty was increasingly non-Lutheran. Michael Birkner suggested that these shifts meant "daily chapel became less meaningful." Incidentally, daily chapel was not required of students during the early 1960s. Furthermore, there were decreasing numbers of Lutheran faculty and board members. Perhaps the most influential factor, though, was the leadership of two consecutive presidents, Glassick and Haaland.

Charles Glassick began his presidency in the summer of 1977. A graduate of Franklin and Marshall College, Gettysburg College's nearby rival and benchmark institution, Glassick had previously served as vice president for academic affairs at the University of Richmond. At Gettysburg, the Glassick Administration was centrally concerned with strengthening academics and fundraising efforts. By all accounts, he succeeded. Glassick's leadership laid a foundation for Gettysburg's rise to national prominence as a liberal arts college, which included an enhanced academic program and a sharper, more aggressive development office effort.

President Riggs credited the consecutive Glassick and Haaland Administrations with playing important roles in changing the college's identity. In fact, six of the eight respondents agreed that the president is the key to shaping and changing the college's identity. Riggs explained Glassick's argument for a different type of faculty at Gettysburg, envisioning a faculty of teacher-scholars. Historian Michael Birkner also recalled Glassick's arrival in 1977. He said, "[Glassick's] goal was 'to wake up a sleepy faculty' and to gain a higher status for Gettysburg as a national liberal arts college, aside from its position as a regional school. Glassick was a pivotal president." Sherman Hendrix, Professor of Biology, also reported a similar record for Glassick. Hendrix understood the Glassick Administration goals to be improving student retention, attracting more qualified students, and changing public perception of the institution. Like other interviewees, Hendrix cited the back-to-back administrations of Glassick and Haaland in the success. Hendrix said, "The move from a regional to a national college was a major critical event in shaping Gettysburg's identity."

With the multitude of change during this administration, Glassick still maintained a degree of affection for the college's Lutheran identity. This religious identity, however, was ebbing with each passing year. Mattson noted that Glassick was Methodist, "though he was supportive of Gettysburg's church affiliation." He was so supportive of this church relationship that he appointed the first Director of Church Relations in 1979 (Glatfelter, 1987). This is both a symbolic and functional staff position that relates directly to the local Lutheran synods. However, by the end of the Glassick Administration, the Director of Church Relations position no longer existed at the college. Ciolino's recollection of Glassick was nearly identical: "He was a Methodist but still supportive of the church affiliation of the college."

Despite Glassick's endorsement of the college's Lutheran heritage, church-college ties would inevitably be loosened during his administration, especially given the administration's agenda. For example, Glassick intended to increase the college's endowment, a prerequisite for joining the upper echelon of colleges and universities. An important component of this strategy was crafting a board that could effectively fundraise. Like other institutions, realigning the college governing board meant changing minimum requirements of Lutheran membership.

Birkner succinctly summarized the president's charge: "[Glassick] wanted to identify trustees who were successful and financially connected, with the intention of increasing endowment and strengthening the college's development efforts." Interviewees, including Ciolino, remarked on Glassick's talent for development work. "Charles Glassick was a fantastic fundraiser," said Ciolino. This talent, combined with a vision for creating an effective fundraising board, fueled Glassick's success and provided his successor with a strong base for further growth.

The Haaland Administration followed Glassick's. President Riggs shared, "Haaland came in 1990 and built on [Glassick's] foundation. He helped move Gettysburg from being a good regional college to an excellent national liberal arts college." Like Glassick, Haaland was also attuned to increasing the flow of philanthropic dollars to Gettysburg College. Mattson, who had served the college during Glassick's tenure, also observed Haaland's arrival in 1990. He noted, "Financial pressures have affected the Board of Trustees. [President] Haaland wanted money on the board. Inevitably, this changes the character of the board. (Haaland) and the college wanted a national, rather than a regional, board." Birkner also recalled Haaland's work in continuing the trajectory set up by Glassick. This leadership combination, Birkner explained, was successful, particularly with securing financially-capable trustees.

In the early years of the college, the Board of Trustees was two-thirds to three-quarters Lutheran (Burtchaell, 1998). These numbers dropped over subsequent years, especially as the college sought new dollars. Looking beyond the Lutheran church and Lutheran donors was not unprecedented for Glassick and Haaland, for former presidents had also realized that financial support might be secured from other sources. For instance, Gettysburg's fifth president, Lutheran pastor Samuel Hefelbower appointed in 1904, encouraged trustees to seek new sources of income (Glatfelter, 1987). His efforts, however, ultimately failed.

Increased philanthropic dollars, as well as board diversification, resulted from the efforts of Glassick and Haaland. Meanwhile, financial support from the Central Pennsylvania and Maryland Synods was shrinking. Though impressive in the aggregate, the contribution of these two synods began to decrease in 1970 from Central Pennsylvania's high of $200,000 in 1969 to $100,000 in 1978; Maryland's high of $68,000 in 1968 had fallen to $24,000 in 1978 (Glatfelter, 1987). Birkner recalled, "With the presidents' goal of diversifying the board in order to increase giving, the board inevitably became less Lutheran. Synod financial support decreased as the perceived Lutheran affiliation diminished. With limited dollars, the area synods increasingly chose to support other things [than Gettysburg College]." Because of his vantage point in the office of institutional research, Sal Ciolino shared a summation of the results of board diversification. Ciolino said:

> The focus on endowment growth has been a response to financial pressures and enhancing Gettysburg's profile. This decision to build the endowment started in the 1980s under Glassick and was carried out by Haaland in the 1990s. Along with this decision and the realization of increased endowment, we no longer described ourselves as 'the first Lutheran college in America located in the rolling hills of Pennsylvania.' Rather, now we were 'a highly selective institution, a suburban D.C. school, affiliated with the Lutheran church.' We also developed specific expectations for our board members: they must solicit gifts, identify leadership donors, and 'be active and sharp.'

Whereas Glassick was generally supportive of the Lutheran relationship despite his being Methodist, Haaland was not. Haaland's attitude was echoed by multiple respondents. Donnella, for instance, said that President Haaland wanted to preserve Gettysburg's Lutheran identity as a natural fit, but added, "[Haaland] had antipathy toward religion, especially as a result of a negative encounter with fundamentalism." Ciolino recalled his "good vision" but also noted "he was not a Lutheran." Birkner described Haaland as "not particularly sympathetic to Gettysburg's Lutheran identity. [Haaland] had less affiliation and affection for Lutheranism than previous presidents." Mattson, in fact, called Haaland "the least Lutheran of Gettysburg's presidents."

Effects of the Haaland Administration are still being observed. His work at increasing the institutional endowment and strengthening the college profile resulted in greater board diversification. Of course, Lutheran representation on the Board of Trustees dipped. To be sure, the impact of Haaland's administration still needs testing. Chaplain Donnella summarized Haaland's work this way: "His resolve was to make Gettysburg College a nationally renowned liberal arts college. He stabilized finances along with the help of the chief development officer, initiated a growth plan for the college, and foresaw the need to diversify the student body, faculty, and staff."

In addition to the two transformative presidents, two chaplains emerge as significant figures that shaped the Lutheran identity of Gettysburg College over the past five decades. While Karl Mattson's contributions are addressed in the discussion of the Center for Public Service in the next section, John Vannorsdall is discussed here. Arriving on campus as chaplain in 1962, Vannorsdall was a dynamic, powerful force who understood the intersection of church and the academy. He also understood the changing culture of the nation in the 1960s and how those shifts would likely affect the church. Upon his arrival, Vannorsdall wrote in the January 1963 alumni bulletin, "The strengthening of religious life on the campus begins with the honest acknowledgement that the Church is a minority movement at work in the changed culture. We cannot depend on past traditions, but are called to work toward dynamic community" (Glatfelter, 1987:925–26). Indeed, societal changes proved to be seismic during the tumultuous Sixties.

Vannorsdall was not the first official chaplain of the college; that was Edwerth Korte, who served the Gettysburg campus community from 1952 until 1960. During Korte's ministry, the grand Christ Chapel, centrally located at the heart of campus, was opened. Ironically, though, during his time at Gettysburg, President Arnold Hanson terminated the policy of compulsory chapel. Before Korte's arrival, the president served the college as the symbolic (and often real) spiritual head of the community, not unlike other colleges of the church. Birkner even called former presidents the "chaplain of the institution." Later, of course, it was the chaplain who officially served this specific capacity.

Vannorsdall's success and influence was due in part to his understanding of campus ministry in the 1960s, as well as the circumstances in which he served. This is to say that, according to Mattson, "John

Vannorsdall was a Lutheran chaplain supported by a very Lutheran president and a Lutheran dean in a context that was much more Lutheran." More than half of the department chairs, for example, were Lutheran. More than forty percent of the students were Lutheran. Within this context was the familiar Lutheran issue of social justice issues. What interest there was about social justice issues in the 1960s tended to center in the chapel, under Vannorsdall's leadership.

Mattson, himself passionate about issues of social justice, remembered his predecessor's similar ministerial focus, one also valued and embraced by the Gettysburg College community. He clarified, "Vannorsdall and [President] Hanson, the president during much of his time here, were very close, and the president supported the chaplain's activities. Under Vannorsdall, social justice and civil rights activities were centered in the chapel." Mattson continued Vannorsdall's leadership on issues of social justice, confirmed by various study interviewees. In 1991, Mattson left the chaplain's office to direct the newly-established Center for Public Service, discussed in the next section.

Two other presidents are worth noting, though their names emerged but twice during the interviews. Arnold Hanson served as president from 1961 to 1977; Kate Will served from 2004-2008. Both were described as sympathetic to the institutional Lutheran identity. Hanson, who had previously served as dean of the College of Arts and Sciences at Cornell University, was described as a "modest, hard-working Lutheran." President during the turbulent 1960s that marked a national change at religiously-affiliated colleges and universities, Hanson generally maintained the institutional relationship between Gettysburg College and the Lutheran church. Chaplain Mattson remembered Hanson as the "last truly Lutheran president." Though not an ordained pastor, Hanson was a Lutheran lay leader.[7] Mattson also recalled Hanson's steadfast support of Chaplain Vannorsdall and his far-reaching campus ministry.

Kate Will's presidency followed the Haaland Administration. Professor Birkner noted that Will seemed "more interested in the Lutheran aspect" than her predecessor. The Will Administration rekindled talk of Lutheran identity preservation, particularly with regard to the college's relationship with the national Lutheran church. Will's overtures to a more pronounced college-church relationship cleared way for the

7. The first non-Lutheran president was Willard Paul, a Presbyterian, who served 1956–1961.

possibility for further identity preservation with Gettysburg's next president, Janet Riggs.

The course President Riggs will chart is yet to be determined: she is the executive of a college historically related to the Lutheran church, a college that some have argued has outgrown that ecclesial relationship. Does the president accentuate or diminish that religious identity amidst the institutional quest to become national and esteemed? When asked who most shapes the college-church identity, Riggs answered with a knowing laugh, "One might say the president. But others might say the entire campus community. I believe the responsibility is dispersed. Our Lutheran heritage has had a very positive impact on our college's focus and values." Six months into her infant presidency, Janet Riggs has many tasks to balance and myriad questions to answer. Among them, what role, if any, will the Lutheran tradition play in the college's future? More to the point, is this question even present among the institution's central agenda?

LAUNCHING THE CENTER FOR PUBLIC SERVICE

Over the last fifty years, the Gettysburg College community has demonstrated a commitment to issues of social justice, public service, and civil rights. Commenting on students' involvement in service and the public good, President Riggs said, "This, I think, can be attributed to our Lutheran heritage. Now Gettysburg is not unique in its commitment to public service, but we were early on in the advocacy of public service and a specific center devoted to public service. [A commitment to public service] is important to who we are." Shepherding this effort through the tumult of the 1960s was Chaplain Vannorsdall, followed by Chaplain Mattson though the 1980s. As detailed in the previous section, these two leaders spoke powerful voices to the listening ears of the campus community, especially with regard to social justice and service issues. Michael Birkner summarized their impact on this specific ministry:

> These two chaplains were the right people at the right time for Gettysburg. Vannorsdall was a mentor, a sounding board for students questioning the power structure, racism, and authority in the 1960s. He provided a haven for the Christian students during this confusing time of the Vietnam War. He maintained a focus on social justice and really spoke to students' needs. He was

a charismatic leader. And Karl Mattson was what was needed in the 1980s. He, too, provided a haven for students and carried on Vannorsdall's commitment to social justice. I want to say this the right way: the current chaplain, Joseph Donnella, doesn't have the same influence now that those previous chaplains had. Perhaps it's because of a changing student body, a changing culture. Perhaps it was because of the separation of the social justice effort from the chaplain's office. In the early 1990s, the Center for Public Service was established and taken from the chaplain's office. Mattson went on to direct that center.

Kim Davidson, the Associate Director of the Center for Public Service, offered an overview of the center in a telephone conversation.[8] She indicated that the Center has no connection with a Lutheran or any other religious organization; rather, it functions as a stand-alone office of the college. Its origin in the chaplain's office, however, is significant. In addition to the theological origins of the Center, an activist's combat death in the Vietnam War also sparked the beginning of the Center for Public Service. Gettysburg College alumnus Stephen Warner's GI insurance proceeds provided the endowment for the establishment of the Center. Initially, the focus of the Center's work was to emphasize and create opportunities for co-curricular community service. Once established, the focus shifted, since the early 2000s, to developing closer, more intentional relationships between service and academics.

Davidson explained that the aim of the programs is "not to do public service so students can feel good about themselves, but rather the focus is public service to address issues of social justice." The focus and tone is intended to be didactic, critical, and reflective. Davidson reported that "way over half" of Gettysburg students are engaged in activities at the center, though currently this specific number is not tracked. Strategies to record this number are in development. According to its website (2009), the Center for Public Service at Gettysburg College "engages students, community members, faculty and staff to facilitate partnerships, education, critical thinking, and informed action. Through these alliances, we aim to foster social justice by promoting personal, institutional, and community change." Students are challenged to think critically and act compassionately through four major program areas that frame the Center's efforts: student leadership, reflective service, service-learning, and immersion projects.

8. The phone call occurred on July 21, 2009.

Until 1991, these programs and efforts were coordinated by and through the Office of the Chaplain. While this office was centrally concerned with the ministry of Word and Sacrament, social justice issues gave focus to the outreach and campus ministry of this office. In 1991, college leaders decided to establish a Center for Public Service to formalize and expand college service-learning programs, which had previously stemmed from the chaplain's office. This separation of public service from the Office of the Chaplain marks the third significant critical event that shaped the Lutheran identity of Gettysburg College. In brief, it appears that this move diminished the influence, centrality, and campus engagement with the chaplain's office. In a sense, the Office of the Chaplain became less relevant on a campus that so valued the public service and social justice issues that the chaplain's office once coordinated.

About the split of public service from the chaplain's office, President Riggs pondered, "This was an important point because it took a key component of the chaplain's office and made it a stand-alone program. This . . . showed the college's commitment to public service." Karl Mattson, chaplain in 1991, was given the choice to remain chaplain or direct the newly-established Center. Mattson chose to make the switch and subsequently demonstrated success in launching and building the Center for Public Service. While the establishment of the Center certainly demonstrated a deep commitment to public service, what effect did this shift have on the chaplain's office and religious life of the campus?

Mattson agreed that social justice issues did give the chaplain's office focus, but he contends that the chaplain's office maintained other priorities, too. The following is how the center originated, in Mattson's own words:

> A small, significant group of students were drawn to this social justice focus at Gettysburg. They still are. In 1991, President Gordon Haaland, the least church-related of Gettysburg presidents during my time, and maybe ever, commissioned a campus study of desirable new initiatives, and a Center for Public Service was the first recommendation. I was given the choice to remain chaplain or become the Director of the Center, and I chose the Center. Some of the programs that had grown up in the chapel followed me to the Center. The chaplain's office and the Center worked very closely together. The idea of the Center was, in part, to make public service more available to the majority of students who did not relate to the chapel. And it worked extraordinarily well.

While certainly well-intentioned "to make public service more available to the majority of students who did not relate to the chapel" and while the center worked "extraordinarily well," the separation of service-learning from the chaplain's office is significant. One must be careful not to impugn Mattson's steadfast ministry and great effort. On the contrary, he continued the important work of Vannorsdall and brought his own gifts to the Gettysburg community. However, the institutional decision to develop a specific office for public service did subtract a significant component of the chaplaincy's ministry.

Provost White described the center's establishment as growing out of the passion of students who took their own desires to make change. "In a real way," he said, "they put their liberal arts to work. I observe that, at Gettysburg anyway, students seem to have redefined or redirected their religious passion to the Center for Public Service." To be sure, students are busy at Gettysburg, engaged in rigorous academics, dynamic social activities, and meaningful service. But as Chaplain Donnella observed, "We are doing good things [at Gettysburg College], but we don't always know why. Are we making the connection between the relationship with the public service and its relationship to God? Less activity and more reflection is what I would like to see." He went on to explain that the college strives for equality and justice distribution and even making God's kingdom known, but that we do not always use religious language to describe this work.

Sal Ciolino, who has served at the college since the early 1970s, disagrees slightly. He interprets the Christian and Lutheran expression of Gettysburg to be lived out precisely through these public service activities. He is correct in his assessment that public service and social justice have been traditionally important to the Lutheran tradition in America. Ciolino points to the Vietnam War protests on Gettysburg's campus as an example of the college supporting social justice issues even when doing this was unpopular in America. He recalled that, during the war, "Gettysburg work was not to shut down protest against the war but to discuss it. Do we separate our faith from the rest of ourselves? Lutherans look to social justice to overcome inequities." Because the Center was an outgrowth of the chapel and the college's Lutheran heritage, Ciolino regards this as an expression of Lutheran identity.

The ELCA Social Statement on Education, "Our Calling in Education," outlines seven expectations for its college and university campus ministries (2007:50–51). They include:

- Being a worshipping community;

- Educating in the faith, which includes create a safe environment for faith discussions;

- Calling students to live out their baptismal vocation;

- Engaging faith and learning;

- Modeling thoughtful and respectful dialogue on controversial issues;

- Providing opportunities for service in Church and society;

- Offering opportunities for friendships, fun, and community life.

In word and deed, Gettysburg College does most of these things in one form or another, and some very well. However, the college does not perform these expectations within a faith-based framework. Rather, this work springs *from* a faith tradition. While Gettysburg's intentions may emanate from its Lutheran tradition, they are not necessarily articulated in Lutheran language and vocabulary. What, if anything, does this reveal about Gettysburg's preservation or diminishment of its Lutheran identity?

While Gettysburg is, in fact, living out some of the fundamentals of Lutheran higher education, the college is not necessarily naming this service as work of the church. In other words, where is God in this serving and learning? In the critical reflection the college asks of students who participate in activities of the Center, do teacher-mentors question students about Christ, faith, and vocation? Given its self-described mission, Gettysburg College would likely consider such questions inappropriate, out-of-bounds. It would seem that a critical link is missing in this church-college relationship with regard to *naming* vocation. The action is essentially present; the theological reflection is not. On one hand, the establishment of the Center for Public Service underscored Gettysburg College's commitment to service-learning; on the other hand, its founding diminished the relevance—or at least the status and popularity among students—of the Office of the Chaplain. This diminishment, it is argued here, contributed to the diminishment of Gettysburg College's Lutheran identity.

THE QUEST TO BECOME A NATIONALLY RECOGNIZED, TOP-RANKED LIBERAL ARTS COLLEGE

Without exception, all interview participants questioned for this study identified Gettysburg College's central pursuit to become a top-ranked, national liberal arts college. Clearly, this institutional goal is known, and by all accounts, embraced by the college community. Certainly those interviewed for the study expressed support of and even pride in this ambitious quest. Evidence—more highly qualified students, a larger endowment, and prestigious inclusion on the widely-read *U.S. News and World Report* annual list of best colleges and universities, to name a few—shows that the college's plan to rebrand itself as a premier liberal arts college is working. While difficult to demonstrate empirically, the college's Lutheran identity seems to have been a trade-off in this shift toward national prestige. So, can an aspiring college be both an elite national school and a college of the church? Or, is fulfilling both of these criteria simply a matter of institutional will?

In all of the interviews, as well as in the literature, several colleges and universities perpetually emerged as being both nationally reputable and meaningfully engaged with their sponsoring church traditions. Particular examples include Wheaton College (Evangelical), Calvin College (Reformed), Valparaiso University (Lutheran),[9] Baylor University (Baptist), and the University of Notre Dame (Roman Catholic), though others certainly exist (Benne, 2001). However, these institutions aspire to be *both* highly regarded and engaged with their churches. Clues show that, while Gettysburg College seeks a strong national reputation, it does so exclusive of its church-related identity.

Self-description is illustrative. Over the past two decades, Gettysburg College decision-makers have chosen to "tone down," as one interviewee said, the institution's Lutheran language in its official publications. Ciolino contends that this change did not diminish the identity, but rather it more accurately described the true climate and culture of the college. He said, "Several years back, Gettysburg [admissions] literature had symbols that inferred or at least created the impression, 'we don't want you if you're not Lutheran.' We changed, or at least toned

9. Valparaiso University is not counted among the twenty-seven ELCA colleges and universities or among the institutions of the Lutheran Church—Missouri Synod. Rather, it is considered to be an independent Lutheran institution.

down this message, as the numbers of references created an image that overstated the relationship." He argued that the linguistic changes provided a more accurate image of the actual relationship and church governance role, emphasizing that the Lutheran language was not omitted but rather reduced in the admissions materials.

Perhaps the best evidence of this reduction in language is found in comparing past and present strategic plans. In June 1971, Gettysburg College published *Decade of Achievement*, a report on institutional progress in the previous decade. Following up on that document with a new plan for the future, the college published that same month *Decade of Decision: A Project for the Growth and Development of Gettysburg College, 1972–1982*. Thirty-six years later, in June 2007, the college published a new, refreshed plan called *Strategic Directions for Gettysburg College*. Contrasting the two documents, one can recognize a change in tone with regard to religious affiliation, or religious engagement, for that matter. Both plans are clear, optimistic, and ambitious. Only the earlier one, though, speaks of itself as a college of the church.

To begin, *Decade of Decision* was a product of the Long Range Planning and Development Committee, appointed by President Hanson in 1969 and comprised of equal members of the board, administration, faculty, and student body. In its preface, the document clearly states that *Decade of Decision* was intended for planning purposes, not fundraising purposes. Thoroughly advocating liberal education as a college keystone, the document addresses three primary areas of the campus community: program, personnel, and facilities. The expressed institutional purpose sounds familiar to today's higher education language: "The College is faithful to its purpose if its graduates, whatever the role in life they choose, continue to be informed, critical, human, and creative individuals, well prepared to act responsibly in the complex world of the future."

The section most affecting Lutheran identity is the document's first section, "Program." The document describes the program as "curricular, non-curricular, and general," components designed to implement the college's purpose. Included in the curricular portion are discussions of "close student-faculty relationships" and development of students' "analytical powers." The authors address religious life, along with athletics and the arts, in the next section, "the non-curricular program." Service and social programs, which were traditionally closely tied with the religious presence on campus, are also discussed in this section.

The planning document describes the Religious Life Program as "entirely voluntary," a program which "affords a dimension and an opportunity otherwise unattainable. The program, formal and informal, ranges from corporate worship to the manifestation of intangible values implicit in the nature of the institution and its mission." The document demonstrated that religious values are integral to the college's educational experience. Most significantly, the document proclaimed in very clear terms the institution's affiliation as a Lutheran college: "Gettysburg Lutheran heritage, as well as its intention to perpetuate that church-relatedness, makes evident the fact that it proceeds 'under God.' Pragmatically, this seems that distinct and significant values are integral to the function and process of the community for learning. Church-relatedness, more specifically the religious life program derivative therefrom, helps to nourish those values." In very unambiguous language, the Gettysburg College of 1971 boldly declared its identity as a Lutheran college.

Thirty-six years later, in 2007, *Strategic Directions for Gettysburg College* makes no reference to the college's religious identity. In fact, the term 'Lutheran' does not appear once, nor does the word 'faith.' The only related reference involves the term spiritual, reflected in the college's core values statement. The statement is the fourth of six declarations, which reads: "[Our core values include] the free and open marketplace of ideas and the exploration of the ethical and spiritual dimensions of those ideas, both indispensable to helping students learn to determine which have lasting value." In the conclusion of the planning document, a brief reference is made to "theologian Samuel S. Schmucker" in a statement about the college's commitment to "advancing the cause of liberal education."

The 2007 planning document is based upon five assumptions: (1) Gettysburg will continue as a residential liberal arts college; (2) Gettysburg is dedicated to excellence; (3) Gettysburg will maintain a total enrollment of approximately 2,600 students; (4) Gettysburg will continue careful financial planning and achievement of balanced budgets; and (5) Gettysburg affirms the value of institutional assessment. SWOT analysis revealed a strength of the college to be its rich history, described boldly in the document this way: "our historical legacy is the most distinctive in the country." Challenges were identified to be changing demographics in the country (especially the Northeast from which the college attracts the majority of its students), making the case for the value of a liberal arts education, and a relatively small endowment (especially compared to the college's aspirant liberal arts institutions).

Aspiring to continue its ascent among the leading liberal arts institutions in the country, the college plans to advance this effort by focusing on four strategic themes: engagement, distinction, access, and connection. Goals supporting the theme of engagement include maintaining an outstanding faculty and staff, enhancing opportunities for student research, offering global learning experiences, and promoting leadership, civic engagement, and community service as key priorities within the co-curricular program. No mention of critical theological reflection appears in this section.

Perhaps the most evocative absence, however, is found in the second theme, distinction. Here, the authors make a compelling case for Gettysburg's long-storied history, especially with regard to the American experience. However, in no place does the planning document reference Gettysburg College as the first Lutheran college in America. Likewise, under the theme of access, which discusses the issue of diversity, any reference to religious diversity is avoided. At the risk of restating the obvious, the college's most recent strategic plan does not include connection or relationship to the historic Lutheran identity of the college, especially when compared to the 1971 planning document. It would seem that Gettysburg College has made systematic institutional decisions to diminish, at least publicly, its relationship to the Lutheran church.

Just as a review of the college planning documents reveals a change in the institution's attitude about its identity over the years, an examination of interviewees' responses provides another perspective on Gettysburg's quest to become a premier liberal arts college. President Riggs, who was provost during preparation of the 2007 strategic plan, described the college's admissions strategy for increasing its profile. To the point, the college transformed its admissions effort, starting in the early 1990s. Included in this strategy was increasing the applicant pool, broadening the geographic reach, increasing diversity, and enhancing the overall academic quality of the student body. Similarly, Weise pointed to the increased hiring of women and minorities during the late 1970s, perhaps not unique to Gettysburg College, as the shift that began to change the face of the college. This shift, he argued, was followed later by expansion of the student body, and later, an increased emphasis on scholarship and decreased attention to teaching.

Provost White echoed this comment. When asked to name significant critical events in the college's history during the past few decades, White named the institution's new emphasis on faculty scholarship. Not only did this emphasis lead to an increased academic profile for the college, but it inevitably diluted the traditional focus on teaching. White şaid, "Traditionally, teaching has been the most important priority of the faculty. But now the emphasis is to use the liberal arts tradition as a foundation to be faculty researchers. This is a shift away from an exclusive focus on teaching."

Such a shift does not necessarily spell the end of close student-teacher relationships; in fact, collaborative student-teacher research can also provide mentoring opportunities. Nevertheless, emphasis on teaching has traditionally been a hallmark of liberal education. Weise added that Gettysburg's aspirant benchmark institutions have the advantage of great faculties, where there is "a lower teaching load . . . and a lower student-teacher ratio, smarter students, more accomplished colleagues, and closer connections with national colleagues."

Mattson also commented on the changing composition of the student body and faculty over the years, "both of whom are markedly less Lutheran than they were in 1975." This phenomenon, according to Mattson, is due primarily to the college's decision to seek a regional and national reputation. As a result, the campus community now more nearly replicates the religious affiliation of the larger region with very significant effect on a diminished college-church relationship. As its cache was more firmly established, the college began to seek more intentionally families who could pay the high tuition, leading to a situation in which the school, as Mattson described, "was in a better position to 'buy' students who could raise the academic student standards." Though not without risk, this strategy is common among colleges seeking to increase their student academic profile.

For Ciolino, the institutional decision to grow the student body was a signal that the college was changing. The plan, which called for a student body expansion from 1,900 to 2,650, consequently called for new facilities, new curricular and co-curricular programs, expansion of the faculty, and the addition of cutting-edge technology. Ciolino also noted an institutional change that resulted in a shift in public perception of the college. In 1975, college decision-makers moved Gettysburg to Division III status in athletics. "This sounds like an odd one, but the move changed us," Ciolino said. The move set the tone that Gettysburg would be more academic, less a "jock school," as Ciolino described. "Prior to that we were, in many circles, perceived as a good Lutheran school that would give a football scholarship."

In the end, these shifts affected the Lutheran identity. Ciolino explained that Gettysburg is different, in general, than other Lutheran colleges, citing its difference in pay,[10] admissions perspective, and percentage of Lutheran students. He added, "My observation of Gettysburg shows that being church-affiliated is not a draw for highly selective students. Ties to synods and parishes are not strong anymore, because people are saying, 'Go to the best school, not the best Lutheran school.'" Review of the Gettysburg plan suggests that the college has fully embraced this notion, and by its own assessment, the plan is working. In both 2008 and 2009, *U.S. News and World Report* named Gettysburg College the forty-ninth best liberal arts college in the country. To this point, Hendrix remarked, "Yes, we made it on the national scene." So, Gettysburg's Lutheran identity appears to have diminished as a trade-off in the quest to become a top-ranked, national liberal arts college. Why? Are these two identities mutually exclusive for this particular college? In any event, while the ties to the Lutheran church have loosened significantly over the past decades, the profile and prestige of Gettysburg College is being firmly cemented.

SUMMARY

The saga of Gettysburg College is reflective of the American story. The ghosts of wars and U.S. Presidents linger in the lore of this college. While Lutheran higher education was not born in Pennsylvania, it was first rooted at the collegiate level in America with the founding of Gettysburg College. This saga over the past forty-five years has been shaped by a founder's lasting vision for a non-sectarian college, by transformative leaders, by the launch of a center devoted to public service, and by an ambitious pursuit to become a nationally-known, top-ranked liberal arts college.

---

10. According to ELCA records, Gettysburg College faculty members were the highest paid among the ELCA colleges and universities in 2008. Gettysburg professors earned an average salary of $101,303, with a total compensation of $132,660. The median totals for all ELCA colleges were $74,134 and $98,400, respectively.

So how has the college changed in forty-five years? Specifically, with regard to its ethos and logos as a Lutheran college, how has Gettysburg College changed from 1965 to today? With regard to its Lutheran identity, the college has changed considerably. Despite signs indicating that the college's Lutheran identity was not particularly robust prior to the 1960s, it was still present and relevant then. After review of the documents, analysis of the interviews, and reflection on physical observations, the ethos of today's Gettysburg as a college of the church, Lutheran or otherwise, is very weak; any presence of logos is essentially non-existent. Hendrix remembered fondly a time in the early 1970s when, as he described it, there was a "high water mark for the vibrancy of faith-based campus life since I've been at Gettysburg. This spirit was active in those days but died a slow death."

Is the Lutheran heritage of Gettysburg College a mere historical artifact, much like the nearby Civil War battlefields? More than one interviewee suggested that underscoring this religious affiliation would threaten to alienate prospective students, especially the large number of Roman Catholic and Jewish students who make up more than fifty percent of the college's student body. Could the college still publicly celebrate this Lutheran identity, or is there simply no capital in such an endeavor? Can the college still be regarded, in certain religious circles anyway, as a Lutheran school without meaningfully functioning as such? This is to say that it would exist as a college of the church in name only.

Ciolino offered this perspective: "What would Gettysburg gain by leaving the church? And what an insult it would be if we did? We're the first Lutheran college founded in America! In an age when church affiliation is not popular, Gettysburg has kept it." The Gettysburg story is still unfolding, and its Lutheran tradition has not disappeared completely. A question remains, one out of the scope of this study but one that is worth answering. Can a top-ranked, nationally recognized liberal arts college also be a well-engaged college of the church that views its religious identity as a central part of the institution? Perhaps the history of Gettysburg College will someday tell.

PART 3

Cross-Case Analysis
and Discussion

7

Cross-Case Analysis

THIS CHAPTER IS CENTRALLY focused on the study's first and second research questions. Using the cross-case analysis deepens understanding and explanation of the study's data and phenomena (Miles & Huberman, 1994). First, are colleges and universities of the Evangelical Lutheran Church in America preserving or diminishing their Lutheran identities? Second, do the isomorphic status drivers of secularization, financial viability, and faculty professionalization affect organizational Lutheran identity at Concordia College, Lenoir-Rhyne University, and Gettysburg College? The third research question is addressed in the next chapter.

At its foundation, institutional isomorphism is the story of people making choices that consequently shape the organizations of which they are a part. The narrative case studies in this dissertation describe if and how institutional change has occurred over a forty-five-year time horizon, and if change has occurred, if the college has preserved or diminished its Lutheran identity over that time period. As *organizations*, how are three specific ELCA colleges and universities treating their institutional identity? As explained in the introduction, this study adopts an organizational perspective, one analyzed through the lens of organizational theory, and is a new take on the ELCA schools.

IDENTITY PRESERVATION OR DIMINISHMENT:
GENERAL INSTITUTIONAL COMPARISONS

Before focusing on the effects of the three status drivers on Concordia, Lenoir-Rhyne, and Gettysburg, it is useful to answer the first research question. Are colleges and universities of the ELCA seeking to preserve or diminish their Lutheran identities? To be sure, the first research question does not seek to answer identity questions universally for all ELCA colleges and universities. The results of a qualitative study are not intended to be generalized. However, the careful selection of the three schools from Benne's typology in Phase I of the study's design suggests that the identity histories of Concordia, Lenoir-Rhyne, and Gettysburg could reveal useful insights about organizational identity at schools in each of the three categories.

Related to the first research question are two sub-questions. What did it mean to be a Lutheran college in the late 1960s and early 1970s, and what does it mean to be one now? Asked another way, what organizational identity or ethos holds these twenty-seven colleges and universities together? In tracing the three sagas in chapters 4, 5, and 6, clear reflections of the Lutheran vision of education, which was outlined in the literature review, appeared throughout the colleges' stories.

In some cases, however, especially in recent years, these characteristics of Lutheran higher education have faded and have occasionally disappeared completely. All three schools demonstrate fierce pride in and insistence upon the liberal arts tradition as a foundation for the educational experience, a basic marker of Lutheran higher education. What is more, all three schools embrace their clear historical beginnings as colleges of the Lutheran church, though Gettysburg described its original relationship to be "Lutheran-related." Most significantly, the differences in expression of institutional Lutheran identity appeared to reside in issues of Lutheran theology and subsequent organizational ethos.

By all accounts observed in this study, Concordia College is aggressively seeking to preserve a decidedly distinctive Lutheran identity. Lenoir-Rhyne University is seeking to preserve a faith-centered educational experience, guided by but not limited to the Lutheran tradition. Gettysburg College is not seeking to preserve an organizational Lutheran identity, but it is not abandoning the rhetoric, albeit very subtle, of Lutheranism's role in its institutional history. So, at the risk of appearing flippant, the answer to the first research question is: Concordia, yes; Lenoir-Rhyne, sort of; and Gettysburg, not really.

First, Concordia scored the highest marks of colleges demonstrating church-relatedness on Benne's typology in Phase I of this study. As the case study revealed, the recurring theme of Concordia's saga is one of clear mission. The extent to which the college took serious, critiqued, memorized, and engaged its simple mission statement was a surprise. At several points during her interview, President Pam Jolicoeur evoked the word "unabashedly" when describing how her institution proclaimed its Lutheran identity. Every person interviewed and all the documents analyzed for this dissertation pointed to the Lutheran tradition as a central bedrock principle of the institution.

Has Concordia made trade-offs with regard to its mission in its quest to achieve this high level of Lutheran identity preservation? For two reasons, Concordia decision-makers have not made trade-offs. First, the basic mission of the school *is to be a Lutheran college*. This self-understanding is simply in the DNA of Concordia College, repeatedly demonstrated through interviewees' comments, analyzed documents, and on-site observations. Second, Lutheran theology and the Lutheran view of higher education supports a diversity of belief and non-belief in the educational experience. In other words, being a Lutheran college and serving a wide variety of non-Lutheran students are not mutually exclusive. Ironically, the open and accepting Concordia is not particularly diverse, rating the highest percentage of Lutheran students among the ELCA colleges.

To be sure, several factors or conditions contribute to Concordia's ability to preserve its Lutheran identity. Among the most important factors is the college's enduring, unwavering commitment to maintaining its relationship with the Lutheran church. Simply said, the college wants to preserve this relationship and sees it as a central part of its mission. Second, that clearly-articulated mission statement is another important factor. Third, strong leadership by college presidents over the past fifty years has ensured that that mission statement would be embraced, affirmed, and galvanized.

Concordia and its community have held a remarkable faithfulness to its mission statement, made manifest in its self-understanding as a college of the Lutheran church that intentionally integrates faith and learning. A final and very significant factor in Concordia's ability to preserve its identity is related to its geographical location in the Lutheran-rich Upper Midwest. To the point, a constant and interested stream of Lutheran students makes up the student body; a high percentage of Lutheran faculty teach these students and support the institutional mission; Lutheran alumni and friends reinvest in the college with financial support and participate in Concordia leadership roles; and an engaged Lutheran synod supports the college's mission as an institution of the church.

Today, very much like in the 1960s, Concordia College students are still required to take religion classes, and these students are taught and mentored by a faculty carefully selected through the filter of a very rigorous and intentional hiring process. The "three questions" discussed in chapter 5 ensure that candidates for the Concordia faculty understand and endorse the college's institutional mission as a college of the church. All of these factors and conditions inspire and create an ethos that is "remarkably Lutheran." While Concordia's geographic location supports its Lutheran identity, the college's intentionality to preserve its organizational identity as a college of the Lutheran church is as essential.

Second, Lenoir-Rhyne data exhibited some of the most interesting and complex implications for organizational identity. Today, as in the 1960s and subsequent decades, the college documents reviewed for this study point to a bold proclamation of institutional Lutheran identity. The term 'Lutheran' is not buried in the highest profile documents—strategic plans, admissions materials, website content, and the mission statement—but rather is featured initially and prominently. The current language also employs a more general Christian nomenclature, in addition to the Lutheran-specific language. Despite its geographic location in the South where Lutherans are sparser than in the Midwest, Lenoir-Rhyne has been able to attract Lutheran students and faculty regionally and nationally. Although a minority at the college, Lutherans along with non-Lutherans still help to support an institutional goal of demonstrating an organizational church-relatedness. Lenoir-Rhyne is a Lutheran college, to be sure, but the interviews, documents, and observations engaged for this study reveal a more generic church-college with *Lutheran tendencies*. The current president, Wayne Powell, envisions a pragmatic approach to the Southern Lutheran college he leads, explaining:

> In the Upper Midwest, a Lutheran college is one which has a heritage in Lutheran traditions and is still today almost completely

Lutheran in its student body and in its theology. In the Southeast a Lutheran college is one which has a heritage as being founded in the Lutheran church but today serves a very broad and diverse group of students. The southeastern Lutheran schools still take a Lutheran approach to higher education by ensuring that spiritual-ity is part of all that happens, but by being open to people of all faiths. Neither model is more Lutheran than the other. Rather, the demographics dictate how Lutheranism is manifested.

Undoubtedly, Powell's understanding of Lutheran higher education in the twenty-first century shapes Lenoir-Rhyne's current position for de-termining its Lutheran identity.

Over the forty-five-year time horizon, Lenoir-Rhyne leaders could have chosen to diminish the Lutheran identity in favor of institutional strategies that would have positioned the school differently in the mar-ketplace. One example offered during the interviews was the case of Lenoir-Rhyne benchmark Elon College, an institution that diminished its church-relatedness, shifted to university status, repositioned itself, and subsequently realized tremendous success. Lenoir-Rhyne did not adopt the strategy of diminishing its church-relatedness, and the president and provost suggested in interviews that the college had no plans, under their leadership, to abandon its church-relatedness. The current strategic plan substantiates this outlook.

Since the university does not record the percentage of Lutheran fac-ulty, no statistical comparison can be made between current and previ-ous Lutheran faculty composition. However, interviewees suggested that fewer Lutheran faculty teach at Lenoir-Rhyne in 2009 compared with the early part of the time horizon. Certainly, the faculty has changed over the last decade and will continue to change due to attrition. One of the themes described in chapter 5, the Lenoir-Rhyne saga, was the Fanning Factor, an assertion that non-Lutheran faculty affirm and sustain a faith-centered, if not particularly Lutheran, climate at Lenoir-Rhyne. Provost Hall insisted that current institutional hiring questions ensure potential faculty candidates understand the mission of Lenoir-Rhyne as a college of the church.

Both Concordia and Lenoir-Rhyne have made intentional decisions to preserve the Lutheran identity of each school. The Commission for Lenoir-Rhyne reported that Lenoir-Rhyne's faith-relatedness is one of the outstanding strengths of the college and that this identity should be preserved in the future. The subsequent institutional strategic plan included "faith development" as the fifth goal of the strategy, though this point is described in terms of the "Christian perspective" and the "church catholic," rather than specifically Lutheran. While the institutional mission statement does prominently feature the term "Lutheran," the connection to its Christian tradition, in a broader sense, appears to be the greater priority for Lenoir-Rhyne.

Nevertheless, Lenoir-Rhyne is at a crossroads with regard to its Lutheran identity. Will the university maintain its commitment to its faith tradition? What part will the Lutheran tradition play in this relationship? President Powell suggested in the interview that the Lutheran identity could be in jeopardy in the near future. Powell said: "Some at L-R are deliberate and some are indifferent [about the Lutheran identity]. The message from the top is one of support for Lutheran identity. Many in the administration and faculty do not care and merely go along because of the party line. It is likely that the next administration may move away from the ELCA." Powell's opinion seems to reflect a theme present in the identity histories of all three schools: college leadership—the administration, governing board, and faculty—all play a role in the preservation or diminishment of organizational identity. For Lenoir-Rhyne, the institutional Lutheran ethos has persisted throughout the years of the time horizon, though there are signs that this Lutheran identity is moving toward a broader, more generic "Christian" or "spiritual" emphasis. The more compelling question is what will happen in the immediate years ahead with regard to organizational identity preservation.

Third, Gettysburg College, like Concordia, revealed data that quite plainly answered the first research question. To be clear, Gettysburg does prize its Lutheran tradition, but only in a strictly historical sense. One would be hard-pressed to find institutional strategies that indicate the college is intentionally seeking to preserve any organizational identity as a school of the Lutheran church. Only one of the interview participants, a faculty member, seemed noticeably hostile toward the idea of Gettysburg kindling its relationship to the Lutheran church. All other participants, at the very least, noted the importance of the Lutheran tradition as an *historical* function.

The recurring theme in the Gettysburg College saga is history. This is to say that significant historical events not only occurred at the college, but the institution places great value on the role of that history in the life of the college. Events and people in American history—the Civil War's Battle of Gettysburg, Lincoln's Gettysburg Address, and Dwight D. Eisenhower—occupy important roles in the lore of the college. Likewise, the history of American Lutheranism also intersects with Gettysburg College, particularly with regard to Schmucker and the development of an assimilated American Lutheran theology. It is no surprise that interviewees and institutional documents repeatedly pointed to Lutheranism as an important historical characteristic of the college.

One cannot overlook the most significant factor in influencing the Lutheran identity of Gettysburg College, a factor that shaped subsequent presidential decision-making and institutional strategic planning. Since the time he founded the college in 1832, Samuel Schmucker envisioned a non-sectarian institution that was merely "Lutheran-related." In analyzing the data and identifying this theme, two related questions surfaced. Is Schmucker's vision a valid *reason* for Gettysburg's current diminished Lutheran identity, or is Schmucker's vision an *excuse* for the identity diminishment?

Clearly, mission statements and founders' intentions at Concordia and Lenoir-Rhyne have been remarkably critical in shaping institutional direction. As the literature explains, mission statements inspire members of the organization and give shape, purpose, and meaning to the organization. Decision-making is a cumulative effect of the previous visions and intentions within the organization; strategic plans are not made in a vacuum but rather are influenced by the organizational ethos. While decision-makers unsympathetic to the Lutheran tradition may have looked for excuses to move away from the institution's church-relatedness, the original organizational mission spelled out in Schmucker's charter is powerful DNA that shapes and reshapes purpose over time.

Over the forty-five-year time horizon, Gettysburg College has changed considerably with regard to its Lutheran ethos. The percentage of Lutheran students had plummeted from approximately fifty percent in 1964, according to Sherman Hendrix, to five percent today. Similarly, the percentage of Lutheran faculty had also fallen to approximately six percent.[1] Hendrix also added, "Gettysburg has moved away from a religion course requirement, and the role of religion has diminished over the years." No religion courses are required at Gettysburg in 2009, replaced

1. Data on Lutheran faculty percentages at Gettysburg College in the 1960s is not available.

by a more general humanities requirement that includes the option to use a religion course to satisfy.

Is it too late for Gettysburg College to reclaim its identity as a Lutheran institution? Practically speaking, it seems unlikely that the college would make any significant institutional course change, reimagining a strategic trajectory that would include a historical relic that it has worked hard to erase, or at least to dim. Presidents over the past few decades, particularly Glassick and Haaland, have aspired for Gettysburg's national recognition and secure position among elite liberal arts colleges. Consequently, the college has indeed realized success with the goal, and a boldly articulated Lutheran identity has not been part of the formula for that success. In fact, some interviewees intimated that emphasizing this historical ecclesial relationship could jeopardize the college's quest for national acclaim among elite small colleges. Institutional documents, specifically the mission statement and the recent planning document, do not include Lutheran identity or any substantive discussion of faith.

Theoretically, the college could still recover or reaffirm pieces of its Lutheran tradition. During her interview, President Riggs, who is an active Lutheran herself, displayed subtle interest in the school's Lutheran relationship. More than one interview participant remarked about Riggs' predecessor's renewed interest in Gettysburg's Lutheran tradition. The framework for a vibrant Lutheran identity to flourish is present at Gettysburg: a strong commitment to the liberal arts, an enduring dedication to public service and social justice, and a remarkably rich Lutheran history. Missing are the integration of faith and learning and an intentional discussion of vocation linking public service to the sacred. Institutional intentionality, sparked and stoked by presidential leadership, is absolutely necessary for this ecclesial relationship to flourish.

As the literature indicates, organizational preservation and diminishment is related to the influence of isomorphic status drivers. The next three sections address the effects of secularization, financial viability, and faculty professionalization observed at the three institutions, especially in relation to organizational preservation and diminishment. While data show all three status drivers at work at all three schools, Concordia leaders appeared more concerned with secularization. This is not to say that secularization has not affected Lenoir-Rhyne and Gettysburg, but rather Concordia decision-makers expressed concern about the effects of secularization on the college's Lutheran identity. Similarly, issues related to financial viability more clearly emerged in the Lenoir-Rhyne data, given that institution's perpetual fiscal challenges. Finally, Gettysburg's quest for national prestige and excellence suggests that faculty professionalization issues continue to be a key status driver with regard to that college's identity.

SECULARIZATION

Simply put, secularization is the separation of life activities from the influences of organized religion (Marsden, 1992). Furthermore, it is the idea that religious authority has diminished, shaped in part by new trends toward inclusiveness and plurality (Arthur, 2001; Demerath, 1998). As explained in the literature review, secularization in American higher education has escalated since the 1960s. The isomorphic status driver of secularization is best illustrated by the mechanism of coercive isomorphism, which results from formal and informal influences of organizations upon other organizations. These influences may be either actual or ceremonial, shaped by cultural expectations in the organizational environment (DiMaggio & Powell, 1983). As a result of conformity toward environmental rituals, norms, and expectations, organizations tend to become increasingly homogenous.

Interview participants at each of the three schools commented on the role of secularization in higher education. Although secularization has occurred at the three institutions, the Concordia community seemed to be most interested in discussing the issue as it relates to the institutional identity, primarily because the phenomenon poses an actual threat to the expressed Concordia mission to function as a college of the church. Whereas secularization tends to push some organizations toward conformity with secular organizations, data suggest that college leaders steered Concordia toward other schools also seeking to preserve their religious identities. In fact, twelve of the fourteen Concordia benchmark colleges and universities are intentional about their religious affiliation, six of them ELCA colleges.[2]

At Concordia, secularization as an isomorphic status driver actually influenced college leaders to defend aggressively against these shaping

---

2. The other two of Concordia's benchmark schools, though not expressly religiously-affiliated today, were founded as Christian schools.

forces. In fact, Concordia's Knutson, Dovre, and Jolicoeur emulated schools they and the governing board perceived to be preserving their Lutheran identity (and in some cases the Reformed and Roman Catholic traditions) in the face of secular change. All of these schools claim publicly to preserve intentionally their church-relatedness. The list includes both Lutheran and non-Lutheran institutions. That Concordia is geographically located within a region of the country heavily populated with Lutherans was another notable factor for its ability to stave off secular influences. In other words, with a critical mass of Lutheran faculty and a majority of Lutheran students, Concordia was in a position to ensure the engagement of a faith-centered curriculum and educational experience, situated within a critical mass of Lutherans.

This is not to say that Concordia has completely escaped secularization over the years. Ernest Simmons noted that the Concordia community has become increasingly diverse over the years, citing a student body population of seventy-eight percent Lutheran when he arrived in the 1970s to the current sixty percent. Nevertheless, this number—sixty percent—is still remarkably high, considering that most of the ELCA colleges and universities record Lutherans as minorities among their student bodies. This diversity, as respondents pointed out, is not a bad development. Professor Per Anderson agreed with Simmons, noting that diversity among Lutherans' theological and social perspectives has increased in recent years. Simmons suggested three manifestations of secularization at the college:

> First, today students don't know the Lutheran tradition as they once did. That is not a pejorative comment but a descriptive one. Students here are very active and socially concerned, but they are not, generally speaking, aware of the Biblical construct or the Catechism. Second, students want to be spiritual but not necessarily religious. They don't seem to have much time for traditional church activities. So, Lutheran colleges haven't changed, but what it means to be a Lutheran student is different than before. Third, changing demographics might affect the campus faith community in the future. Will this increased plurality be forced upon Concordia? How religiously diverse can and should Concordia be?

In his book, Simmons (1998) calls identity a process. For Simmons, organizational identity is an evolving process, shared and supported by all members of the community. "Identity," he says, "must be everybody's business or it is not identity at all but rather a nostalgic veneer preserved by anachronistic sentimentality" (Simmons, 1998:22). Because its college community is so heavily populated with engaged Lutherans interested in the ecclesial identity, Concordia has been able to make this identity process an institutional priority even as secularization looms.

To Simmons' point, all who are involved in the campus community must have a role. Simmons said, "The president must affirm the faith tradition, the Board has to be engaged with it, and the faculty has to see it as valid. When faculty is engaged, though, we have to be careful to distinguish between the lectern and the pulpit." Concordia's preservation of its tradition comes out at the hiring of faculty. President Dovre did not mandate that all faculty be Lutheran, but he did insist that at least one Lutheran be in the final pool of candidates. His rationale was that the faculty must know the Lutheran tradition. In this instance, Concordia leaders worked to combat the influence of secularization by striving to maintain a critical mass of Lutherans among the campus community.

Dovre noted the effect of secularization on Concordia's Lutheran identity, citing three examples. First, he suggested that the diminished role of *in loco parentis* was a direct result of secularization. This phenomenon, however, is in no way exclusive to Concordia. Rather, the decline of *in loco parentis,* replaced by the professionalization of student life, began in the 1960s and affected the entire landscape of American higher education. Second, Dovre noted the diminished numbers of Concordia faculty, staff, and students who participate in campus worship on a regular basis. Third, he pointed to the hiring of a more religiously diverse faculty. In the 1970s, Dovre expanded the faculty, and this new spate of hiring involved less consideration of religious values than before. Subsequently, for perhaps the first time in its history, Concordia began to employ a faculty less familiar with the Lutheran identity, ethos, and logos of the college. Dovre suggested that increased diversity in religious affiliation of the Concordia community, the growth of individualism, the growth of overall affluence, and higher material expectations of the college and its people reflected the broader culture and the effects of secularization during his administration.

Likewise, Faculty Assembly Chair Dawn Duncan recognized the effects of secularization upon the Concordia identity. However, her outlook confirms that Concordia has responded to secular forces differently from Lenoir-Rhyne and Gettysburg. In other words, Concordia decision-makers have found a way to use secularization as a rallying cry for the campus community to defend vigorously the college's Lutheran identity. Duncan offered this perspective:

> If anything, I think secularization has confirmed Concordia's Lutheran identity. As a postcolonial theorist, I understand particularly well how people hold onto an identity that is threatened, finding ways to live that identity in the midst of others. For instance, my husband remarks that I was never so Irish-American or Catholic until I found myself among so many Norwegian Lutherans. I recognize the truth of that statement, because I find myself needing to educate and contextualize as I share my perspective on issues, since I may come from a different perspective. Concordia plays an important role, from the local to global secular world, as we share a particular faith-based, Norwegian heritage perspective on learning and acting in the world.

Has the status driver of secularization affected Concordia College's Lutheran institutional identity? In sum, secularization, interpreted as a threat to the institutional identity, has actually caused campus leaders to rally around the mission and to push against secular forces, thus preserving or maintaining the Lutheran organizational identity.

Next, has secularization affected the Lutheran identity of Lenoir-Rhyne? According to President Powell, "Of course" secularization has influenced the college. The president cited the diversity of backgrounds and beliefs and the subsequent changing demographics as examples of these effects. Specifically, he referenced a trend he has observed at Lenoir-Rhyne since his arrival a decade ago: the dwindling number of Lutheran faculty, many of whom are not committed to the church. Professor of Religion David Ratke agreed, referencing recent discussions with some faculty members who were ignorant of the university's Lutheran heritage or dismissive of it. Since federal guidelines changed in the 1970s regarding public higher education funding, religiously-affiliated colleges and universities have had to rethink the way they populate their faculties. What is more, demographic shifts continue to favor diversity of faculty, staff, students, and board members in the increasingly changing higher education landscape.

Powell also suggested another effect of secularization on the university; namely, that the status driver has actually reshaped Lutheranism itself, especially in the context of how college students in the twenty-first century engage faith and learning. Powell said, "In the traditional sense of Lutheran identity, it is essential to have a large Lutheran faculty. In the changing world, Lutheranism takes on a new meaning and can be enhanced regardless of the denomination of the faculty." Powell continued by suggesting that Lutheran colleges and universities are still quite relevant in American higher education, but that these schools must redefine the meaning of Lutheranism to address the needs of the changing faculty and student body. Said Powell, Lutheran identity is worth preserving "in the context of the needs of the next generations." So, secularization has affected the way Lenoir-Rhyne perceives its mission as a university of the Lutheran church, one sensitive to a changing demographic population.

Although it cannot be argued effectively that an institution can completely stop the effects of secularization with any strategy, Lenoir-Rhyne, like Concordia, has attempted to respond to the fewer number of Lutherans on campus by encouraging a dialogue among the college community about Lutheran organizational identity. Lenoir-Rhyne has found success at encouraging its non-Lutheran faculty members to engage and affirm the university's church-relatedness, an idea called the Fanning Factor. Part of this notion is represented by Richard Von Dohlen, retired philosophy professor, who perpetually participated in the college-church dialogue during his three decades at Lenoir-Rhyne. In an article called "Strangers in Luther Land," Von Dohlen described the paradoxical nature, inherent tension, and potential rewards of teaching and mentoring at a Lutheran college as a person from a non-Lutheran faith tradition.

While the overall number of Lutheran students has decreased since the 1960s to a 2008 level of sixteen percent, the institutional ethos has also changed, declined. Secularization could be a contributing factor in a portion of this diminishment: no more required weekly chapel attendance, the loosening of religious curricular requirements, and the anecdotal decline of participation of students in campus religious activities, observed by Weisner and Yoder in this study's interview data. Pastor Weisner also offered an insightful observation of how secularization has affected current students at Lenoir-Rhyne, especially in relation to the students for which Larry Yoder provided ministry in the 1970s. Weisner said:

> The dissolution of the family has sent us students not from church-related homes. I see four categories of students that we have. First, we have students from homes where faith is not cherished, but the student wants to know more. This is the group in which I have

most often baptized students. Second, we have students who come from very church-related families but aren't engaged. These might be the P.K.s.[3] Third, we have the students where faith comes with them and grows along the way at college, but they don't publicly demonstrate it. Fourth, some just don't care at all about issues of faith. I hope I have a good relationship with everybody. I try to show the love of Christ.

With regard to emulation of other colleges and universities, secularization has shaped Lenoir-Rhyne's strategic planning. Several of Lenoir-Rhyne's benchmark institutions are not religiously-affiliated at all. Although Lenoir-Rhyne's Powell and Hall did not identify a specific institutional benchmark list, Hall explained that the university loosely follows the member schools of the New American Colleges and Universities (ANAC). This national consortium includes twenty selective, small-to-mid-size independent colleges and universities, fitting the general profile its board and administration now aspires for Lenoir-Rhyne University. The members are a mix of religious and non-religious schools, including three Lutheran schools.

The emulation patterns demonstrated by Lenoir-Rhyne, however, are more directly influenced by fiscal issues, discussed in the next section. Despite the university's diverse list of benchmarks, church-related and not, Provost Hall insists that Lenoir-Rhyne will maintain its strong ecclesial ties. He said, "We are shooting for a model similar to Elon [University],[4] but we will be ultimately different than Elon, because we want to maintain our Christian tradition. Elon has not done that."

In light of the interview, document, and observational data, Gettysburg College and its Lutheran identity have been most affected by secularization. To be clear, this secularization is best demonstrated by the schools it has chosen to emulate, as well as the status driver of faculty professionalization, discussed later. Of the seven schools identified by Gettysburg as either benchmark or aspirant schools, none express an intentional religious affiliation, though three were founded with religious affiliation. Instead, all proclaim a deep commitment to an esteemed, highly selective, rigorous liberal arts experience, hallmarks for which

3. P.K. is a common abbreviation for "pastors' kids," a part of the vernacular on the Lenoir-Rhyne campus.

4. Elon University is one of the member schools of ANAC, the New American Colleges and Universities.

Gettysburg strives. Coercive isomorphic forces have nudged Gettysburg toward the homogenized field of elite—and decidedly secular—liberal arts colleges with which it measures itself and aspires to emulate.

Interview respondents provided examples of secularization. For example, Michael Birkner cited declining attendance in chapel and the decline of overt religious programming on campus, including student activities. Additionally, Birkner pointed to a change in the curriculum, moving to a "loose religious model." Sherman Hendrix also noted the change in the Gettysburg religious course requirement. He explained, "The old curriculum had students taking two religion courses from professors with a Lutheran identity. Now the religion requirement is gone and replaced by a more general humanities requirement that includes the option to use a religion course to satisfy." Further, Hendrix suggested that the role of religion has diminished over the years at Gettysburg.

Perhaps the most visible sign of secularization's impact on Gettysburg College is expressed in the quiet emptiness of the vast Christ Chapel, the towering, sprawling church that sits in the center of the campus. With Gettysburg's changing campus community, the usefulness of the chapel as a house of worship became less and less important. Has secularization affected the Lutheran identity of Gettysburg? Since secularization has affected the elite, national liberal arts colleges to which Gettysburg aspires, Gettysburg has also diminished its Lutheran identity in the emulation and modeling process.

The forces of secularization exerted on the three college identities have affected the institutions' ethos and outlook. Clearly, each of the schools has been influenced in some way by secular forces, though some more than others. Secularization affected the schools differently, sparking Concordia's enthusiasm to align itself with colleges that rebuke the secular, and fueling Gettysburg toward an exclusively secular organizational field. Fitting the pattern it has generally demonstrated throughout this study, Lenoir-Rhyne falls somewhere between Concordia and Gettysburg.

FINANCIAL VIABILITY

Small colleges and universities like Concordia, Lenoir-Rhyne, and Gettysburg, all liberal arts in character, face perpetual financial challenges (Breneman, 1994). Although the focus of this study was not to conduct in-depth analysis of institutional financial health and fiscal management, part of the dissertation does focus on how each schools' financial viability affects, if at all, organizational isomorphic behavior and treatment of institutional identity. The status driver of financial viability is best illustrated by the mechanism of mimetic isomorphism. When the environment is uncertain and the goals are ambiguous, organizations model themselves on other organizations perceived to be healthy and strong (DiMaggio & Powell, 1983; March & Olson, 1976).

Modeling other organizations that are considered to be viable is a response to uncertainty and can yield a useful template for borrowing best practices and implementing innovative ideas (DiMaggio & Powell, 1983). A contemporary example is the strategy of the beleaguered (but solvent) Ford Motor Company to emulate the best practices of the successful Toyota and Honda automobile manufacturers. New or challenged organizations routinely seek successful models upon which to build (Kimberly, 1980).

Because of its geographic location in the Lutheran-rich Upper Midwest where ELCA students, faculty, and staff are abundant, Concordia has minimized the effects of secularization brought about by a diminishment of Lutheran critical mass in its college community. Like the vast majority of similar schools, Concordia is a tuition-driven school. President Jolicoeur explained, "Our admission potential is better in the upper Midwest. Our Lutheran identity is important here, and there are lots of people [regionally] who know and like that." When asked if her college has been forced to make trade-offs for the sake of financial viability at the expense of its Lutheran identity, Jolicoeur answered, "No, we haven't had to. But that doesn't mean we won't make changes in our strategy. For example, we may actually decide to be smaller as a student body, moving from, for example, 2,800 to 2,500 students." Jolicoeur suggested this possible strategy as a way of helping to improve four-year graduation rates and student retention.

Former President Dovre echoed Jolicoeur's perspective. About the issue of trade-offs, Dovre insisted that Concordia has not made fiscal trade-offs at the expense of Lutheran identity, saying, "We have the gift of being located in a land of many Lutherans, and even the non-Lutherans like us, given the strong ecumenical tradition and spirit of the region. Location has also been helpful in terms of Concordia's fundraising efforts, including high numbers of alumni and Lutherans familiar with the college." Dovre also explained that financial viability issues played a significant role, particularly in the 1970s, when institutions wished to retain eligibility for federal funds. Since hiring needed to be non-discriminatory with respect to religious affiliation, many institutions initially gave up on the matter of institutional mission and identity. According to Dovre and Jolicoeur, Concordia did not, has not, and will not.

This is not to say that Concordia leaders have held financial viability issues completely at bay. A challenge Concordia has faced since the 1960s is balancing its mission of preserving the organizational Lutheran identity, while also involving non-Lutherans on the governing board and in philanthropic efforts. With regard to institutional development efforts, Jolicoeur explained, "We have created new opportunities to add new wealthy non-Lutheran donors and are creating new roles for the wealthy people interested in and engaged with the college. I am aware of other Lutheran colleges that have changed their board requirements for development purposes. We will not." Provost Krejci echoed Jolicoeur's notion, saying, "We never have discussed changing those [board] requirements [to diminish the number of Lutherans] in favor of policies that would build a wealthier board."

If Concordia looks to its benchmark colleges for models of best practices, the interview and document data do not evidence this. No interview participant, including the presidents, commented on fiscal benchmarking and best practices. Whether mimetic isomorphic behavior is happening at Concordia is unclear. Rather, Concordia's benchmarking is attuned primarily to schools intentionally preserving their religious identities. When asked about Concordia's benchmarking best practices or business models of other schools, Professor Emeritus Engelhardt responded, "Concordia has always tried to be a good steward of what it has been given and has always tried to balance its budgets. I assume business management is a matter of Christian vocation, and I think Concordia has attempted to be true to that understanding."

Professor Duncan, the Chairperson of the Faculty Assembly, offered an astute, measured outlook on how issues of financial viability have shaped Concordia with regard to homogenization. When asked how other institutions have influenced Concordia's fiscal decision-making, Duncan, like the other interviewees, did not cite specific schools and strategies. Instead, respondents described an independent institution, one almost insular and protected by its own Lutheran predominance and geographic location. In addition to her role on the Faculty Executive Committee, Duncan also serves on the Strategic Budget Committee, which has provided her insight into the college's financial attitude and actions. Duncan reported: "I would say that our Lutheran identity has had a positive impact on our financial status at a time when others are reeling. Rather than the college being reactionary, with finances being the power player, we have remained active so that we can provide good stewardship in financial matters. We are cautious rather than greedy, avoiding undue risk; yet we faithfully and thoughtfully invest in programs that will continue to strengthen the college learning community. There are steady hands at the helm."

Does the status driver of financial viability affect the Lutheran identity of Concordia? Data show that Concordia College has not been forced to make fiscal trade-offs for the sake of preserving organizational identity. The college has not revised requirements for governing board membership that would diminish Lutheran membership (clergy or layperson) in favor of including wealthy, influential non-Lutherans. It is unclear whether revising board membership would actually create a broader and wealthier board while simultaneously preserving the organizational identity. Instead, Concordia leaders have found alternative ways to engage meaningfully non-Lutheran volunteers. Given its position and geography, Concordia simply has not had to make these trade-offs.

One of the four themes uncovered at Lenoir-Rhyne was its struggle with financial challenges. In independent interviews, respondents repeatedly cited these challenges, particularly the 1991 financial crisis. The strategic plans, *Strategy for the Seventies* and 2009's *University Rising*, address institutional resolve toward fiscal responsibility and financial stability. A basic key to the mimetic isomorphic process is that organizational uncertainty is a powerful force that encourages imitation. Faced with uncertainty brought on by issues of financial viability, Lenoir-Rhyne leaders have begun to look to similar schools, members of the New American Colleges and Universities.

It is important to note, however, that Provost Hall also said, "I have never been a big supporter of institutional benchmarking." Powell also chose not to comment in detail on institutional benchmarking. That such high-level administrators did not elaborate on the practice of benchmarking and organizational emulation (formal or informal) suggests that it is not currently a widely used Lenoir-Rhyne practice. Lenoir-Rhyne uses no official institutional benchmark or aspirant list. It can be safely concluded that Lenoir-Rhyne decision-making is not as dependent upon benchmarking as are Concordia and especially Gettysburg.

Interestingly, interview and document data both point to Lenoir-Rhyne's efforts to identify and adapt a workable business model. However, no data directly show that the university has intentionally sought successful business models at other successful schools, aspirant or otherwise. Instead, the institutional benchmarks, which the president and provost reluctantly described as such, are ANAC members. In a follow-up telephone conversation, Provost Hall noted that these ANAC schools were chosen primarily on "academic and curricular" grounds.

Rufus Moretz, retired Professor of Religion who had been on faculty for nearly forty years, spoke with great candor about financial issues and Lenoir-Rhyne's future. Moretz said:

> I think financial issues are having a significant impact on the general direction of the institution. In my view the current administration would like to move away from the shared governance pattern of the past 40 years toward a business model as a more efficient means of managing the resources of the institution. Shared governance means that faculty have a large share in determining curriculum, and they do not often quickly reach consensus. Shared governance gives to faculty a large share in decisions about who is to be hired and who is to be continued. A business model would make such decisions mainly on the basis of efficiency with potential negative consequences for the kind of institution Lenoir-Rhyne has been during the forty-plus years I have observed it both as a student and as a faculty member. Its history with the liberal arts and Lutheran heritage could be negatively impacted if the institution turns in this direction.

Has the status driver of financial viability affected Lenoir-Rhyne's Lutheran institutional identity? The answer is mixed. On one hand, Lenoir-Rhyne, an institution occasionally beset by fiscal challenges, has chosen to model itself after ANAC institutions, albeit loosely and unofficially. Some of these schools are not religiously-affiliated. On the other hand, the university has chosen to preserve its Lutheran identity and religiosity based primarily upon two factors: mission and financial viability. While functioning as a college of the church is a publicly professed aim of Lenoir-Rhyne, a university commission found that the institution's religious affiliation is a strength, which could potentially attract students, donors, and volunteers interested in such an educational experience. Said another way, there is capital in Lenoir-Rhyne's decision to accentuate its faith-centered, if not exclusively Lutheran, character. As President Powell explained, "We see the connection to the church as a strength both programmatically and financially. It is part of our uniqueness."

Compared with Concordia and Lenoir-Rhyne, Gettysburg College is in the most enviable financial position, based on endowment values alone. Its endowment, after the 2008 economic downturn, was valued at approximately $190 million,[5] compared with $80 million for Concordia and $50 million for Lenoir-Rhyne. In the president's annual budget update on February 18, 2009, Riggs referenced the ailing economy and distressed higher education environment while offering assurance of the college's overall strong position. Riggs said, "In spite of the challenges we all face in this environment, I remain encouraged by the continuing strong Board enthusiasm for the College's fundamental mission. Gettysburg remains in a relatively strong position because of their support and wise counsel and a long-time institutional practice of prudent financial management."

Given its aspirations, Gettysburg's endowment is currently lacking. In order to compete with the elite private liberal arts colleges among whom Gettysburg envisions itself, the college must sharply increase its endowment. Although Gettysburg has traditionally been tuition-driven, President Riggs foresees an increasing reliance on philanthropic cash flow, which is particularly sensitive to the economic environment. Riggs explained that Gettysburg alumni are increasingly more diverse in their income and will be looked to for increased support of the college. According to Riggs, increased development activities will be important in the future."

When asked what Gettysburg most closely evaluates in its benchmarks, Riggs said,

> (We look at) best practices and their reputations as excellent liberal arts colleges. And they all have big endowments, especially in comparison with ours. With more financial resources, they can attract students by providing strong financial aid packages, and

5. As of May 31, 2008, before the economic recession, the Gettysburg College endowment approximated $255 million. Lenoir-Rhyne's endowment was valued at an estimated $62 million and Concordia's at $80 million. These numbers are reported by the ELCA Division for Vocation and Education.

more money is available for academic programs. Following that, you also have the opportunity for lower student-to-faculty ratios. And these schools also can provide more frequent sabbaticals for faculty. Generally, these colleges are in a better position to do these things. Financial resources have a lot to do with that.

In sum, the issue of financial viability has affected Gettysburg's Lutheran institutional identity, evidenced in the revision of its governing board membership requirements. College leaders sought to build a wealthier and more influential Board of Trustees, which would theoretically make possible the expansion of the institutional endowment, critical for entry into the upper echelon of elite liberal arts colleges. Currently, there is no minimum requirement for Lutherans on the board, except for the seat occupied by the Bishop of the Southeastern Synod.

FACULTY PROFESSIONALIZATION

The third status driver, faculty professionalization, is best characterized as the normative mechanism of institutional isomorphic change. As the literature review explained, the widespread phenomenon of professionalization of faculty and administrative roles at colleges and universities increased during the seismic shifts of the 1960s. In fact, normative isomorphic organizational change stems primarily from professionalization (DiMaggio & Powell, 1983). A primary threat to organizational identity with regard to professionalization is the trend of faculty to choose, ultimately, loyalty to profession and discipline over loyalty to institution and mission. The professionalization of the faculty has already occurred; how a particular institution responds to professionalization influences on organizational identity is ongoing and diversely addressed.

The Concordia saga revealed the aggressiveness with which the college maintains hiring practices intended to preserve institutional mission. Specifically, the Concordia hiring process includes three questions, one of which queries the candidate's familiarity with and endorsement of the organizational mission. To be clear, faculty professionalization has occurred at Concordia College, and professors are accomplished scholars who are engaged externally and internally with their disciplines.

Simultaneously, these faculty members are quite committed to the Concordia mission, while also balancing engagement with colleagues in their disciplines and fields. On one hand, faculty professionalization is pushing Concordia toward homogeneity with the larger academy, a body that honors and acknowledges faculty engaged in scholarship. On the other hand, the college is pushing back against professionalization forces, attempting to preserve a faculty equally loyal to the college mission.

Two faculty members and one staff member reflected upon faculty professionalization and organizational identity at Concordia. While Concordia has successfully maintained a well-respected faculty of teacher-scholars, it has also maintained a remarkably strong college-church identity. Despite the college's ability to manage both tasks, these three interviewees did suggest that the effort is not easy nor is it without risk. Duncan noted that the competing pressures and multiple tasks required of faculty do, at times, undermine the professor's ability to faithfully serve the mission of the college and the engagement with the discipline. She noted, "It is up to us to know our limits and to openly discuss these competing pressures with our colleagues and leaders so that our energies can be harnessed and our gifts most productively used. I keep working on this balance."

Campus Pastor Leiseth, though not a faculty member obliged to a particular departmental discipline, also indicated that "professionalization pressures" pose a challenge to a faculty member's ability to serve faithfully within the Lutheran college environment. She said, "One of our theological beliefs is that we are finite creatures created with a need for rest and Sabbath. The pressure on faculty members is enormous, and there is a critical issue at Concordia with faculty and administration finding room for restorative time." While much energy and dedication is invested in the mission of the college and one's discipline or department, Concordia faculty and staff seem to be at capacity. Leiseth added, "There isn't time for reflection and deep relationships. There isn't time for restoration. There isn't time for worship. This will become more and more critical if it is not resolved."

Engelhardt also pointed to the tension, saying, "If faculty members become fully absorbed in professional issues, they might not have time or energy to engage in the question of Lutheran identity or in fostering Lutheran education ideals." Since the 1970s, Concordia College administrators, as well as strategic planning documents, have called for greater attention to scholarly engagement of their faculty, advancing this institutional effort with financial support. Identified again and again in

Concordia's identity history, bringing to the classroom and laboratory—indeed to the profession—a Lutheran understanding of vocation is the solution to reconciling professional demands and organizational loyalty.

At Lenoir-Rhyne, demonstration of faculty scholarship and engagement with professional organizations, including publishing and speaking and conference attendance, is a relatively new expectation. Lenoir-Rhyne has traditionally focused on teaching and mentoring throughout its history, and according to the administrators and planning documents, these foci will continue to be of fundamental importance. With the college's recent movement to university status, as well as the related demands of faculty professionalization on the higher education landscape, Lenoir-Rhyne leaders have begun in recent years to establish new, expanded expectations for tenured faculty.

Teaching, discovering, application, and integration are active and vibrant ways of benefitting students and the university. Provost Hall said, "For our university, we need to do what helps the faculty to become better teachers. We are larger than that notion of publish or perish. It is a model that allows our faculty to remain vibrant and engaged and still maintains the student as the center of our identity and our mission." Alternatively, since his arrival at Lenoir-Rhyne, Hall has prioritized the need for faculty scholarly engagement within their disciplines and professional organizations.[6]

Part of Hall's initiatives, endorsed by the president and other administrators, has been to ensure that all faculty members receive an annual $750 allotment for professional activities, whether they use it or not. As a result, the university observed a significant increase of faculty allotment expenditures on research agendas and conference attendance during the 2008 academic year. Most of this participation was recorded among the liberal arts faculty and included edited books, published articles, and presentations.

About faculty participation in professional organizations and research activities, Hall asserted, "It is easy to be insulated at a small school, and we are trying to overcome that. One goal of the strategic plan is to double the funding so that eventually all faculty are engaged in external scholarship in their disciplines' communities or in other areas of

6. During the past decade, even before Hall's arrival, Lenoir-Rhyne administrators had already begun to identify the need to increase funding for faculty's professional engagement.

professional development appropriate to our mission." What is more, the three criteria for the university's tenure review for faculty are teaching and mentoring, research development, and service.

Five Lenoir-Rhyne interview respondents reiterated this new university emphasis. Joe Smith and Andrew Weisner noted the increase in both institutional funding and encouragement for involvement in the disciplines' communities. Bill Mauney, Dean of the College of Professional and Mathematical Studies (a large and important Lenoir-Rhyne academic school), reported that the participation rate among the faculty in his school is in the eighty to ninety percent range, and that the overall institutional rate is increasing. Mauney claimed, "Faculty cannot be excellent unless they have external engagement with their disciplines. The prime mission for faculty here is teaching, but they must be good at research, too. Research is part of our vocation as faculty members."

Larry Yoder said that "participation is necessary so as to keep pace with innovation and thinking, especially with other Lutheran and similar colleges." Marsha Fanning evoked the need for cross-intellectual activities, particularly in the sciences, of which her discipline is biology. She said, "Research focus in the sciences has been related to student research. Presentations, teaching, and mentoring are all priorities. Faculty must stay current. My work with ABLE (Association of Biological Lab Education) helps my teaching perspectives."

Comparatively, Gettysburg displayed a more sophisticated, comprehensive, and long-standing engagement with faculty professionalization. Riggs said, "We think that's really important. It's good for Gettysburg's reputation. It's good professional development. And it's good for what they bring back to campus. This regular participation preserves intellectual vitality." At Gettysburg, the general institutional ideal of mission and purpose shifted over the past three decades from an exclusive focus on teaching to one of scholarship and research in order to compete with and establish an association with elite national liberal arts colleges. Provost White indicated that Gettysburg had experienced a shift to galvanizing the liberal arts tradition as a foundation for nurturing faculty researchers and creative artists. "This is a shift away from an exclusive focus on teaching," he said.

Professor Char Weise, the elected head of the Gettysburg faculty, was perhaps the most critical respondent, suggesting that an emphasis on the college's religious tradition threatens its quest to become a nationally respected liberal arts college. Instead, faculty involvement in external professional activities is vital, as Weise said, because "of personal fulfillment, being an active member of a scholarly community outside the college, it benefits students and makes a better faculty." Institutional funding has been made available to the faculty for these purposes for years, evidenced by the scholarship produced at Gettysburg over the last two decades. Long-time chaplain Karl Mattson reiterated that these faculty endeavors are "extremely important" to the institution.

Michael Birkner, like Weise, also displayed candor, saying, "Faculty professional involvement supports the effort by setting objectives for faculty. The college says, 'Go out and meet your peers and bring the information back to the classroom.' You don't get tenure unless you're an active scholar at Gettysburg." Sherman Hendrix, a senior professor on faculty since the 1960s, said:

> In each of our fields of expertise, it is expected by the institution that faculty keep connections in their various fields. There are expectations that this participation happens, seen in criteria for tenure and promotion. This profile on faculty external participation in professional organizations and activities was raised or emphasized in the seventies but more so in the eighties. Its importance exploded in the 1990s. Teaching and mentoring is the primary focus. There is great pressure—probably for any faculty member—to manage both well. The junior faculty at Gettysburg may disagree [that teaching and mentoring are the primary focus], especially as they compete for tenure.

To compare Weise's outlook as the junior faculty with Hendrix's perspective as a senior faculty, it is clear to see the dynamic faculty environment at Gettysburg. Hendrix, who is a self-described sympathizer of the college's Lutheran identity, stands in sharp contrast to Weise, who expressed no interest in preserving or even acknowledging publicly Gettysburg's Lutheran identity.

At each of the three institutions, faculty professionalization has affected organizational Lutheran identity inasmuch as faculty loyalty to discipline surpasses loyalty to institutional mission. Indeed, the professionalization of the faculty is a new reality for colleges and universities. While the Concordia faculty has also experienced professionalization, the college has also boldly and aggressively emphasized its Lutheran mission. The effect of professionalization on Lenoir-Rhyne is unclear, especially since institutional emphasis on systematic external engagement with academic disciplines is a relatively recent phenomenon. Diminishment of Gettysburg's Lutheran identity as a result of faculty professionalization is clearly demonstrated, particularly given the institution's broadened and rigorous expectations for its faculty.

SUMMARY

Although the answers were being considered, crafted, and foreshadowed in the case studies of the three schools, chapter 7 specifically and summarily answered the first two central research questions of this study. First, regarding the question of preservation and diminishment at ELCA colleges, the answers are mixed. Concordia College is intentionally seeking to preserve its Lutheran identity, evidenced by the efforts of successive administrations, by the cooperation and affirmation of an engaged campus community, and by close attention to an enduring mission statement and focused strategic plan.

Lenoir-Rhyne is systematically preserving its identity as a religiously-affiliated institution, where vocation and faith development are prioritized. Despite its strong ties to the North Carolina synod and a fairly robust Lutheran faculty, the Lutheran component appears to be less privileged than a general Christian perspective, reflective of the demographics of the faculty, staff, and student body at this small, southern Lutheran university.

According to members of the campus community, strategic planning documents, and the institutional mission statement, Gettysburg College is clearly not seeking to preserve its Lutheran identity in any functional way. This is not to say that the college does, on occasion, refer to its founding as a non-sectarian, Lutheran-related institution. For all intents and purposes, Gettysburg has realized great success in repositioning itself as a nationally-recognized, elite liberal arts college. A Lutheran identity, as Gettysburg leaders have envisioned over the past thirty years, plays no pragmatic role in this formula.

Second, do the status drivers of secularization, financial viability, and faculty professionalization affect Lutheran institutional identity at Concordia, Lenoir-Rhyne, and Gettysburg? Again, the answers are mixed. Secularization has affected all of higher education, especially since the 1960s. The three schools in this study have responded differently to these forces, and their Lutheran identities have similarly been influenced diversely. Financial viability is a perpetual concern for all three of these colleges, and the majority of those like them, whether they are wealthy or not. However, because of institutional fiscal health and long-range institutional planning, the three schools' Lutheran identities have been affected differently by the response to finances. Faculty professionalization, like the other two status drivers, has also affected most, if not all, American colleges and universities. These forces have affected the three schools in this study insofar as faculty loyalty to academic discipline surpasses loyalty to institutional mission. The third research question, how and why identity preservation is being planned, is answered in the next chapter.

8

Discussion

Conclusions, Implications, and Summation

THE CASE STUDIES IN this work were intended to chronicle or record the sagas of three schools over a forty-five-year time horizon and evaluate the data (Guba & Lincoln, 1988). The products of this effort were three recent cases of these schools' treatment of their organizational Lutheran identities.

Accordingly, the organization of this chapter will follow the same general structure as chapter 2, the literature review, observing the following section headings: conclusions related to institutional theory, conclusions related to organizational literature, conclusions related to governance literature, and conclusions related to Lutheran higher education literature. Finally, the chapter concludes with implications for application, suggestions for future research, and final summary statements on the study's three central research questions.

CONCLUSIONS RELATED TO INSTITUTIONAL THEORY LITERATURE

- The three schools in this study are not completely self-contained and/or are influenced and rely upon external organizations and environments for planning and emulation.

- Isomorphic status drivers did influence organizational Lutheran identity at the schools in this study, though in diverse ways.

- Although it occurred at two schools in this study, institutional emulation of other organizations did not always threaten organizational identity: homogeneity with other schools occurred on the basis of institutional aspirations, including religiously-affiliated colleges, financially viable colleges, and elite liberal arts colleges.

- Isomorphism was best demonstrated by Gettysburg College in its pursuit to emulate a small, elite organizational field.

- Applying theories of isomorphism to the three schools in this study is problematic, because the organizational fields are dynamic and not well-defined.

Regarding the issue of Lutheran organizational identity, Concordia, Lenoir-Rhyne, and Gettysburg all exhibit signs of isomorphic change over the forty-five-year time horizon. Theories of isomorphism suggest that organizations do not change by responding to the environment but rather emulating—and adapting to—institutional norms, protocols, and best practices of the perceived leading organizations. Both Concordia and Gettysburg use institutionally-identified benchmark lists; Gettysburg even differentiates its benchmarks into three categories: like (currently similar characteristics), reach (aspirant), and watch (colleges seeking to emulate Gettysburg) schools.[1]

Concordia looks to like-minded benchmark colleges that preserve their religious affiliation, including ELCA colleges (Augustana, Gustavus Adolphus, and Luther) and non-Lutheran institutions (Calvin, Elon, St. Benedict). In this case, Concordia's Lutheran identity was actually strengthened by mimetic isomorphic factors. Gettysburg's "like" colleges are similar in composition, and its reach colleges are the more elite, more highly selective, wealthier colleges it aspires to be like (Dickinson, Franklin and Marshall, Swarthmore, and Williams colleges). Although Lenoir-Rhyne does loosely benchmark based upon ANAC members (including Elon, Belmont, Pacific Lutheran, and Susquehanna Universities),

---

1. Sal Ciolino asked that I not identify all of Gettysburg's benchmarks, particularly distinguished into the three categories. To maintain congruency among the schools, this study does not identify a complete list of each schools' benchmarks.

administrators played down the notion that the university uses the practice systematically.

Collectively, the twenty-seven ELCA colleges and universities turned out to be difficult to imagine as an isomorphic model because it is not clear which schools are the leaders in the organizational field. Moreover, the three schools addressed in this study emulate (or at least observe) institutions both inside and outside of the ELCA organizational field, and these fields widely vary. Nevertheless, examining the institutional change of Lutheran colleges and universities through the lens of isomorphism is important and useful for understanding how these institutions comprehend themselves, how they envision their futures, and how they plan institutional direction.

Pfeffer and Salancik (1978) offered the resource dependence model, arguing that successful organizations must first adapt externally, and then internally, in seeking resources and legitimacy from their environment. Although it also fits the mimetic isomorphic mechanism, the resource development model is also present in Gettysburg's pursuit of repositioning itself as an elite, national liberal arts college, an effort demanding legitimacy. According to its present strategic plan, adaption to and emulation of its aspirant benchmarks moves Gettysburg closer to its desired identity but farther from its Lutheran identity. Whether these two notions are mutually exclusive is suggested later in this chapter as a recommendation for future research.

All three schools show that secularization has affected the ethos, curriculum, and outlook of the institution, though Concordia leaders demonstrated the greatest resolve to combat secular forces against organizational Lutheran identity. Likewise, all three institutions had experienced the effects of professionalization of their faculty composition, workload, and focus, with Gettysburg's identity being most changed by this status driver. Relatively recently, Concordia and Lenoir-Rhyne have begun to emphasize aggressively the importance of measurable faculty engagement with external communities within their disciplines; Concordia's effort began more than twenty years ago and Lenoir-Rhyne's in the last decade. Significant professionalization of Gettysburg's faculty began as part of the plan to transform the faculty in the 1970s.

While Concordia has been able to build a faculty that is both professionally engaged and generally supportive of the organizational Lutheran identity, Lenoir-Rhyne's record is a bit too premature to determine. Thus far, Lenoir-Rhyne has managed to balance faculty professionalization trends while also preserving its relationship with the church. The university is at a crossroads as the faculty continues to change in the coming years due to attrition. Gettysburg, on the other hand, has built a strong and esteemed professionalized faculty in its pursuit of a coveted liberal arts cachet, but has diminished its Lutheran identity in the process. This is an example of normative isomorphism negatively affecting the organizational Lutheran identity. Interview respondents and documents alike pointed to a widely-held, if not loudly spoken, notion that being an elite college and church-related are mutually exclusive.

CONCLUSIONS RELATED TO ORGANIZATIONAL LITERATURE

- Mission statements of the three schools in this study play an influential role in determining the direction of the institution and inspiring organizational members to endorse and affirm the mission and identity.
- Organizational identity is defined and reinforced by the way the internal participants interpret the organization and its mission.

During the process of data collection, it became very clear that mission statements played surprisingly significant roles in the institutional lives of the three schools in this study. During the research design process of this dissertation, my methodologist cautioned against focusing so sharply on organizational mission statements, as they are often obligatory, superficial, and ultimately insignificant. To his point, mission statements are not infallible; they are products of each organization's members and are endpoints rather than starting points. In this study, the three schools demonstrated remarkable attention to and engagement with their mission statements, especially Concordia College. This revelation was a watershed in the development of the three case studies, giving direction to the identification of themes and critical events.

Mission statements of colleges and universities of all institutional types appear to be a requirement for either legitimizing the institution, articulating a shared vision for the institution, or both (Morphew & Hartley, 2006). In the case of the three schools examined here, mission statements do just this: they legitimize and institutionalize the leaders' vision and rally organizational members toward a shared institutional vision. At Concordia, the venerable twenty-eight-word mission statement has been, since its development some fifty years ago, regularly and systematically parsed, studied, and critiqued and has been unequivocally affirmed and embraced by three Concordia presidents. In this effort, members of the Concordia community have understood the purpose and vision outlined in the statement and have subsequently endorsed and been inspired by it. The statement—along with leadership that emphasized the statement's centrality and relevance and a college community that was receptive to the statement's message—has shaped the trajectory and identity of Concordia.

While Lenoir-Rhyne and Gettysburg did not demonstrate the same extreme level of engagement with the mission statement as did Concordia, these schools still did engage and depend upon their statements, as evidenced by interviewee responses and documents. At least half of the Lenoir-Rhyne respondents pointed to the university's stated mission to "clarify personal faith" as "an institution of the North Carolina Synod of the Evangelical Lutheran Church in America." Moreover, the statement is broad enough to speak of faith development generally, despite its specificity as a university of the Lutheran church. While Lenoir-Rhyne has appeared to preserve its Lutheran identity, the university seems more interested in preserving its identity as a faith-based, religiously-affiliated school.

Gettysburg's mission statement, like Concordia's, is succinct but descriptive: "Gettysburg College, a national, residential, undergraduate college committed to a liberal education, prepares students to be active leaders and participants in a changing world." Every Gettysburg interview respondent expounded upon the college's chief goal, a derivative of the basic mission, to reposition itself as an elite, nationally-recognized liberal arts college. Nowhere in this mission statement or in the related current institutional planning document is mention of a Lutheran or any faith-related identity. All three schools reflected their level of Lutheran identity in their mission statements, which in turn reinforced members' interpretation of the organization's mission and identity.[2]

2. It is worth reiterating that mission statements, while influential, are products of organizations, organizational ethos, organizational members, and organizational leaders. In this study, missions appeared to significantly drive behaviors within the organizations,

CONCLUSIONS RELATED TO GOVERNANCE LITERATURE

- More than any other factor, the leadership of governing boards, presidents, and other senior administrators was essential in preserving or diminishing organizational Lutheran identity at all three schools in this study.

Embracing a mission statement and seeking to preserve or diminish organizational identity do not simply happen by accident. Leadership determines such courses of action. One respondent in the study argued that critical mass is the only significant factor that determines Lutheran organization identity; I strongly disagree with this claim. Indeed, critical mass (or at least numerous influential organizational members who affirm the identity and placed in key roles) does act as an important ingredient in the preservation of Lutheran identity. But clear and confident leadership that steers the institution toward such an identity is paramount.

Moreover, case study data presented in this dissertation suggest that presidential leadership is particularly crucial in shaping organizational identity. More than half of interview participants at three schools pointed to the president as the single person who sets the tone for organizational identity. Concordia's Lutheran identity is so ingrained due in large part to three consecutive presidential administrations over a more than 50 year period. Similarly, Lenoir-Rhyne's presidents have strongly affirmed the university's church-related identity, especially over the forty-five-year time horizon examined in this study. The four decade trend of Gettysburg's shift away from its church-relatedness is due primarily to the leadership of two of its effective and articulate presidents. That Gettysburg's current president, as well as her predecessor, appears somewhat interested in reconnecting *in some way* to the college's institutional Lutheran identity is worth noting.

Provosts also proved to be important indicators of institutional intentions to preserve or diminish Lutheran identity. Since provosts typically work closely with faculty, their attitudes and outlooks on institutional identity are closely observed by professors. Concordia's provost clearly offered one of the most articulate, well-informed perspectives on Lutheran higher education of all the people interviewed for this study. Amazingly, he is an active Roman Catholic! When the governing board, president,

---

especially with regard to institutional ethos and strategic decision-making.

and provost support the Lutheran institutional identity, a powerful and prevailing message is broadcast to the campus community about what the organization values and aspires to be.

The Lenoir-Rhyne provost, a Baptist who had previously served at a Baptist university that had also prioritized preserving its ecclesial relationship, was not particularly well-informed about Lutheran higher education. In fact, he said as much during the interview. However, the provost did make clear that Lenoir-Rhyne has every intention to maintain its strong relationship with the church and would continue to nurture its faith-centered mission. Student faith exploration and development, he explained, would remain a basic institutional goal.

·Gettysburg's provost, a fairly young faculty member, agreed with the other respondents who encouraged the de-emphasis of Gettysburg's church-related background. He also strongly advocated the college's repositioning strategy. A self-described non-Lutheran Protestant, the provost responded that he could not properly describe what it means to be a Lutheran college, describing it as a "secular college." He was particularly interested in underscoring the new institutional emphasis on faculty scholarship in its pursuit to be a liberal arts college of national repute. Moreover, the provost's outlook reflected the prominent sentiment among the Gettysburg interviewees.

Governing boards also played a role in the identity equation. The Boards of Trustees at Lenoir-Rhyne and Gettysburg voted to lower the minimum number of Lutherans serving on the schools' governing boards for purposes of diversification. Although the reasons for this revision to membership policy are valid and defensible—diversification to include wealthy donors, influential figures, and volunteers who can provide specific expertise to the board—these moves diminished Lutheran identity.

Lenoir-Rhyne has actually maintained a policy requiring one quarter of its Board of Trustees be Lutheran *clergy*, so the diminishment at Lenoir-Rhyne is much less in comparison to Gettysburg, which eliminated any minimum Lutheran requirement. Despite the policy reducing the minimum number of Lutherans on the governing board, Lenoir-Rhyne still ranks among the ELCA schools that still have Lutheran membership requirements for the board. The decision by Gettysburg leaders to make this revision was related to factors in pursuing its institutional repositioning strategy, which called for, among other things, a wealthier, more ·influential board that could significantly raise the college endowment.

CONCLUSIONS RELATED TO LUTHERAN HIGHER EDUCATION LITERATURE

- On-going, intentional, systematic discussions involving the broad institutional community affect organizational Lutheran identity preservation and diminishment.

- Diverse models, or expressions, of Lutheran identity emerged at all three schools in this study.

Robert Benne's typology matrix of religiously-affiliated colleges and universities was quite accurate in sorting and identifying the three schools examined in this study. The six criteria used to place the twenty-seven colleges and universities upon the spectrum of church-relatedness helped to locate Concordia, Lenoir-Rhyne, and Gettysburg in categories that, according to the case study narratives, accurately depicted their expression of institutional Lutheran identity. While a critical mass of Lutherans, or at least a significant number of Lutherans and non-Lutherans committed to the tradition, is extremely important, preservation of Lutheran identity at the three schools was dependent upon the institution's *intentionality* of preserving the identity.

At Concordia and Lenoir-Rhyne, the two schools that demonstrated an intentionality to preserve Lutheran identity, systematic and ongoing institutional conversations involving a significant number of organizational members were an annual priority. Along with the critical mass issue, the intentional, ongoing discussion and instruction regarding vocation, the meaning of Lutheran higher education, and the purpose of a Lutheran college are the basic ingredients to preserving Lutheran identity. The reason for each institution's decision to preserve or diminish its Lutheran identity appears to be reflected in the leadership (president and governing board, particularly), mission statement, strategic plan, and original institutional purpose.

Concordia boasts a majority of Lutherans among its campus community, and sustained deliberate and enduring systematic instruction about the purpose and value of functioning as a college of the Lutheran church. Lenoir-Rhyne is populated by a Lutheran minority as well as a dynamic community of non-Lutherans devoted to the ideal of a faith-centered educational experience. Moreover, the university maintains an ongoing institutional effort to dialogue about Lutheran higher education.

Gettysburg, on the other end of the spectrum, records almost no Lutherans among the faculty or student body and encourages no systematic discussion about Lutheran higher education.

All three schools demonstrate different expressions of Lutheran identity: Concordia's is robust and undeniable; Lenoir-Rhyne's is more generic (meaning less specifically Lutheran) but no less genuine; and Gettysburg's is historical and ambivalent, at best. Concordia's saga is one marked by clear mission to live as a college of the Lutheran church. Lenoir-Rhyne's saga is shaped by geography, a Southern school that values a spiritual, faith-centered student experience. Gettysburg's saga is a tale of history, its Lutheran identity lingering somewhere in the organizational folklore, an identity perhaps never fully endorsed from its beginning.

IMPLICATIONS FOR THEORY, POLICY, AND PRACTICE

This dissertation's case studies and conclusions yield potential implications for theory, policy, and practice. Theoretical implications emerge for both the institutional and organizational literature bodies. First, isomorphism, part of institutional theory, partially framed this study. More specifically, the three isomorphic status drivers—secularization, financial viability, and faculty professionalization—universally affect institutions of higher education. This study provides insight on how three schools responded to the status drivers with regard to their institutional identity. For Lutheran higher education scholars, the case studies suggest how ELCA schools can respond to isomorphic pressures.

Second, in conceptualizing this study, I envisioned the role of Lutheran identity through the lens of organizational theory, a new way of examining the ELCA schools. This study adds to the literature on Lutheran higher education, related organizational identity issues, and institutional mission of the ELCA colleges and universities. Speaking more broadly, the study also adds to organizational literature on planning and mission related to other niche, mission-specific schools, including military colleges, single-sex colleges, HBCU[3] institutions, other religiously-affiliated colleges, and other non-ELCA Lutheran colleges and universities.

Policy implications are suggested for colleges and universities, particularly for governing boards, presidents, and other chief administrators.

3. Historically Black Colleges and Universities.

The three institutions in this study demonstrated diverse levels of identity preservation and diminishment, based upon their own sets of rationale. Interpretation of mission and execution of strategic plans programmed how decision-makers interviewed in this study chose to address organizational Lutheran identity. The results offered here demonstrate policy implications for individual schools seeking to reclaim or de-emphasize a component of the institution's traditional or original identity. Qualitative methods used in this study have provided a compelling narrative of preservation or diminishment, which could shape decision-makers' policy decisions to preserve, sustain, reclaim, or diminish institutional identity.

Based primarily upon interview participants' responses, implications for practice focus on the ELCA, college and university administrators, and mission-specific institutions. For the ELCA Division for Higher Education, the case studies demonstrate the potential for different expressions, or models, of Lutheran identity at the twenty-seven ELCA colleges and universities. The evaluation of different models, as the literature suggested, could provide a resource for the ELCA's engagement with colleges it has determined to be "less Lutheran" in recent years. Furthermore, the study could offer pragmatic suggestions about the character of organizational Lutheran identity and the criteria for determining a college's Lutheranness.

For institutions, the study's practical implications could show administrators and governing boards the importance of intentionality and planning in the process of organizational identity preservation and diminishment. Participants' responses, in particular, reveal the importance of engagement and ongoing conversation with the campus community. Practically speaking, the ELCA colleges and universities as a collective body could discover new, innovative ways to communicate their value, arguing more effectively to prospective families why Lutheran colleges and universities are worthwhile. For mission-specific, niche schools, the study demonstrates three detailed narrative examples of the advantages, disadvantages, trade-offs, and rewards of preserving or diminishing organizational identity.

SUGGESTIONS FOR FUTURE RESEARCH

The scope of this study was quite specific, seeking to determine how three specific ELCA schools are handling their organizational identity and whether particular environmental factors influence this identity. Because the study followed a qualitative research design, the results are not intended to be generalized. Still, the study addresses these specific issues but raises questions about other mission-specific colleges and universities. Generally, further related research could reveal more useful data about this small, but significant niche field of higher education institutions.

A longitudinal qualitative study featuring a larger sample of the ELCA colleges and universities, or even a quantitative, survey-based study of all twenty-seven ELCA institutions, would likely expand the data and understanding of identity preservation and diminishment. Are *all* ELCA institutions addressing issues of organizational identity, and if so, why? In a broader sense, a study sampling religiously-affiliated colleges and universities, as well as other mission-specific, niche schools (military colleges, single-sex colleges, and HBCU institutions) might look at organizational identity preservation and diminishment. Why, if at all, are these institutions seeking to sustain their specialized identities? What strategies do these schools use to achieve this goal? What are the trade-offs in favor of a niche identity?

Specific to research in Lutheran higher education and other religiously-affiliated schools, a quantitative, qualitative, or mixed methods study focused on the relevance and viability of these schools could reveal valuable data for strategic planning, resource development, governance, and mission. A focused study on the future of the ELCA colleges and universities, particularly with regard to financial viability, could also yield interesting results for both the institutions and the national church. Anecdotally, at least five of these ELCA institutions face dire financial challenges, and in fact, ELCA-related Waldorf College essentially collapsed in 2009 and was purchased to function as a non-Lutheran, for-profit institution. Presumably, an even larger population could be served if research on religiously-affiliated schools were to include an expanded sample of kindergarten-to-high school institutions.

A final area of recommended research emerged from Gettysburg's data. Can a college be perceived as both religiously-affiliated and elite, or are these two distinctions perceived to be mutually exclusive in the higher education arena? To focus the work even more precisely, the question could be posed to colleges similar to Gettysburg: good schools aspiring to emulate elite liberal arts colleges already firmly positioned and perceived as national, elite liberal arts colleges.

RESEARCH QUESTIONS AND ANSWERS: A SUMMATION

- Are colleges and universities of the Evangelical Lutheran Church in America preserving or diminishing their Lutheran identities?

Though not generalizable, the data of this study suggest that three of the twenty-seven schools in this body are addressing Lutheran organizational identity in different ways. Concordia College is aggressively seeking to preserve its Lutheran identity, an effort evident during this study's 45-year time horizon. What is more, college leaders aspire for Concordia to be the ELCA college most clearly and confidently expressing its Lutheran ethos. This institutional characterization is a result of a Lutheran critical mass, perpetual engagement with a cogent mission statement, and steady presidential leadership.

Lenoir-Rhyne University is seeking to preserve its identity as a religiously-affiliated institution, offering a faith-centered and spiritually enriched educational experience and maintaining a healthy relationship with the Lutheran church. Without continued strong leading Lutheran voices among the campus community—especially the governing board, the president, and the faculty—Lenoir-Rhyne will likely continue to emphasize a more generic (and less specifically Lutheran) ethos of Christian spirituality and faith-centeredness. Organizational leadership, mission interpretation, and strategy will determine this future trend.

Gettysburg College, arguably the most academically prestigious of the twenty-seven ELCA institutions, is on its way to becoming a nationally recognized liberal arts college by design, though it has achieved this distinction at the expense of its Lutheran identity. To be clear, this ecclesial relationship was never fully imagined to be a partnership in which the church played a significant role in the life of the college. Still, the Lutheran tradition did shape the early curriculum, as the school was an incubator for Lutheran clergy and church leaders. Today, the organizational identity is treated as a part of the college's history, important institutional lore but no more privileged than Gettysburg's connection to Lincoln and the Civil

War. Subtle signals suggest Gettysburg's interest in reclaiming at least a fraction of its Lutheran tradition, evidenced by renewed participation in ELCA events and recent overtones of presidential interest (by Presidents Will and Riggs) in rekindling the college-church relationship.

- Do the status drivers of secularization, financial viability, and faculty professionalization affect Lutheran institutional identity at these colleges and universities?

Particularly since the 1960s, secular forces have significantly affected higher education. Concordia, Lenoir-Rhyne, and Gettysburg have each responded differently to these pressures, and their Lutheran organizational identities have also been diversely affected. Concordia leaders reacted by bolstering the mission as a college of the Lutheran church and engaging the campus community through ongoing instruction and conversation about this mission. Lenoir-Rhyne has responded similarly, though not with the same intensity. Both Concordia and Lenoir-Rhyne have insisted that their presidents be Lutheran. By the self-description of interviewees and the indications of planning documents, Gettysburg has become a secular college, perhaps echoing its original non-sectarian charter.

Like most similar American colleges and universities, this study's three schools face perpetual fiscal challenges. Corroborated by institutional planning documents, Concordia leaders insist that the college has not made identity trade-offs for the sake of fiscal viability, including revision of governing board membership requirements. Of the three schools, Lenoir-Rhyne has demonstrated the sharpest financial struggle, but the college has generally sustained its Lutheran identity when it could have chosen to emulate secular models. The university has also maintained minimum requirements for Lutherans on its governing board. Despite being the wealthiest of the three schools, Gettysburg has eliminated a Lutheran requirement for its governing board, populating its Board of Trustees with wealthy and well-connected volunteers better positioned to raise substantial funds for the college.

Faculty professionalization, like the other two status drivers, has also affected most, if not all, American colleges and universities. These forces have affected the three schools in this study as faculty loyalty to academic discipline surpasses loyalty to institutional mission, demonstrated across a number of interviews. Concordia has maintained rigorous hiring standards that have sustained a faculty that is simultaneously high-quality and supportive of the Lutheran organizational identity. Lenoir-Rhyne has maintained a faith-related, Christian identity, though its faculty has become less and less Lutheran. Gettysburg has built a very high-quality, heavily engaged faculty, but one that is generally disinterested, and occasionally hostile to the Lutheran organizational identity.

- If the colleges and universities described in my case studies are seeking to preserve their Lutheran identities, why and how are they planning this preservation?

First, Gettysburg's decision to diminish its Lutheran identity is based upon several reasons. First, the governing board and presidents have chosen this strategy. Second, the planning documents, the one from the 1970s as well as the current plan, have called for an aggressive and focused strategy to reposition Gettysburg. The data suggest that Gettysburg decision-makers believe robust religious identity and an elite, selective, national status are mutually exclusive characteristics. Third, the original college charter, envisioned and prepared by Samuel Schmucker, called for Gettysburg's establishment as a non-sectarian school.

On the other hand, Concordia and Lenoir-Rhyne demonstrated evidence of organizational Lutheran identity preservation. Why have these schools chosen this path? Similarly, they both interpret a bold, strongly articulated Lutheran identity to be at the center of their organizational mission. Furthermore, Concordia has shown great success in attracting Lutherans, students and faculty alike, to be part of the campus community. Lenoir-Rhyne is seeking to preserve its Lutheran identity—and more precisely its faith-relatedness—because institutional research has shown that doing so is in the university's best fiscal interest. In other words, there is potential capital in emphasizing its relationship to the church, attracting interested students, faculty, staff, volunteers, and donors.

How are Concordia and Lenoir-Rhyne planning this preservation? Both institutions have been led by presidents (selected by dedicated and informed governing boards) who have, over the past half-century, made choices that have privileged the Lutheran perspective, logos, and ethos as the dominant institutional ideology at their colleges. Concordia has followed this course guided by an effective mission statement, systematic campus dialogue about Lutheran higher education, a good relationship with the Lutheran church, and valuable institutional planning documents. Lenoir-Rhyne has pursued a strategy to sustain its relationship to the church using similar tactics, though its identity, shaped by the institution's changing demographics, appears to be moving toward a more generic Christianity, framed by a Lutheran framework.

LAST THINGS

This study examined three Lutheran colleges through the lens of organizational and institutional theories, building three narratives of preservation and diminishment of Lutheran identity over a 45-year period. Taking a fresh organizational approach to ELCA colleges and universities, the study treated these schools as *organizations* with missions, strategies, leaders, and identities. With ever-growing pressures facing small colleges and universities, clear and confident articulation of organizational identity is more and more important in the crowded marketplace of higher education. An institution's self-understanding of its identity—whether a Lutheran college, military school, all-female university, HBCU, or Episcopal seminary, just to name a few—is a vital ingredient in fully developing its intended educational experience for students, professional environment for faculty and staff, and societal relevance in developing citizens for service in the world.

Afterword

Pamela Jolicoeur

Pamela Jolicoeur served as President of Concordia College from 2004 until her untimely death in 2010. She was the leader of the College at the time the research underlying this book was being conducted. Pam's gifts were rich and diverse. She was both a practitioner and a herald of excellence. She saw the excellence in our community and called us to do our best and be our best—to overcome our "militant modesty" and to live out our possibilities for excellence.

Another of Pam's gifts was her conception and practice of leadership. For Pam, leadership was not about having all the right answers but about having the right questions, not about having a detailed road map but about setting the general direction, not about an exclusive cadre of leaders but about an engaged commons, not about scarcity but about abundance, not about accepting someone else's vision for our future but about framing our own, not about hierarchy but about abundance and not about uniformity but about diversity. And so our community was refreshed and leadership became a community function and not a solo performance.

Pamela enriched Concordia's understanding of Vocation and mission. In doing so she reflected her own spiritual journey from the Holy Orders of her early life to the impulse of grace which would frame her midlife understanding of Vocation. As a college president she kept asking the vocational question which shapes Concordia's mission. She enriched and expanded that conversation with her intellectual and relational capacities.

In so doing, she rallied the community around the foundation of our institutional being, *Soli Deo Gloria.*

Paul J. Dovre
President Emeritus
Concordia College

Appendix A

Colleges and Universities of the ELCA*

COLLEGE OR UNIVERSITY	LOCATION	YEAR FOUNDED
Augsburg College	Minneapolis, MN	1869
Augustana College	Rock Island, IL	1860
Augustana College	Sioux Falls, SD	1860
Bethany College	Lindsborg, KS	1881
California Lutheran University	Thousand Oaks, CA	1959
Capital University	Columbus, OH	1850
Carthage College	Kenosha, WI	1847
Concordia College	Moorhead, MN	1891
Dana College	Blair, NE	1884
Gettysburg College	Gettysburg, PA	1832
Grand View College	Des Moines, IA	1896
Gustavus Adolphus College	St. Peter, MN	1862
Lenoir-Rhyne University	Hickory, NC	1891
Luther College	Decorah, IA	1861
Midland Lutheran College	Fremont, NE	1883
Muhlenberg College	Allentown, PA	1848
Newberry College	Newberry, SC	1856
Pacific Lutheran University	Tacoma, WA	1891
Roanoke College	Salem, VA	1842

Appendix A

COLLEGE OR UNIVERSITY	LOCATION	YEAR FOUNDED
St. Olaf College	Northfield, MN	1874
Finlandia University	Hancock, MI	1886
Susquehanna University	Selinsgrove, PA	1858
Texas Lutheran University	Seguin, TX	1891
Thiel College	Greenville, PA	1866
Wagner College	Staten Island, NY	1883
Wartburg College	Waverly, IA	1852
Wittenberg University	Springfield, OH	1845

*The financially-beleaguered Waldorf College, one of the ELCA institutions, was sold to a for-profit organization in 2009, severing its formal relationship with the ELCA.

Appendix B

Phase I Sorting and Analysis Worksheet for Case Study Site Selection (Benne, 2001)

COLLEGE OR UNIVERSITY	CHAPEL ATTENDANCE POLICIES*		INSTITUTIONAL GOVERNANCE				PERCENTAGE OF LUTHERAN STUDENTS****		PERCENTAGE OF LUTHERAN FACULTY		DEPENDANCE UPON THE CHURCH*****		TOTAL
			PRESIDENTIAL SELECTION POLICIES**	BOARD MEMBERSHIP POLICIES***									
Augsburg College *Minneapolis, MN*	Pro-tected time (Tues/R—Thurs)	3	Must be ELCA	2/3 Lutheran	3	34.2%	3	Not tracked	1	C	2	12
Augustana College *Rock Island, IL*	Protected (T)	2	Must be Lutheran or ecumenically related	35% (14 of 40) from geo synods	2	21.9%	2	Not tracked	1	D	1	8
Augustana College *Sioux Falls, SD*	Protected (M-F)	3	Must be Lutheran	Majority Lutheran	2	46.0%	3	Not tracked	1	C	2	11
Bethany College *Lindsborg, KS*	Protected	2	Must be ELCA	No stipulation	2	19.9%	2	Not tracked	1	C	2	9
California Lutheran University *Thousand Oaks, CA*	Protected (Weekly)	2	"Shall usually be a member of the ELCA"	Majority Lutheran	2	19.7%	2	Not tracked	1	C	2	9

COLLEGE OR UNIVERSITY	CHAPEL ATTENDANCE POLICIES*		INSTITUTIONAL GOVERNANCE			PERCENTAGE OF LUTHERAN STUDENTS****		PERCENTAGE OF LUTHERAN FACULTY		DEPENDANCE UPON THE CHURCH****		TOTAL
			PRESIDENTIAL SELECTION POLICIES*	BOARD MEMBERSHIP POLICIES***								
Capital University *Columbus, OH*	Protected (W)	2	No provision	30% Lutheran	2	14.6%	2	Not tracked	1	C	2	9
Carthage College *Kenosha, WI*	Protected (MWF)	3	Must be Lutheran or ecumenically related	1/3 Lutheran	2	18.3%	2	Not tracked	1	C	2	10
Concordia College *Moorhead, MN*	Protected (M-R)	3	Must be ELCA	85% Lutheran	3	53.0%	3	Not tracked	1	A	4	14
Dana College *Blair, NE*	Protected	2	"In harmony with policies of ELCA"	60% Lutheran	2	21.5%	2	Not tracked	1	C	2	9
Finlandia University *Hancock, MI*	Protected (Twice weekly)	3	Must be Lutheran	None, but predominantly Lutheran	2	29.8%	3	Not tracked	1	C	2	11
Gettysburg College *Gettysburg, PA*	Not protected (Sunday only)	1	No provision	2 elected by the ELCA	1	5.1%	1	Not tracked	1	D	1	5
Grand View University *Des Moines, IA*	Protected (T)	2	Must be Lutheran	Majority Lutheran	2	14.1%	2	Not tracked	1	C	2	9

COLLEGE OR UNIVERSITY	CHAPEL ATTENDANCE POLICIES*		INSTITUTIONAL GOVERNANCE			PERCENTAGE OF LUTHERAN STUDENTS****		PERCENTAGE OF LUTHERAN FACULTY		DEPENDANCE UPON THE CHURCH*****		TOTAL
			PRESIDENTIAL SELECTION POLICIES**	BOARD MEMBERSHIP POLICIES***								
Gustavus Adolphus College *St. Peter, MN*	Protected (Daily)	3	Must be ELCA	8 Lutheran pastors	3	50.3%	3	Not tracked	1	B	3	13
Lenoir-Rhyne University *Hickory, NC*	Protected (W)	2	Must be Lutheran	Majority Lutheran	2	16.0%	2	Not tracked	1	C	2	9
Luther College *Decorah, IA*	Protected (Daily)	3	Must be Lutheran	60% Lutheran	3	49.8%	3	Not tracked	1	B	3	13
Midland Lutheran College *Fremont, NE*	Protected	2	Must be ELCA	32-39% Lutheran based upon total membership	2	40.0%	3	Not tracked	1	C	2	10
Muhlenberg College *Allentown, PA*	Not protected	1	No provision	3 seats for 3 bishop to assign	1	6.0%	1	Not tracked	1	D	1	5
Newberry College *Newberry, SC*	Protected (T)	2	Must be ELCA	No stipulation	2	13.1%	2	Not tracked	1	D	1	8
Pacific Lutheran University *Tacoma, WA*	Protected (MWF)	3	Must be Lutheran	At least 49% (18 of 37); 3 must be pastors, 3 bishops	2	25.2%	3	Not tracked	1	B	3	12

COLLEGE OR UNIVERSITY	CHAPEL ATTENDANCE POLICIES*	INSTITUTIONAL GOVERNANCE		PERCENTAGE OF LUTHERAN STUDENTS****	PERCENTAGE OF LUTHERAN FACULTY	DEPENDANCE UPON THE CHURCH*****	TOTAL
		PRESIDENTIAL SELECTION POLICIES**	BOARD MEMBERSHIP POLICIES***				
Roanoke College *Roanoke, VA*	Protected (T) — 2	Understand r/ship of college with Lutheran church	No stipulation but positions are held — 2	7.6% — 1	Not tracked — 1	C — 2	8
St. Olaf College *Northfield, MN*	Protected (Daily) — 3	Must be ELCA	Majority Lutheran — 3	40.8% — 3	Not tracked — 1	B — 3	13
Susquehanna University *Selinsgrove, PA*	Not protected during the week — 1	Ability to sustain partnership with Lutheran church	No stipulation — 2	12.9% — 2	Not tracked — 1	C — 2	8
Texas Lutheran University *Seguin, TX*	Protected (MWF) — 3	Elected "consistent with the policies of the ELCA"	Majority Lutheran — 2	25.6% — 3	Not tracked — 1	C — 2	11
Thiel College *Greenville, PA*	Not protected — 1	Must be ELCA	3 members from 3 related synods — 2	8.5% — 1	Not tracked — 1	C — 2	7
Wagner College *Staten Island, NY*	Not protected — 1	No provision	No stipulation — 1	1.9% — 1	Not tracked — 1	D — 1	5
Waldorf College+ *Forest City, IA*	Protected (MWF) — 3	Must be Lutheran	Majority Lutheran — 2	34.5% — 3	Not tracked — 1	C — 2	11

COLLEGE OR UNIVERSITY	CHAPEL ATTENDANCE POLICIES*		INSTITUTIONAL GOVERNANCE		PERCENTAGE OF LUTHERAN STUDENTS****		PERCENTAGE OF LUTHERAN FACULTY	DEPENDANCE UPON THE CHURCH*****		TOTAL
			PRESIDENTIAL SELECTION POLICIES**	BOARD MEMBERSHIP POLICIES***						
Wartburg College *Waverly, IA*	Protected (MWF)	3	Must be Lutheran	60% Lutheran	2	36.5%	3	Not tracked	1	C	2	11
Wittenberg University *Springfield, OH*	Protected (TR)	3	No provision	Majority Lutheran	2	15.9%	2	Not tracked	1	C	2	10

1: Accidentally Pluralist (1–5)   2: Intentionally Pluralist (6–10)   3: Critical Mass (11–15)   4: Orthodox (16–20)

*None of the colleges or universities require chapel attendance, thus no schools received a value of 4. 1=Unprotected; 2=Single chapel offering; 3=Multiple weekly chapel offerings.

** According to the ELCA Office of Vocation and Education, January 2005.

*** Presidential Selection and Board Membership are combined to represent governance and assigned a composite score.

**** A composite of all Lutheran students, including non-ELCA students, according to the ELCA Office of Vocation and Education, Fall 2007. 1=<10%; 2=11%–25%; 3=26%–75%; 4=>75%.

***** College and university respondents self-described institutional relationship with the church by using one of four of Benne's descriptions. A describes a close relationship; D a distant.

+ Waldorf College ceased to function as a college of the ELCA in 2009.

Appendix C

Typologies of Church-Related Colleges Matrix (Benne, 2001)*

	ORTHODOX	CRITICAL-MASS	INTENTIONALLY PLURALISTIC	ACCIDENTALLY PLURALISTIC
Major divide	The Christian vision as the organizing paradigm		Secular sources as the organizing paradigm	
Public relevance of Christian vision	Pervasive from a shared point of view	Privileged voice in an ongoing conversation	Assured voice in an ongoing conversation	Random or absent in an ongoing conversation
Public rhetoric	Unabashed invitation for fellow believers to an intentionally Christian enterprise	Straightforward presentation as a Christian school but inclusive of others	Presentation as a liberal arts school with a Christian heritage	Presentation as a secular school with little or no allusion to Christian heritage
Membership requirements	Near 100% with orthodoxy tests	Critical mass in all facets	Intentional representation	Haphazard sprinkling
Religion/theology department	Large, with theology privileged	Large, with theology as flagship	Small, mixed department, some theology, but mostly religious studies	Small, exclusively religious studies
Religion/theology required courses	All courses affected by shared religious perspective	Two or three, with dialogical effort in many other courses	One course in general education	Choice in distribution or an elective
Chapel	Required in large church at a protected time daily	Voluntary at high quality services in large nave at protected time daily	Voluntary at unprotected times, with low attendance	For few, on special occasions

220

Ethos	Overt piety of sponsoring tradition	Dominant atmosphere of sponsoring tradition—rituals and habits	Open minority from sponsoring tradition finding private niche (dominantly secular atmosphere)	Reclusive and unorganized minority from sponsoring tradition (dominantly secular atmosphere)
Support by church	Indispensable financial support and majority of students from sponsoring tradition	Important direct and crucial indirect financial support; at least 50% of students	Important focused, indirect support; small minority of students	Token indirect support; student numbers no longer recorded
Governance	Owned and governed by church or its official representatives	Majority of board from tradition, some official representatives	Minority of board from tradition by unofficial agreement (autonomously owned and governed)	Token membership from tradition (autonomously owned and governed)

*Though this table represents Benne's complete typology matrix, my study will utilize only the ones that correspond with the selected objective criteria.

Appendix D

Selected Interview Guide Questions:
Loren Anderson, Pacific Lutheran University

1. What does it mean to be a Lutheran college?

   In 1975, at my very first conference focused on discussing Lutheran college identity, a speaker answered the identity question this way: "At Lutheran colleges, we are free to ask the question, 'What does it mean to be a Lutheran college.'" At first I found that answer disappointing, but it has stayed with me all this time. There is great wisdom in that answer.

   There is no critical mass of Lutherans in the Pacific Northwest which is, often called the "none zone," describing the absence of any dominant faith tradition. So here at PLU, we talk often about the notion of vocation. Lutheran higher education calls us to engage students by asking them the larger questions of life, including "what am I called to do?" This has been a powerful organizing feature at PLU over the years. We also talk regularly about the faith and reason dialogue and the education of the whole person. Our campus ministry is strong and staffed by two Lutheran pastors.

2. Name two or three critical events—turning points—during the last 40 to 45 years that have significantly shaped PLU's Lutheran institutional identity.

   I think back to the early 1990s when the university created its first institutional long-range plan. The community came together to reflect systematically about identity. We took two years discussing, and the conversation helped us come to a new clarity about our Lutheran identity. The community found there was strong interest and support for its Lutheran identity, we evolved a fresh institutional rhetoric to describe it. The conversation helped us express our identity in fresh ways with more inclusive language.

3. What are the primary goals, or mission, of PLU?

    Our mission statement came out of the language planning process in the 1990s. It is well known by many members of the campus community: "The mission is to educate students for lives of thoughtful inquiry, service, leadership, and care—for other persons, for their community, and for the earth."

4. How would you describe the overall faith community at PLU? PLU's "Lutheranness?"

    The student body is 25 percent Lutheran and this reflects strong and positive relationships with our ELCA congregations. Thirty percent of our students identify themselves from other Christian denominations, and it splinters from there. The faith community is incredibly diverse and eclectic. Traditionally, many in the Pacific Northwest describe themselves as not religious but spiritual.

5. Martin Luther makes a (very!) unexpected appearance at PLU. What might he say about the Lutheran ethos, or "way of life," of your campus community?

    I believe that if he stayed a couple of days, he'd be quite impressed. Luther's theology and writings on education appeal to the best instincts of the academy. PLU embodies these instincts.

6. Has secularization affected PLU's Lutheran identity? If so, how?

    The short answer is "yes." PLU's understanding of its identity and mission reflects our context and our location here in the Pacific Northwest. Our focus on vocation as a central element in our identity is one reflection of that context.

7. It is widely held that small colleges and universities face perpetual financial pressures. Sometimes colleges and universities seek to emulate other schools believed to offer healthy models in order to manage financial viability. How, if at all, has the struggle to remain financially viable affected PLU's Lutheran identity?

Our concern is to be academically distinctive, and this includes our Lutheran distinction. I say, "Let's claim our Lutheran tradition in a way that sets us apart."

8. The more uncertain the relationship between means and ends, the greater the extent to which an organization will model itself after organizations it perceives to be successful. Given this notion, which college or university(ies)' business model, best practices, or accomplishments does PLU seek to emulate, or at least pay attention? Why these colleges?

We benchmark against a group of 16 institutions that includes some schools in the Pacific Northwest, some Lutheran schools, and some member of the Associated New American Colleges.

9. In you judgment, what is the relationship, if any, between preserving a lively, robust Lutheran identity and maintaining a critical mass of Lutheran faculty?

Given where we are located, we do not believe that critical mass is the issue. Rather, we seek to hire faculty who want to be at a faith based or value centered teaching university. I am encouraged by the new faculty that we are hiring. They are interested in and open to understanding the Lutheran tradition of higher education. Our faculty development programs seek to deepen and expand that understanding.

10. Do you believe PLU is deliberately seeking to preserve its Lutheran identity? If so, why? How is it planning this preservation?

Yes, because it is who we are.

Appendix E

Interview Guide for Presidents

1. What brought you to this college/university community?

2. What does it mean to be a Lutheran college?

   a. What do you think is the difference, if any, between Lutheran colleges and universities and other schools?

   b. Name three advantages, if any, of a Lutheran college or university educational experience.

   c. Name three disadvantages, if any.

3. How would you describe the overall faith community at this college/university?

   d. What most shapes the faith community here at this college/university?

   e. What role, if any, should the president, chaplain, and faculty play in developing the faith community of a college/university?

   f. Who do you believe has the greatest power in and responsibility for shaping the relationship between the college/university and the ELCA?

4. How would you describe the "Lutheranness" of your college/university?

   g. Do you believe Lutheran colleges and universities have become "less Lutheran" over time (specifically since the mid-1960s)?

    h. If so, how?

    i. Martin Luther makes a (very!) unexpected appearance at this college/university. What might he say about the Lutheran ethos, or "way of life," of your campus community?

5. What are the primary goals, or mission, of this college/ university?

6. Name two or three critical events—turning points—during the last 40 years that have significantly shaped the college/university's Lutheran institutional identity.

7. Has secularization affected your college/university's Lutheran identity?

    j. If so, how?

    k. Can you give me specific examples of this secularization?

8. It is widely held that small colleges and universities face perpetual financial pressures. Sometimes colleges and universities seek to emulate other schools believed to offer healthy models in order to manage financial viability. How, if at all, has the struggle to remain financially viable affected the college/university's Lutheran identity?

    l. Has the college/university chosen to make trade-offs for the sake of financial viability at the expense of its Lutheran identity?

    m. If so, name examples of these trade-offs.

    n. The more uncertain the relationship between means and ends, the greater the extent to which an organization will model itself after organizations it perceives to be successful. Given this notion, which college or university(ies)' business model, best practices, or accomplishments does your college/university seek to emulate, or at least pay attention?

    o. Why are these colleges and universities this college/university's benchmarks?

9. In you judgment, what is the relationship, if any, between preserving a lively, robust Lutheran identity and maintaining a critical mass of Lutheran faculty?

p. How would you describe the importance of faculty and administrative staff participation in trade and professional organizations?

q. Is faculty participation in these organizations an institutional priority?

r. What is the rate or frequency of this participation among the faculty in such organizations?

s. Is it the job of a faculty member at a Lutheran college or university to foster the ideals of Lutheran higher education?

t. In addition to teaching and mentoring, faculty members often face pressure to manage many tasks: publishing, research, committee service, and membership in professional organizations, to name a few examples. Do these "professionalization pressures" pose a threat to a faculty member's ability to serve faithfully within the Lutheran college environment?

10. Do you believe your college/university is deliberately seeking to preserve its Lutheran identity?

u. If so, why?

v. How is it planning this preservation?

11. In 2009, are Lutheran colleges still relevant in the landscape of American higher education?

w. Is this Lutheran identity worth preserving?

ADDITIONAL QUESTIONS SPECIFIC TO PARTICIPANTS' PROFESSIONAL ROLES

Interview Guide Questions for Current Presidents

1. How would you describe the financial dependence of the college/university upon the ELCA or Lutheran synod?

a. If this represents a recent change (increase or decrease in financial support), what effect has this made on the relationship between the college/university and the ELCA or synod?

    b. How would you describe the college/university's dependence upon the ELCA or Lutheran synod for its religious identity?

2. What are the most significant sources of income for this college/university?

3. Which Lutheran colleges or universities have effective models for Lutheran institutional identity? Why?

4. How would you describe the role of a faculty member at a Lutheran college?

Appendix F

Interview Guide for Provosts and Academic Deans

1. What brought you to this college/university community?
2. What does it mean to be a Lutheran college?
   a. What do you think is the difference, if any, between Lutheran colleges and universities and other schools?
   b. Name three advantages, if any, of a Lutheran college or university educational experience.
   c. Name three disadvantages, if any.
3. How would you describe the overall faith community at this college/university?
   d. What most shapes the faith community here at this college/university?
   e. What role, if any, should the president, chaplain, and faculty play in developing the faith community of a college/university?
   f. Who do you believe has the greatest power in and responsibility for shaping the relationship between the college/university and the ELCA?
4. How would you describe the "Lutheranness" of your college/university?
   g. Do you believe Lutheran colleges and universities have become "less Lutheran" over time (specifically since the mid-1960s)?

    h. If so, how?

    i. Martin Luther makes a (very!) unexpected appearance at this college/university. What might he say about the Lutheran ethos, or "way of life," of your campus community?

5. What are the primary goals, or mission, of this college/university?

6. Name two or three critical events—turning points—during the last 40 years that have significantly shaped the college/university's Lutheran institutional identity.

7. Has secularization affected your college/university's Lutheran identity?

    j. If so, how?

    k. Can you give me specific examples of this secularization?

8. It is widely held that small colleges and universities face perpetual financial pressures. Sometimes colleges and universities seek to emulate other schools believed to offer healthy models in order to manage financial viability. How, if at all, has the struggle to remain financially viable affected the college/university's Lutheran identity?

    l. Has the college/university chosen to make trade-offs for the sake of financial viability at the expense of its Lutheran identity?

    m. If so, name examples of these trade-offs.

    n. The more uncertain the relationship between means and ends, the greater the extent to which an organization will model itself after organizations it perceives to be successful. Given this notion, which college or university(ies)' business model, best practices, or accomplishments does your college/university seek to emulate, or at least pay attention?

    o. Why are these colleges and universities this college/university's benchmarks?

9. In you judgment, what is the relationship, if any, between preserving a lively, robust Lutheran identity and maintaining a critical mass of Lutheran faculty?

  p. How would you describe the importance of faculty and administrative staff participation in trade and professional organizations?

  q. Is faculty participation in these organizations an institutional priority?

  r. What is the rate or frequency of this participation among the faculty in such organizations?

  s. Is it the job of a faculty member at a Lutheran college or university to foster the ideals of Lutheran higher education?

  t. In addition to teaching and mentoring, faculty members often face pressure to manage many tasks: publishing, research, committee service, and membership in professional organizations, to name a few examples. Do these "professionalization pressures" pose a threat to a faculty member's ability to serve faithfully within the Lutheran college environment?

10. Do you believe your college/university is deliberately seeking to preserve its Lutheran identity?

  u. If so, why?

  v. How is it planning this preservation?

11. In 2009, are Lutheran colleges still relevant in the landscape of American higher education?

  w. Is this Lutheran identity worth preserving?

ADDITIONAL QUESTIONS SPECIFIC TO PARTICIPANTS' PROFESSIONAL ROLES

Interview Guide Questions for Current Provosts/Academic Deans

1. How would you describe the role of a faculty member at a Lutheran college?

2. In your judgment, can non-Lutheran (or even non-Christian) faculty members serve the ideals of a Lutheran educational experience?

3. How important is a critical mass of faculty to maintaining and building a strong Lutheran institutional identity?

4. In Phase I of this study, I researched which ELCA colleges and universities maintain a record of the percentages of its Lutheran faculty, similar to its recording of Lutheran students. However, not a single school records that number anymore. What do you make you this?

Appendix G

Interview Guide for Faculty Assembly Chairpersons

1. What brought you to this college/university community?
2. What does it mean to be a Lutheran college?
   a. What do you think is the difference, if any, between Lutheran colleges and universities and other schools?
   b. Name three advantages, if any, of a Lutheran college or university educational experience.
   c. Name three disadvantages, if any.
3. How would you describe the overall faith community at this college/university?
   d. What most shapes the faith community here at this college/university?
   e. What role, if any, should the president, chaplain, and faculty play in developing the faith community of a college/university?
   f. Who do you believe has the greatest power in and responsibility for shaping the relationship between the college/university and the ELCA?
4. How would you describe the "Lutheranness" of your college/university?
   g. Do you believe Lutheran colleges and universities have become "less Lutheran" over time (specifically since the mid-1960s)?

    h. If so, how?

    i. Martin Luther makes a (very!) unexpected appearance at this college/university. What might he say about the Lutheran ethos, or "way of life," of your campus community?

5. What are the primary goals, or mission, of this college/university?

6. Name two or three critical events—turning points—during the last 40 years that have significantly shaped the college/university's Lutheran institutional identity.

7. Has secularization affected your college/university's Lutheran identity?

    j. If so, how?

    k. Can you give me specific examples of this secularization?

8. It is widely held that small colleges and universities face perpetual financial pressures. Sometimes colleges and universities seek to emulate other schools believed to offer healthy models in order to manage financial viability. How, if at all, has the struggle to remain financially viable affected the college/university's Lutheran identity?

    l. Has the college/university chosen to make trade-offs for the sake of financial viability at the expense of its Lutheran identity?

    m. If so, name examples of these trade-offs.

    n. The more uncertain the relationship between means and ends, the greater the extent to which an organization will model itself after organizations it perceives to be successful. Given this notion, which college or university(ies)' business model, best practices, or accomplishments does your college/university seek to emulate, or at least pay attention?

    o. Why are these colleges and universities this college/university's benchmarks?

9. In you judgment, what is the relationship, if any, between preserving a lively, robust Lutheran identity and maintaining a critical mass of Lutheran faculty?

p. How would you describe the importance of faculty and administrative staff participation in trade and professional organizations?

q. Is faculty participation in these organizations an institutional priority?

r. What is the rate or frequency of this participation among the faculty in such organizations?

s. Is it the job of a faculty member at a Lutheran college or university to foster the ideals of Lutheran higher education?

t. In addition to teaching and mentoring, faculty members often face pressure to manage many tasks: publishing, research, committee service, and membership in professional organizations, to name a few examples. Do these "professionalization pressures" pose a threat to a faculty member's ability to serve faithfully within the Lutheran college environment?

10. Do you believe your college/university is deliberately seeking to preserve its Lutheran identity?

u. If so, why?

v. How is it planning this preservation?

11. In 2009, are Lutheran colleges still relevant in the landscape of American higher education?

w. Is this Lutheran identity worth preserving?

ADDITIONAL QUESTIONS SPECIFIC TO PARTICIPANTS' PROFESSIONAL ROLES

Interview Guide Questions for Current Faculty Assembly Chairpersons

1. How would you describe the role of a faculty member at a Lutheran college?

2. In your judgment, can non-Lutheran (or even non-Christian) faculty members serve the ideals of a Lutheran educational experience?

3. How would you describe the importance of Lutheran identity to the college/university?

4. How important is a critical mass of faculty to maintaining and building a strong Lutheran institutional identity?

Appendix H

Interview Guide for Chaplains/Campus Pastors

1. What brought you to this college/university community?
2. What does it mean to be a Lutheran college?
   a. What do you think is the difference, if any, between Lutheran colleges and universities and other schools?
   b. Name three advantages, if any, of a Lutheran college or university educational experience.
   c. Name three disadvantages, if any.
3. How would you describe the overall faith community at this college/university?
   d. What most shapes the faith community here at this college/university?
   e. What role, if any, should the president, chaplain, and faculty play in developing the faith community of a college/university?
   f. Who do you believe has the greatest power in and responsibility for shaping the relationship between the college/university and the ELCA?
4. How would you describe the "Lutheranness" of your college/university?
   g. Do you believe Lutheran colleges and universities have become "less Lutheran" over time (specifically since the mid-1960s)?

    h. If so, how?

    i. Martin Luther makes a (very!) unexpected appearance at this college/university. What might he say about the Lutheran ethos, or "way of life," of your campus community?

5. What are the primary goals, or mission, of this college/university?

6. Name two or three critical events—turning points—during the last 40 years that have significantly shaped the college/university's Lutheran institutional identity.

7. Has secularization affected your college/university's Lutheran identity?

    j. If so, how?

    k. Can you give me specific examples of this secularization?

8. It is widely held that small colleges and universities face perpetual financial pressures. Sometimes colleges and universities seek to emulate other schools believed to offer healthy models in order to manage financial viability. How, if at all, has the struggle to remain financially viable affected the college/university's Lutheran identity?

    l. Has the college/university chosen to make trade-offs for the sake of financial viability at the expense of its Lutheran identity?

    m. If so, name examples of these trade-offs.

    n. The more uncertain the relationship between means and ends, the greater the extent to which an organization will model itself after organizations it perceives to be successful. Given this notion, which college or university(ies)' business model, best practices, or accomplishments does your college/university seek to emulate, or at least pay attention?

    o. Why are these colleges and universities this college/university's benchmarks?

9. In you judgment, what is the relationship, if any, between preserving a lively, robust Lutheran identity and maintaining a critical mass of Lutheran faculty?

p. How would you describe the importance of faculty and administrative staff participation in trade and professional organizations?

q. Is faculty participation in these organizations an institutional priority?

r. What is the rate or frequency of this participation among the faculty in such organizations?

s. Is it the job of a faculty member at a Lutheran college or university to foster the ideals of Lutheran higher education?

t. In addition to teaching and mentoring, faculty members often face pressure to manage many tasks: publishing, research, committee service, and membership in professional organizations, to name a few examples. Do these "professionalization pressures" pose a threat to a faculty member's ability to serve faithfully within the Lutheran college environment?

10. Do you believe your college/university is deliberately seeking to preserve its Lutheran identity?

u. If so, why?

v. How is it planning this preservation?

11. In 2009, are Lutheran colleges still relevant in the landscape of American higher education?

w. Is this Lutheran identity worth preserving?

ADDITIONAL QUESTIONS SPECIFIC TO PARTICIPANTS' PROFESSIONAL ROLES

Interview Guide Questions for Current College Chaplains

1. How would you describe the financial dependence of the college/university upon the ELCA or Lutheran synod?

a. If this represents a recent change (increase or decrease in financial support), what effect has this made on the relationship between the college/university and the ELCA or synod?

     b. How would you describe the college/university's dependence upon the ELCA or Lutheran synod for its religious identity?

2. Which Lutheran colleges or universities have effective models for Lutheran institutional identity? Why?

3. In your judgment, is this college/university "more or less Lutheran" now than when it was when you arrived? Please explain.

Appendix I

Interview Guide for Institutional Memory Participants

1. What brought you to this college/university community?
2. What does it mean to be a Lutheran college?
   a. What do you think is the difference, if any, between Lutheran colleges and universities and other schools?
   b. Name three advantages, if any, of a Lutheran college or university educational experience.
   c. Name three disadvantages, if any.
3. How would you describe the overall faith community at this college/university?
   d. What most shapes the faith community here at this college/university?
   e. What role, if any, should the president, chaplain, and faculty play in developing the faith community of a college/university?
   f. Who do you believe has the greatest power in and responsibility for shaping the relationship between the college/university and the ELCA?
4. How would you describe the "Lutheranness" of your college/university?

g. Do you believe Lutheran colleges and universities have become "less Lutheran" over time (specifically since the mid-1960s)?

h. If so, how?

i. Martin Luther makes a (very!) unexpected appearance at this college/university. What might he say about the Lutheran ethos, or "way of life," of your campus community?

5. What are the primary goals, or mission, of this college/university?

6. Name two or three critical events—turning points—during the last 40 years that have significantly shaped the college/university's Lutheran institutional identity.

7. Has secularization affected your college/university's Lutheran identity?

j. If so, how?

k. Can you give me specific examples of this secularization?

8. It is widely held that small colleges and universities face perpetual financial pressures. Sometimes colleges and universities seek to emulate other schools believed to offer healthy models in order to manage financial viability. How, if at all, has the struggle to remain financially viable affected the college/university's Lutheran identity?

l. Has the college/university chosen to make trade-offs for the sake of financial viability at the expense of its Lutheran identity?

m. If so, name examples of these trade-offs.

n. The more uncertain the relationship between means and ends, the greater the extent to which an organization will model itself after organizations it perceives to be successful. Given this notion, which college or university(ies)' business model, best practices, or accomplishments does your college/university seek to emulate, or at least pay attention?

o. Why are these colleges and universities this college/university's benchmarks?

9. In you judgment, what is the relationship, if any, between preserving a lively, robust Lutheran identity and maintaining a critical mass of Lutheran faculty?

    p. How would you describe the importance of faculty and administrative staff participation in trade and professional organizations?

    q. Is faculty participation in these organizations an institutional priority?

    r. What is the rate or frequency of this participation among the faculty in such organizations?

    s. Is it the job of a faculty member at a Lutheran college or university to foster the ideals of Lutheran higher education?

    t. In addition to teaching and mentoring, faculty members often face pressure to manage many tasks: publishing, research, committee service, and membership in professional organizations, to name a few examples. Do these "professionalization pressures" pose a threat to a faculty member's ability to serve faithfully within the Lutheran college environment?

10. Do you believe your college/university is deliberately seeking to preserve its Lutheran identity?

    u. If so, why?

    v. How is it planning this preservation?

11. In 2009, are Lutheran colleges still relevant in the landscape of American higher education?

    w. Is this Lutheran identity worth preserving?

ADDITIONAL QUESTIONS SPECIFIC TO PARTICIPANTS' PROFESSIONAL ROLES

Interview Guide Questions for Institutional Memory Participants

1. Please describe to me your role and responsibilities at the college/university, and when you served there.

2. How would describe the changes that have occurred, if any, at the college/university in the past 40 years?

3. Describe the Lutheran ethos of the college/university during the 1965-1975 era. If it helps to pinpoint a specific year, describe 1969.

4. Was chapel required for members of the college/university community?

   a. Describe chapel and the attendance then.

   b. Who came to chapel?

   c. What happened in chapel?

5. Tell me about the faculty then.

   d. Was the majority of faculty Lutheran, or was it even an issue of discussion?

6. How has the institution's response to financial pressures affected Lutheran identity?

7. In your judgment, is your college/university "more or less Lutheran" now than during the 1965-1975 era?

   e. How?

   f. Why?

Appendix J

Document List

CENTRAL DOCUMENTS FOR ANALYSIS

- Institutional Mission Statements
- Strategic Plans (circa 1965-1975)
    - Concordia: *A Blueprint for Concordia College*
    - Lenoir-Rhyne: *Strategy for the Seventies*
    - Gettysburg: *Decade of Decision*
- Current Strategic Plans
    - Concordia: *Strategic Plan—2005-2010* (as well as other items in the *Blueprint* series)
    - Lenoir-Rhyne: *University Rising*
    - Gettysburg: *Strategic Directions for Gettysburg College*

SUPPLEMENTAL DOCUMENTS FOR CONTEXT AND BACKGROUND

- College Histories
    - Concordia: *On Firm Foundation Grounded*
    - Lenoir-Rhyne: *Fair Star*
    - Gettysburg: *A Salutary Influence*

Appendix J

- Admissions Materials
- Fact Books and Various Campus Visitor Literature
- Campus Maps
- Websites

Appendix K

Institutional Mission Statements

CONCORDIA COLLEGE

The mission of Concordia College is to influence the affairs of the world by sending into society thoughtful and informed men and women dedicated to the Christian life.

LENOIR-RHYNE UNIVERSITY

In pursuit of the development of the whole person, Lenoir-Rhyne University seeks to liberate mind and spirit, clarify personal faith, foster physical wholeness, build a sense of community, and promote responsible leadership for service in the world. As an institution of the North Carolina Synod of the Evangelical Lutheran Church in America, the university holds the conviction that wholeness of person, true vocation, and the most useful service to God and the world are best discerned from the perspective of Christian faith. As a community of learning, the university provides programs of undergraduate, graduate, and continuing study committed to the liberal arts and sciences as a foundation for a wide variety of careers and as guidance for a meaningful life.

Appendix K

GETTYSBURG COLLEGE

Gettysburg College, a national, residential, undergraduate college committed to a liberal education, prepares students to be active leaders and participants in a changing world.

Appendix L

Document Analysis Guiding Questions

GUIDING QUESTIONS FOR DOCUMENT ANALYSIS:

- When was the mission statement written?
- Has it changed over time?
- Does the mission statement include the word Lutheran?
- Succinctly, what main goal does the mission statement express?
- What are the main points—the basic outline—of the mission statement?
- When were the former and current strategic plans written?
- Do the strategic plans (former and current) include the word Lutheran?
- Do the strategic plans (former and current) proclaim an explicit Lutheran relationship?
- Do the former and current strategic plans differ with regard to the treatment of Lutheran identity? If so, how?
- Does the language indicate a move toward or away from the Lutheran heritage?
- What does the former strategic plan emphasize?
- What does the current strategic plan emphasize?
- What are the main points—the basic outline—of the former and current strategic plans?

Appendix M

Brief Institutional Profiles of Concordia, Lenoir-Rhyne, and Gettysburg*

	CONCORDIA COLLEGE	LENOIR-RHYNE UNIVERSITY	GETTYSBURG COLLEGE
Location	Moorhead, MN	Hickory, NC	Gettysburg, PA
Founding Year	1891	1891	1832
President (years in office)	Pamela Jolicoeur (4)	Wayne Powell (6)	Janet Morgan Riggs (0)**
Total FTE Students	2,776	1,360	2,451
Total FTE Faculty	218	128	229
Comprehensive Fees	$30,280	$31,220	$46,830
Endowment Value***	$80 million	$62 million	$255 million
Voluntary Support	$9.4 million	$6.8 million	$11 million
Faculty Doctorates****	77%	78%	91%
Student : Faculty Ratio	13:1	12:1	10:1

*Information as of February 2009 for FY 2008-2009
**Riggs had served as interim president, however, since summer 2008.
***At the end of FY 2008
****All ranks

Bibliography

Albert, S. & Whetten, D. (1985). Organizational identity. In Cummings, L. L. & Staw, B.M. (Eds.). *Research in organizational behavior, Vol. 7* (pp. 263–95). Greenwich: JAI.

Aldrich, H. (1979). *Organizations and environments*. Englewood Cliffs, NJ: Prentice-Hall.

Arthur, J. (2001). Changing patterns of church college identity and mission. *Westminster Studies in Education*, 24, 137–43.

Ashforth, B. & Mael, F. (1989). Social identity theory and the organization. *Academy of Management Review*, 14, 20–39.

Ashforth, B. & Mael, F. (1996). Organizational identity and strategy as a context for the individual. *Advances in Strategic Management*, 13, 19–64.

Barbour, I. (1997). *Religion and science: Historical and contemporary issues*. San Francisco: Harper San Francisco.

Benne, R. (2003a). Integrity and fragmentation: Can the Lutheran center hold? In Richard Cimino (Ed.). *Lutherans today: American Lutheran identity in the 21st century* (pp. 206–21). Grand Rapids: Eerdmans.

Benne, R. (2003b). *Ordinary saints: An introduction to the Christian life*. Minneapolis: Fortress.

Benne, R. (2001). *Quality with soul: How six premier colleges and universities keep faith with their religious traditions*. Grand Rapids: Eerdmans.

Benne, R. & Christenson, T. (Fall 2008). Point/counterpoint: What it means to be a "college of the church." *Intersections*, 28, 12–20.

Birkner, M. (2006). *Gettysburg college: The campus history series*. Chicago: Arcadia.

Bolman, L. & Deal, T. (2003). *Reframing organizations: Artistry, choice, and leadership* (3rd ed.). San Francisco: Jossey-Bass.

Bommer, M. & Janaro, R. (February 2005). An integrative planning model for college and university programs. *Planning for Higher Education*, 33 (2), 4–14.

Breneman, D. (1994). *Liberal arts colleges: Thriving, surviving, or endangered?* Washington, DC: Brookings.

Breneman, D. (2008). "How we got here." Chapter in a forthcoming book.

Bunge, M. (Summer 2006). Our calling in education: Working together to generate a strong social statement on public schools, Lutheran schools and colleges, and the faith formation of children and young people. *Intersections*, 23.

Bunge, M. (Summer 2002). Renewing a sense of vocation at Lutheran colleges and universities: Insights from the project at Valparaiso University. *Intersections*, 14, 11–18.

Burtchaell, J. (1998). *The dying of the light: The disengagement of colleges and universities from their Christian churches.* Grand Rapids: Eerdmans.

Byars, L. (1991). *Strategic management, formulation, and implementation: Concepts and cases.* New York: HarperCollins.

Center for public service. (2009). Retrieved May 18, 2009, from http://www.gettysburg.edu/about/offices/college_life/cps/about_cps/

Chell, E. (1998). Critical incident technique. In Symon, G. & Cassell, C. (Eds.). *Qualitative methods and analysis in organizational research: A practical guide* (pp. 51–72). Thousand Oaks, CA: Sage.

Chell, E. & Adam, E. (1994). Exploring the cultural orientation of entrepreneurship: Conceptual and methodological issues. Discussion Paper 94-7, School of Business Management, University of Newcastle upon Tyne.

Christenson, T. (Summer 2005). Education as a Christian (Lutheran) calling. *Intersections,* 21, 28–32.

Christenson, T. (2004). *The gift and task of Lutheran higher education.* Minneapolis: Fortress.

Cimino, R. (2003). *Lutherans today: American Lutheran identity in the twenty-first century.* Grand Rapids: Eerdmans.

Clark, B. (1972). The organizational saga in higher education. *Administrative Science Quarterly,* 17, 178–84.

Clark, B. (1975). *The distinctive college: Antioch, Reed, and Swarthmore.* Chicago: Aldine.

Coffey, A. & Atkinson, P. (1996). *Making sense of qualitative data.* Thousand Oaks, CA: Sage.

Collins, J. & Porras, J. (1994). *Built to last: Successful habits of visionary companies.* New York: Harper Business.

Cooley, C. (1902). *Human nature and the social order.* New York: Scribner.

Council of ELCA-Related College and University Presidents. (2009). Annual Meeting Report.

Creswell, J. (2007). *Qualitative inquiry and research design: Choosing among five approaches.* Thousand Oaks, CA: Sage.

Creswell, J. (1994). *Research design: Qualitative and quantitative approaches.* Thousand Oaks, CA: Sage.

Dacin, M. T. (February 1997). Isomorphism in context: The power and prescription of institutional norms. *The Academy of Management Journal,* 40 (1), 46–81.

Demerath, N., Hall, P., Schmitt, T. & Williams, R. (Eds.). (1998). *Sacred companies: Organizational aspects of religion and religious aspects of organizations.* New York: Oxford.

Demers, C. (2007). *Organizational change theories: A synthesis.* Thousand Oaks, CA: Sage.

DiMaggio, P. (1988). Interest and agency in institutional theory. In. L. Zucker (Ed.). *Institutional patterns and organizations.* Cambridge: Ballinger.

DiMaggio, P. & Powell, W. (1983). The iron cage revisited: Institutional isomorphism and collective rationality in organizational fields. *American Sociological Review,* 48, 147–60.

Dovre, P. (Ed.). (2002). *The future of religious colleges.* Grand Rapids: Eerdmans.

Dovre, P. (2006). The Lutheran calling in education: Context and prospect. *Intersections,* 23, 15–21.

Dovre, P. (2009). *Holy restlessness: Reflections on faith and learning.* Minneapolis: Augsburg.

Duke, D. (1995). *The school that refused to die*. Albany, NY: State University of New York Press.

Dutton, J. & Dukerich, J. (1991). Keeping an eye on the mirror: Image and identity in organizational adaptation. *The Academy of Management Journal*, 34 (3), 517–54.

Edge, J. (October 2004). The need for strategic planning in academia. *T.H.E. Journal*, 32 (3), 40–43.

Engelhardt, C. (1991). *On firm foundation grounded: The first century of Concordia College*. Moorhead, MN: Concordia College.

Erickson, E. (1964). *Insight and responsibility*. New York: Norton.

Erickson, F. (1986). Qualitative methods in research on teaching. In M.C. Wittock (Ed.). *Handbook of research of teaching*. New York: Macmillan.

Estenek, S., James, M., & Norton, D. (December 2006). Assessing Catholic identity: A study of mission statements of Catholic colleges and universities. *Catholic Education: A Journal of Inquiry and Practice*, 10 (2), 199–217.

Evangelical Lutheran Church in America Task Force on Education. (2007). *Our calling in education: A Lutheran study*. Published by the ELCA.

Fennell, M. (1980). The effects of environmental characteristics on the structure of hospital clusters. *Administrative Science Quarterly*, 25, 484–510.

Fidler, B. (1989). Strategic management: Where is the school going? A guide to strategic thinking. In B. Fidler & G. Bowles (Eds.). *Effective Local Management of Schools: A Strategic Approach*. Harlow, UK: Longman.

Fisher, B. (1974). *Small group decision making: Communication and the group process*. New York: McGraw-Hill.

Fisher, J. (1991). *The board and the president*. New York: MacMillan.

Freedman, J. (2004). Presidents and trustees. In R. Ehrenberg (Ed.). *Governing academia* (pp. 9–27). Ithaca, NY: Cornell University Press.

Gioia, D. (1998). From individual to organizational identity. In D. Whetten & P. Godfrey (Eds.). *Identity in organizations: Building theory through conversations* (17–31). Thousand Oaks, CA: Sage.

Gioia, D. & Thomas, J. (1996). Identity, image and issue interpretation: Sensemaking during strategic change in academia. *Administrative Science Quarterly*, 40, 370–403.

Glatfelter, C. (1987). *A salutary influence: Gettysburg College, 1932–1985*. Mechanicsburg, PA: W& M.

Gritsch, E. (1994). *Fortress introduction to Lutheranism*. Minneapolis: Fortress.

Guba, E. & Lincoln, Y. (1988). *Effective evaluation: Improving the usefulness of evaluation results through responsive and naturalistic approaches*. San Francisco: Jossey-Bass.

Hamilton, N. (2006). Faculty professionalism: Failures of socialization and the road. *Liberal Education*, 92 (4), 14–21.

Hannan, M. & Freeman, J. (1977). The population ecology of organizations. *American Journal of Sociology*, 82, 929–64.

Hatch, M. & Cunliffe, A. (2006). *Organizational theory: Modern, symbolic, and postmodern perspectives*. Oxford: Oxford University Press.

Hatch, M. & Schultz, M. (2004). The dynamics of organizational identity. In M. Hatch & M. Schultz (Eds.). *Organizational identity: A reader* (377–403). New York: Oxford University Press.

Hawley, A. (1968). Human ecology. In D. Sills (Ed.). *International Encyclopedia of the Social Sciences* (pp. 328–37). New York: Macmillan.

Heugens, P. & Lander, M. (2009). Structure! Agency! (and other quarrels): A meta-analysis of institutional theories of organization. *Academy of Management Journal,* 52 (1), 61–85.

Hermalin, B. (2004). Higher education boards of trustees. In R. Ehrenberg (Ed.). *Governing Academia* (pp. 28–48). Ithaca, NY: Cornell University Press.

Holsti, O. (1969). *Content analysis for the social sciences and humanities.* Reading, MA: Addison-Wesley.

Ingram, R. (1993). *Governing independent colleges and universities: A handbook for trustees, chief executives, and other campus leaders.* San Francisco: Jossey-Bass.

Ireland, R. & Hitt, M. (1992). Mission statements: Importance, challenge, and recommendations for development. *Business Horizons,* May–June 1992, 34–42.

Jodock, D. (2002). The ELCA college and the church: Strengthening the partnership. Keynote address at "Here We Stand: A Gathering of ELCA College and Seminary Presidents and Bishops of Regions 3 & 5." Minneapolis, August 19, 2002.

Kaplan, G. (2004). How academic ships actually navigate. In R. Ehrenberg (Ed.). *Governing academia* (pp. 165–208). Ithaca, NY: Cornell University Press.

Kerr, C. & Gade, M. (1989). *The guardians: Boards of trustees of American colleges and universities.* Washington, DC: Association of Governing Boards.

Kirk, J. & Miller, M. (1986). *Reliability and validity in qualitative research.* Thousand Oaks, CA: Sage.

Kimberly, J. (1980). Initiation, innovation and institutionalization in the creation process. In J. Kimberly & R. Miles (Eds.). *The organizational life cycle* (pp. 18–43). San Francisco: Jossey Bass.

Krathwohl, D. (1998). *Methods of educational and social science research: An integrated approach* (2nd ed.). Long Grove, IL: Waveland.

Kvale, S. (1996). *Interviews: An introduction to qualitative research interviewing.* Thousand Oaks, CA: Sage.

LeCompte, M. & Preissle, J. (1993). *Ethnography and qualitative design in educational research* (2nd ed.). San Diego: Academic Press.

Lincoln, Y. and Guba, E. (1985). *Naturalistic inquiry.* Newbury Park, CA: Sage.

McGuinness, A. (2005). The states and higher education. In P. Altbach, R. Berdahl, & P. Gumport (Eds.). *American higher education in the twenty-first century: Social, political, and economic challenges* (pp. 198–225). Baltimore: Johns Hopkins University Press.

March J. & Olsen, J. (1976). *Ambiguity and choice in organizations.* Bergen, Norway: Universitetsforlaget.

Marsden, G. & Longfield, B. (Eds.). (1992). *The secularization of the academy.* New York: Oxford University Press.

Marshall, C. & Rossman, G. (2006). *Designing Qualitative Research* (4th ed.). Thousand Oaks, CA: Sage.

Maxwell, J. (2005). *Qualitative research design: An interactive approach* (2nd ed.). Thousand Oaks, CA: Sage.

Mead, G. (1934). *Mind, self, and society.* Chicago: University of Chicago Press.

Meyer, J. (1983). Institutionalization and the rationality of formal organizational structure. In J. Meyer & W. Scott (Eds.). *Organizational environments: Ritual and rationality* (pp. 261–82). Thousand Oaks, CA: Sage.

Meyer, J. & Rowan, B. (1977). Institutionalized organizations: Formal structures as myth and ceremony. *American Journal of Sociology,* 83 (2), 340–63.

Miles, M. & Huberman, A. (1994). *Qualitative data analysis: An expanded sourcebook* (2nd ed.). Thousand Oaks, CA: Sage.

Mitroff, I. & Kilmann, R. (1980). On organizational stories: An approach to the design and analysis of organizations through myths and stories. In R. Kilman, et al, (Eds). *The management of organizational design.* (p. 676). New York: North Holland.

Mizruchi, M. & Fein, L. (1999). The social construction of organizational knowledge: A study of the uses of coercive, mimetic, and normative isomorphism. *Administrative Science Quarterly, 44,* 653–83.

Morey, M. & Piderit, J. (2006). *Catholic higher education: A culture in crisis.* New York: Oxford University Press.

Morphew, C. (2002a). Steering colleges and universities toward distinctive missions. CHEPA Governance Seminar. p. 6.

Morphew, C. (2002b). A rose by any other name: Which colleges became universities. *The Review of Higher Education, 25* (2), 207–23.

Morphew, C. & Hartley, M. (May/June 2006). Mission statements: A thematic analysis of rhetoric across institutional type. *The Journal of Higher Education, 77* (3), 456–71.

Muilenberg, G. (1997). An Aristotelian twist to faith and reason. *Intersections,* Summer 1997, 8–11.

Nelson, C. (1975). *The Lutherans in North America.* Philadelphia: Fortress.

Nicholson, G. & Kiel, C. (2007). Can directors impact performance? A case-based test of three theories of corporate governance. *Corporate Governance, 15* (4), 585–608.

Niebuhr, H. (1956). *Christ and culture.* New York: Harpers.

Norris, J. & Boatmon, E. (1990). *Fair star: A centennial history of Lenoir-Rhyne College.* Virginia Beach: Donning.

Northouse, P. (2007): *Leadership: Theory and practice.* Thousand Oaks, CA: Sage.

Olson, S. (Fall 2006). Vocation and the vocation of a Lutheran college: Cows, colleges, and contentment. *Intersections, 24,* 5–11.

Pacifica Synod of the ELCA. (2008). Who we are. Retrieved May 12, 2008 from http://www.pacificasynod.org/who.htm.

Parsons, T. (1960). *Structure and process in modern societies.* Glencoe, IL: Free Press.

Patton, M. (1990). *Qualitative evaluation and research methods* (2nd ed.). Newbury Park, CA: Sage.

Perrow, C. (May 2000). An organizational analysis of organizational theory. *Contemporary Sociology, 29* (3), 469–76.

Pettigrew, A. (1979). On studying organizational cultures. *Administrative Science Quarterly, 24* (4), 570–81.

Pfeffer, J. & Salancik, G. (1978). *The external control of organizations: A resource dependence perspective.* New York: Harper & Row.

Porter, M. (1996). What is strategy? *Harvard Business Review, 4134,* 59–79.

Pusser, B. & Turner, S. (2004). Nonprofit and for-profit governance in higher education. In R. Ehrenberg (Ed.). *Governing Academia* (pp. 235–57). Ithaca, NY: Cornell University Press.

Riley, N. (2005). *God on the quad: How religious colleges and the missionary generation are changing America.* New York: St. Martin's.

Schulze, L. (2002). An affirmation of the generation of an ELCA social statement on education. *ELCA Division for Higher Education and Schools of the ELCA,* June 2002.

Schwehn, M. (1993). *Exiles from Eden: Religion and the academic vocation in America.* Oxford: Oxford University Press.

Schwehn, M. (1999). A Christian university: Defining the difference. *First Things*, May 1999, 25–31.

Schwehn, M. (2002). Lutheran higher education in the twenty-first century. In P. Dovre (Ed.). *The future of religious colleges: The proceedings of the Harvard Conference on the future of religious colleges October 6–7, 2000* (pp. 208–23). Grand Rapids: Eerdmans.

Simmons, E. (1998). *Lutheran higher education: An introduction.* Minneapolis: Augsburg.

Solberg, R. (1985). *Lutheran higher education in North America.* Minneapolis: Augsburg.

Solberg, R. (1997). What can the Lutheran tradition contribute to Christian higher education? In R. Hughes and W. Adrian (Eds.). *Models for Christian higher education: Strategies for survival and success in the twenty-first century* (pp. 71–81). Grand Rapids: Eerdmans.

Steele, C. (1988). The psychology of self-affirmation: Sustaining the integrity of the self. In *Advances in experimental social psychology.* (Vol. 21, pp. 261–302). New York: Academic Press.

Stensaker, B. & Norgard, J. (2001). Innovation and isomorphism: A case-study of university identity struggle 1969–1999. *Higher Education*, 42 (4), 473–92.

Stimpert, J., Gustafson, L. & Sarason, Y. (1998). Organizational identity within the strategic management conversation. In D. Whetten & P. Godfrey (Eds.). *Identity in organizations: Building theory through conversations* (pp. 83–98). Thousand Oaks, CA: Sage.

Strauss, A. & Corbin, J. (1998). *Basics of qualitative research: Techniques and procedures for developing grounded theory.* Thousand Oaks, CA: Sage.

Trexler, E. R. (2003). *High expectations: Understanding the ELCA's early years, 1988–2003.* Minneapolis: Augsburg Fortress.

Wagner, J., Stimpert, J., & Fubara, E. (September, 1998). Board composition and organizational performance: Two studies of insider/outsider effects. *Journal of Management Studies*, 35 (5), 655–77.

Weber, M. (1952). *The Protestant ethic and the spirit of capitalism.* New York: Scribner.

Yin, R. (1984). *Case study research: Design and methods.* Newbury Park, CA: Sage.

Zemsky, R., Wegner, G. & Massy, W. (2005). *Remaking the American university: Market-smart and mission-centered.* New Brunswick, NJ: Rutgers University Press.

Index

Index